MARY CAROL
Best Wishes
Gary W Suffern

PACIFIED ZONE

GARY W. SUFFERN

PublishAmerica
Baltimore

First printing

ISBN: 1-4137-3077-9
PUBLISHED BY PUBLISHAMERICA, LLLP
www.publishamerica.com
Baltimore

Printed in the United States of America

CONTENTS

CHAPTER 1
DEATH AND DESTRUCTION

We dropped into a previously cut landing zone. My heart was racing and sweat ran down my body under the jungle fatigues and field pack. I looked down from the chopper into wind blown trees and high grass. We hit hard, and everyone jumped off and ran to the outer perimeter of the clearing.

I followed the training lieutenant and watched his moves and heard his commands. I was on my second training day in Viet Nam. The heat was causing me to feel light headed. I looked around in a fog. *Was I really here?* Everything was quiet now. No firing from the enemy. Must be what the lieutenant called a "cold landing zone."

My breathing calmed down, and I looked around. The engineer troops were spread out all around the landing zone into the tree line. I looked up watching the infantry helicopters approach. Two companies of infantry were coming in on this mission. I watched in slow motion as the choppers landed and took off, disgorging their troops.

The green clothed troopers ran to our line and farther into the jungle. As the last troop carrier left, a big Chinook supply chopper landed to off load additional supplies. Once the first Chinook left, another came in to drop more supplies. *This isn't so tough*, I thought as I watched the pilot flare to land. *WOOSH, BANG*, a streak of orange flashed right in front of me and hit the chopper.

Heat from the explosion ripped back toward me and washed over our position. I was slammed to the ground, the wind knocked out of me. I struggled to breathe and inhaled the most god-awful smell of burnt flesh and fuel and god knows what else. Gunfire erupted all over the perimeter, and confusion crushed me like an avalanche. I could see fire and tracers and orange streaks going in all directions. Men were yelling for help and medics; we were so close to the landing zone the men were getting hit by exploding ammunition on the burning chopper.

I couldn't breathe; I couldn't move. All I could do was watch men dying. Bodies were lying everywhere. *Look, it's the lieutenant I came in with.* "Get up," I said. He just laid there face down in his bloody uniform. Smoke was clouding the landing zone like a fog. My eyes were watering from the burning acidic fuel and sweat running off my head under the steel pot helmet. I began to shake uncontrollably as if I was freezing. I was hearing loud explosions in the distance.

"Sir, would you care for some refreshment?" Came a voice far, far away. I was pulled into another place. On a plane, going home? October 6, 1969? I could hear jet engines. Was I back on the plane to the world after my last wounding? I was, a few hours earlier, face down in mud and rain under a mortar attack, wasn't I?

"Sir, would you care for some refreshment?" Came the same voice, only closer now. *Wake up. Wake up.* I opened my eyes and looked around. Up to my right was a stewardess with a refreshment cart offering any kind of drink. Now I remembered where I was.

Elevation of 37,000 feet, and off to the first reunion with my company from Viet Nam. Heading southeast in a Continental 707, to meet who knows who from the company and to what welcome. It's been 25 years since I last saw them and I'm a little leery of what I'm getting myself into. I hadn't heard from my best friend, Lieutenant Steve Tomlinson, since several weeks after my last wounding and medevac back to the world. I really didn't know how the men thought about me, their company executive officer.

Over the months since I was called and invited to the reunion, I could think of many reasons why I couldn't go, but the anxiety was always there under the surface. I waffled so many times my wife finally said I had to go, or I would never forgive myself. I had to go to at least to see Tomlinson, whom I later found out was having similar misgivings. As I listen to the drone of jet engines, I drift off, back to the time of my youth, prior to death and destruction.

October 1966, I was midway through my senior year at Long Beach State University, California. The Viet Nam War had been going on for several years and the Draft was hanging over everyone's head, day by day. My roommate, Russ Clark, was a private pilot and had decided to enter the delayed enlistment program with the Air Force. He talked me into joining him on a drive to the recruiter's office in downtown Long Beach.

I had not given much thought to joining the military after graduation, but in those days I wasn't concentrating on much, other than my fiancée and getting out of school with a degree. So when Russ suggested the Air Force delayed enlistment program, I went along. Russ showed me how to read flight instruments and gave me a short explanation on flying, so I would be ready for the flight aptitude test.

The recruiter was glad to get two for his quota sheet. One week later, the recruiter called to say our results were in from the testing. We piled into Russ's 1955 Oldsmobile and raced to the recruiter's office, confident we had secured our spot in the Air Force program. Russ was devastated to find he had failed the written portion of the pre-flight testing by misreading the instrument panel of the test. I had passed with flying colors and let him know it all the way back to the apartment. This meant I was locked into the delayed program as of December 1966.

When we arrived at the apartment, the mail had been delivered, and I was greeted with a draft notice with an enlistment date of November 28, 1966. I called the recruiter in Long Beach to find out if he could notify the draft board of my position with the Air Force. His reply was,"Tough shit, G.I." He suggested, with my scores on the testing, that I check with the Army recruiter about getting into the Officer Candidate School. The Army turned out to be the only option as all other branches of the service were full at that time.

I did go to the local draft board and plead my case but was told my country needs me now and the appeal was denied. So I went to the Army recruiter and had to take their test, which turned out to be the same aptitude test as the Air Force. The recruiter, informed me a week later I had qualified for Officer Candidate School and could guarantee a spot for me only if I enlisted for three years.

I was given three choices for Officer Candidate School with two required to be combat related. So first I chose Engineers, then Artillery, and finally Armor. After watching the nightly news for so many years and seeing what the infantry was getting a dose of, I decided that wasn't for me.

Everything began to happen rapidly then. I first notified all my class professors of my withdrawal from school, several were probably glad to see me go, and prepared for the big day at the main induction station at Los Angeles. November 18, 1966 was a day of sadness and the beginning of this adventure. Ellen Taylor, my fiancée, drove with me to the induction station, and we parted until first leave, eight weeks later.

The day began at 6 AM [0600 hours military time) and was spent taking the same written test again, stripping for a complete physical, getting sworn in as a servant for Uncle Sam, and then waiting until about 6 PM [1800 hours) for the bus ride to our first stop: basic training. Basic training was at Fort Ord, California. We recruits packed onto the Greyhound Bus.

I was to hand carry the paperwork for all the "Swinging dicks" as the induction sergeant put it, and deliver them to whoever met us at the fort.

7

Everyone was bushed after the long day in Los Angeles, so we all snored our way along. We arrived at the gates of Fort Ord about 2 AM [0200 hours). The fort is a little northeast of the ocean town of Monterey, near the famous Pebble Beach Golf Course. When we finally came to a stop, a sergeant came aboard and told everyone to stay put while I was taken off with the paperwork. I thought, *This isn't so bad*, after I had heard all the horror stories about the first day in basic training.

The sergeant showed me where to stand in a painted area under lights on the tarmac. He then re-entered the bus and gave everyone five seconds to exit. While everyone was trying to get off they were met with as loud and nasty verbal abuse as the sergeant and his aids could muster. WELCOME TO THE US ARMY. After everyone was off, we were "marched" to a building where we filled out a post card to send home to whomever saying we got to our destination in one piece, and we were now the property of Uncle Sam.

Then it was off to our assigned barracks with a corporal escort and to the supply building for bedding. Reveille, military time to get up, came fast with only a few hours sleep. Getting us ready for combat, I guess. I wanted to stay out of trouble, so along with everyone else with the same idea, immediately got up and shaved, dressed, and was ready for the corporal when he came in banging the trash cans and blowing his little whistle. The corporal, who was a pretty good Joe compared to other ranking persons with authority, started explaining what was coming for the day and where to go for chow. We all fell out to the street into a make shift formation and marched to the mess hall.

After chow, we were taken to the supply building for our first issue of army clothing. In one large duffel bag, we had to stuff one Class "A" uniform, four sets of utility fatigues, two pairs of boots, socks, and underwear. Then it was back to the induction barracks (this was where new recruits waited to be assigned to their individual companies) and change into our new army fatigues and package our civilian clothes for shipment back home.

These we wouldn't need for quite a while, as we were restricted to the training company area due to meningitis quarantine. While we were inspecting our new duds, I began talking to the recruit in the next bunk and found out we had tried out for the same semi-pro football team. His name was Dave Escarsega and became my friend through training and beyond.

That second day, in the afternoon, we met our drill instructor and were informed our barracks would be going to Bravo Company, Third Battalion, Third Brigade for our training. Staff Sergeant Nichelson was to be our drill instructor with Buck Sergeant Persichetti as his assistant. SSGT Nichelson wanted to get a head start on training, so he showed us the proper procedures for military bearing and close order drill. We had several days to practice before we were to move to the company area.

SSGT Nichelson preferred to get a head start on the other drill instructors, so his platoon would shine throughout the cycle. This did make a difference, and we remained at the top of the company most of the cycle.

SSGT Nichelson definitely followed the Drill Instructors Creed:

I AM A DRILL SERGEANT DEDICATED TO TRAINING NEW SOLDIERS AND INFLUENCING THE OLD. I AM FOREVER CONSCIOUS OF EACH SOLDIER UNDER MY CHARGE AND BY EXAMPLE WILL INSPIRE HIM TO THE HIGHEST STANDARDS POSSIBLE. I WILL STRIVE TO BE PATIENT, UNDERSTANDING, JUST AND FIRM. I WILL COMMEND THE DESERVING AND ENCOURAGE THE WAYWARD. I WILL NEVER FORGET THAT I AM RESPONSIBLE TO MY COMMANDER FOR THE MORALE, DISCIPLINE, AND EFFICIENCY OF MY MEN AND THEIR PERFORMANCE WILL REFLECT AN IMAGE OF ME.

At the end of the week, we moved to Bravo Company, which was housed in a new multi-story concrete building. The training company consisted of a company commander, training officers, a first sergeant (we all called him "Blinky" because of a nervous tick of his eyes), drill sergeant instructors, their assistants and several company clerks, a mess sergeant and his assistants, and the supply sergeant.

The first day SSGT Nichelson picked six men from the platoon of trainees to be placed in the positions of acting platoon guide (staff sergeant rank), an assistant platoon guide (buck sergeant rank) and four squad leaders (corporal rank). I was picked to be the leader of the first squad and allowed to pick someone for my assistant. I picked Dave Escarcega as my assistant. We leaders were bunked in separate rooms from the rest of the platoon.

The main body of the platoon was bunked in a large room we called a bay. The bay was large and had double, bunk-bed style, metal-framed bunks on both sides. There was room for forty men in the bay. Wall lockers were between the bunks, and foot-lockers were on the floor at the head of each bunk. A rifle rack was located in the middle of the bay about halfway down the floor.

My squads' responsibility was to maintain the bay, making it ready for inspection everyday. The first day I lined up my squad in the bay and told them in as stern instruction as I could think of, that the bay was going to be ready for inspection every day and it was our responsibility, no one else's, to see that it was. If anyone didn't do his job, he would be sorry. That did get their attention and I never had to resort to action, although I nearly lost my position the very next day.

The next day was to be our first inspection of the cycle, so at reveille, I shooed everyone out of the bay to finish up. I decided to stay behind with several of my men to finish up while the company fell out for the first formation. I told my assistant Dave Escarcega to stand at the head of the squad and report everyone in the first squad as present or accounted for. After the formation, Sergeant Perschetti came up to the bay and told me to get my ass down to the Drill Sergeant's office.

I was feeling pretty good about taking the initiative to stay up there. When I arrived at the office, all I got was a dose of yelling from SSGT Nichelson for not being at formation. I was ordered to the front leaning rest position (push-up position) where I stayed for 30 minutes while the rest of the company went to the mess hall for morning chow. Luckily for me, I was in good shape having played sports for the past six years and had no problem with the position, which aggravated SSGT Nichelson. I was finally ordered to report to the mess sergeant for Kitchen Police (KP).

Another favorite physical punishment was called the "Dying Cockroach" position. This order was mostly given while we were in line going to the mess hall. The cadre in charge would order the position to whoever was caught looking around or anything other than standing at attention in line and being mute. The "Dying Cockroach" position consisted of the trainee lying on his back and stretching his arms and legs straight up.

This position you had to hold until told to recover. Mean while everyone behind you moved by you to the mess hall. The more you aggravated the cadre the longer you stayed in the position. The first few days many trainees were seen in the "Dying Cockroach" position. The rest of that day I spent working in the mess hall thinking how stupid I was for not asking SSGT Nichelson before doing what I did. I figured I would be out in the bay with the rest of the troops when I was finally released from KP.

That evening, after night mess, SSGT Nichelson called me to the Drill Sergeant's office. I was expecting the worst.

"Well, Private, have you learned anything from today's activities?" SSGT Nichelson asked.

"Yes, Sergeant, and I'm ready to move my gear to the bay."

SSGT Nichelson laughed and said, "You're not moving to the bay yet. I like your initiative and want you to pick another assistant. I'm moving Private Esgarcega to the second squad as their leader."

"Well," I said, feeling more back to normal, "I pick Private Di Muro."

"He'll be the third squad leader," SSGT Nichelson said,"Now pick another."

I thought for a minute, "Private Larry Jones."

"Jones will be the fourth squad leader. I decided to change all the others I picked but you and make Private Hollis the acting platoon guide and Private Niechlanski the assistant platoon guide. Now double time back to the barracks," SSGT Nichelson said.

Boy, did I. I was higher than a kite. Dodged a bullet. I didn't like losing three of my best squad members but staying the first squad leader felt great. I picked Private Horton to be my assistant. From then on, it was inspections, close order drill, dismounted drill, short arm drill, medical shots, marches, first aid training, field mess training, physical training, basic rifle marksmanship, M-14 rifle classroom training, bayonet training, chemical, biological and radiological training, close combat course, individual tactical training, hand to hand combat, rocket launcher training, obstacle course, automatic rifle training, hand grenade training, M-79 grenade launcher, mortar, recoilless rifle, machine-gun and 45- caliber pistol training all while learning how to low crawl through anything the sergeants could think of.

Of course the low crawl training did come in handy when under attack in a rice paddy full of human waste and muck. One day we were to crawl under barbed wire that was only eighteen inches off the ground and criss crossed for about 50 meters. While crawling with field packs, helmet, and rifles, we were under live fire from a machine-gun and simulated mortars.

All of us acting sergeants and corporals had to crawl first to show the rest of the platoon how to do it. We had done it once before and not under live fire. It was tough moving under those circumstances, and no one knew if he could do it until the time came. All of us made it through and then each squad went through one at a time. My job was to follow behind, without my pack and rifle, and help anyone who might have a problem.

As the squad started, everything was ok at first, until the mortars started going off. Several of the troopers froze, and I had to crawl next to each one and talk them into continuing. I only had to crawl back twice before the squad was finished. Only one of the trainees from the platoon refused to crawl and caught hell from the drill instructors.

GARY W. SUTTERN

During the cycle, we had several trainees who were trying to get a deferment for one reason or another, and they were pretty much ignored by the rest of us. One night, about half way through the cycle, I was awakened by one of my men.

He wanted me to go with him to see something. We went to the latrine where I found one of our platoon members lying in a pool of blood. He had slit his wrist with a straight razor. I sent the squad member down to the orderly room to tell the NCO on duty to call for help.

I called for help from the platoon guide and his assistant to bring towels to try to stop the flow of blood from the guy's wrists. The straight razor was lying next to him in the shower area. He was still breathing, but I couldn't get him to wake up. I could hear the ambulance coming, and several minutes later medics were there and took him to the hospital. We were never told how he did and never saw him again. Rumor had it he had three girlfriends in New York City, and all three were pregnant.

Graduation day finally arrived on February 3, 1967. I was promoted from private E-1 to private E-2, which increased my pay from $60 a month to $75. I also was awarded the sharp shooter's badge and good conduct ribbon along with everyone else. Ellen was able to drive up for the parade ceremony. She came with her Grandmother Zella. It was good to see them, if only for a few hours. SSGT Nichelson had a job for me that afternoon so the visit was cut short.

After a few days I was ordered to report to Pre OCS Infantry, across the post at Fort Ord, so much for the guaranteed OCS branch if you enlist. Private Jones was also ordered to the infantry; he was expecting to go to Engineer OCS. We trucked over to the infantry company by a deuce-and-a-half and got settled in.

Here I ran into the first example of friction between the branches of the service. One of the privates in my platoon had been in the Navy for several years and couldn't take the shipboard duty due to extreme seasickness. He asked for a transfer out of the Navy to the Army. The only way they would let him go was for him to accept a reduction in rank from E-4 to E-1. He still had several years on his enlistment, so he took it.

After four weeks of training, Private Jones and I were ordered to the orderly room to see the first sergeant. I knew I hadn't done anything to get into trouble so when he told us to report to the mess sergeant and relieve the KP troops, I was disheartened. We were to start map and compass training that day and to miss even one day made it hard to catch up. After the mid-day mess

12

was over the first sergeant entered the mess hall and told us to get packed. We were to report to the Battalion Headquarters to pick up our new orders to Combat Engineer training at Fort Leonard Wood in Missouri.

Jones and I were hooting and hollering. We double-timed back to the barracks and packed faster than ever before and then double-timed to the Battalion Headquarters. After being processed out, we were free the rest of the day until our flight at mid-night to Saint Louis, Missouri. We hotfooted it over to the Enlisted Men's Club (EM Club) to catch up on our beer drinking we'd missed while in basic. Somehow, we made it to the airport and caught our flight. We were both pretty looped and slept all the way. We landed at dawn to a cold, windy, stormy day.

We were directed to a two engine DC-3 for our flight to the post airport. The plane must have been of early World War Two vintage for some of the seats were ripped, and there were two seats on either side of the isle. We were both hung over as were a good many of the passengers. As we taxied to the runway, barf bags were passed out by the attendant. Apparently, she had been through these kinds of rides before.

We took off sideways because of the strong wind and had a very turbulent ride the entire trip. Several passengers became violently ill and spread their barf around the cabin. It was all I could do to keep from joining in. I looked around the cabin and most of the troops were green. Finally, we began to slow down and drop our elevation.

What a relief to see the woods coming slowly up to us. I could see the snow patches and smoke stacks of the fort buildings were belching thick blue black smoke, my first encounter with coal burning stoves. We made our first approach to land and since I had flown in small planes with Russ back in Southern California, I thought I was ready for the landing.

We touched down on the runway and began to slide to the right and then left. I could see what looked like ice on the tarmac as we raced down the runway. As we continued, the tail swung back and forth and several times I thought we were going off the runway. The pilot finally accelerated the engines, and we took off sideways again.

Several more troops barfed again and "Oh shit" was heard all over. We circled the airport several times, and I began to think how nice it would be back at Saint Louis. But that wasn't to be, and the pilot took us in for another try. This time we landed and managed to stay down and taxi to the terminal, a Quonset hut. I was sure the pilots were shaking as much as we were.

We got off the smelly plane and walked with rubber legs to the Quonset hut terminal. The wind was blowing a gale, and snowflakes were starting to fall. I smelled something foreign to me, a strong, heavy odor like sulfur. I asked the soldier at the terminal desk, "What's that stink?"

"Why, where you from, boy, ain't you ever smelt coal burning? Welcome to good old Fort Leonard Wood," he said with a big toothy grin.

I showed him our orders and asked, "Where do we go from here?"

He pointed up the road and said we were about a mile from the Third Battalion Headquarters. So Jones and I got our duffel bags and decided to walk. Before starting we dug into our bags and got out our overcoats. I believe I hadn't been this cold in my life. Jones neither. He was from San Diego, California.

We walked slowly up the road and finally got our legs back. This was mid-February 1967, and the trees were dead looking with dried leaves still clinging to the branches. These were oak trees and I wasn't used to that either. I wasn't happy to be there.

Only time and good friendship in meeting new people from all across the United States would remedy the blues. We got to the headquarters and because we were early for our assignment, we were ordered to Charlie Company and told to change into our fatigues and police the area of cigarette butts and any other trash. We had been told by the first sergeant, because we were of E-2 ranking and the first to arrive for the cycle and had been acting squad leaders in basic, we would lead there too.

We went to the assigned barracks and stowed our gear. It was good to get out of the Class "A" uniforms. Apparently we weren't fast enough for the corporal in charge because he came looking for us and chewed our butts off. After our cleanup was over, we were told to stay in the barracks until midday chow at 1200 hours. Things were looking up.

Jones and I were feeling pretty good about the leadership positions and back at the barracks, while kicking back on our bunks, we were reminiscing about the good old days in basic, now that we were veterans.

In walks the first sergeant yelling, "What the hell are yo two doin' layin' on yo bunks with yo boots on? Dint yo mama tech yo nothin' at home, boys? Get yo gear and repot to Alpha Company on the double, their cycle starts tomorrow, there's room fo yo hicks."

We grabbed our gear from the wall lockers and footlockers and hustled over to Alpha Company. We were the last to arrive here and were stuck in the second platoon. The barracks was full of troops by now, and we received a cold reception as some were already figuring on using the open space for their own. We were both assigned to the fourth squad by the drill instructor,

Sergeant First Class Troxell. (This sergeant was to become my platoon sergeant when I was commissioned a second lieutenant and returned to this same company six months later.)

These barracks were of World War Two vintage made of stick frame and heated by a coal-burning boiler. Our squad was on the second floor. Jones and I got settled in and began our training the next day. During the first week, several trainees were giving the squad leaders trouble. I went down to the acting platoon sergeants' room after a day of problems to offer my help to keep the unruly ones in line.

The acting platoon sergeant thanked me for the offer and said he felt he and his squad leaders could manage. He also said he was surprised I came to him and his assistant as they were just discussing the probable trouble-makers and I was mentioned.

I asked why, and he said just from my looks. I told him looks don't mean anything, it's actions that count. He agreed and thanked me for the offer.

I had to lean on some of my fellow trainees to get them to co-operate with the platoon leaders and after the eight weeks of training, we all graduated. I was promoted to E-3, private first class.

This bumped my monthly pay up to $90.00 and gave me my first stripe on the uniform. It also gave me my first taste of actual authority over lower ranks. I had to wait several weeks for my assignment to OCS, and I was assigned to a holding company where we were sent to different training companies or sites to work. Several times, I was in charge of a squad.

While waiting for my orders, Ellen and I were trying to decide on our wedding plans. I was supposed to get a thirty-day leave after the end of the last training, and we were going to get married then. The Army had other plans and kept me at Fort Leonard Wood while they decided my next assignment. Finally the orders arrived, and I was to report to Fort Belvoir, Virginia for the start of OCS at the Engineer Regiment. With the assignment came a two-week leave, so Ellen and I decided to try to get married during that time.

She made the arrangements at home in Anaheim and sent out the invitations to friends and relatives. I flew to my parents' home in Las Cruces, New Mexico, and drove my mom and aunt out to California for the wedding. We were married on a Saturday, May 13, 1967 and spent three days on our honeymoon in Laguna Beach until I had to leave for the East Coast.

I drove to Fort Belvoir and found an apartment for Ellen where she could live after she completed her school year. I reported to the Officer Candidate

Regiment where I was assigned to a holding barracks to wait for the next cycle to begin. I had been promoted to the rank of sergeant, E-5, and my pay had been increased to $354.00 a month.

CHAPTER 2
OFFICER COMMISSION

At Officer Candidate School orientation, all the new candidates were introduced to their respective tactical officers, and we were informed of the company we would be assigned. I was assigned to Alpha Company, fourth platoon. There were 120 candidates assigned to each company, 60 to each platoon with the expectation of graduating less than 50 by the end of the 23 week training period. The first and second platoons were the upper classmen who were now in their junior class phase. This means they had completed twelve weeks of training and seen their upper class graduate the week before.

As soon as the orientation time was over, the harassment began with the arrival of our upper classmen. At OCS, a candidate starts off as a smack bean—restricted to the regimental training area for at least twelve weeks with no privileges, no respect or time of his own, and a shaved head so everyone resembles everyone else. So you are smacked in and look like a bean.

A candidates' first twelve weeks consists of mainly military drilling in marching, physical training to prepare you for the proficiency testing every week, combat field training for under fire situations, and an escape and evasion course to be taken during hell week at Fort A.P. Hill, Virginia during the eleventh week of training (if you make it that far). All during this time, you are constantly harassed by your upper classmen who just love to surround each candidate and yell orders from each side.

All the orders are different and each time you try to comply with an order you are yelled at by the other upper classmen for not complying with his orders. This caused ringing in the ears and a headache. I guess the pressure was to simulate being under fire from explosives during combat. (I suffered the same physical effects in Viet Nam during such combat.) At least in combat you're not being given orders, you are expected to *give* orders.

Push-ups and low crawling on the company gravel were the order of the day. It was the job of the upper classmen to indoctrinate each new candidate to the normal procedures of each day at the regiment, and to help weed out the poor candidates, who in their opinion, were not worthy of being an officer in the US Army. As if they were any smarter at knowing this than the next person. Just because they had made it to this level in their cycle didn't. It only showed how much harassment they had endured and could dish out to the next cycle. Not all the upper classmen were harassment happy.

I vowed not to pass this harassment on to my under classmen if I got to the upper class level. The reason I make note of this is you don't get to OCS until you go through several written tests, oral boards at each level of training (basic, advanced, pre OCS training and a recommendation from each company commander and battalion commander you were under.) Also at the time I went through OCS, you were required to have completed at least two years of college.

During the 23 weeks of training, not only did you have to pass your classroom training and observations from the tactical officers, but you also had to pass the evaluation of your fellow candidates every two weeks. So you had to be on your best behavior and co-operation around everyone. Even those you could not stand at first. Everyone was in the same boat and the quickest way to get booted out of OCS was to cause problems with your fellow candidates. Everyone was instructed to observe his fellow candidate in every aspect of training so as to give the fairest evaluation at each review. These evaluations were kindly known as BAYONET SHEETS, so called because if enough candidates zeroed in on the same candidate in a negative review that could mean the end of his training at the regiment.

One of the fastest ways of being dropped from the regiment during the first weeks was a bad bayonet sheet from your classmates or upper classmen. The tactical officers had the last say on your dismissal but during the first twelve weeks it seemed to be left to the upper classmen more than the tactical officers.

I had better clarify what I mean by tactical officers before we proceed. The tactical officer was either a first or second lieutenant with only one or two years experience in the Army themselves, only just beginning to find their own way in the military. Our lead tactical officer was a first lieutenant who had remained at the regiment after his graduation and had been there for fourteen months. He was promoted after his first year in rank as a second lieutenant (which is were you start when commissioned). The first lieutenant was ok and treated everyone fairly.

The other officer was a second lieutenant who had recently graduated from the Armor OCS Regiment and had prior military training as a drill instructor. He liked to treat everyone like dirt and continued to do so the entire 23 weeks, so much for the tactical officers.

During the first few weeks, my ears constantly rang from the yelling of the upper classmen and the lack of sleep. Many nights the platoon was awakened by upper classmen and battalion officers who were chasing someone from another company who was bringing in unauthorized food or was on a mission of some sort and had been off the regimental boundaries.

During the early weeks of training, military procedures were taught during meal time with eating an incentive to learn. Many days the entire table of underclassmen went without food until we learned the correct orders of certain maneuvers, such as marching in formation or correct military procedure in requesting a specific item. This is why food, also known as pogy bait, was smuggled into the company area during the dead of night.

Several times, during my days as an upperclassman, while assigned as a battalion level officer, I would respond to a commotion caused by other upperclassmen who were chasing an underclassman carrying pogy bait. In one incident, the upperclassmen from Bravo Company had caught their under class with a laundry bag full of hamburgers. I made the upper class give the bag back to the under class and leave the barracks.

Another time a White Elephant (large white food catering truck that delivered food to the field sites cadre) was caught backed up to the window of a company in the Third Battalion. The entire under class nearly were expelled for that mission.

During our underclass days, the upperclass would issue us missions we were expected to carry out. One such mission was to beautify our lawn and barracks exterior. Several of us on the lawn team decided to raid the post golf course for green sod. The golf course was across the street from our parade grounds. So in the dead of night several of us made our way to the golf course and acquired some sod.

The next morning, while we were in training, a military police officer, looking for the sod, happened to see it in the form of our new lawn. Our company commander was contacted, and we were told to return the sod that night, under cover of darkness, or we would be in deep trouble. Apparently the day after we took the sod, the commanding general of Fort Belvoir and some congressmen had played a round of golf and made the discovery. I suppose we disrupted their game.

During the first twelve weeks, Ellen arrived, and I could only see her once a week for a few minutes. Each platoon was expected to have a flag guidon and since she could sew I talked her into making us a real nice flag. This we carried everywhere to identify our platoon.

At our eleventh week, we were transported down to Camp AP Hill for hell week. By this time our platoon had suffered about a 50% reduction. Each week the candidate leadership positions were changed to give everyone the chance to be in that role.

During hell week, the candidate who was placed in the platoon leader position decided to play god. He must have been sleeping during the previous ten weeks when the words co-operation were so commonly used. He used his authority to command everyone to do his bidding. Several times during forced marches he was offered the use of a jeep instead of marching with the rest of us. He chose the jeep, and we chose the bayonet sheets.

During hell week, we had decided to leave the flag back at the barracks, as we had no need to identify ourselves there and didn't want to get it soiled. One of our candidates had been bayoneted out the Friday we left and apparently took the flag as a souvenir. This really pissed us off when we returned.

We learned infantry formations and maneuvers while bivouacked in the hills. Hell week was in August, and it was hot and muggy. At the last of the week, we were to go through an escape and evasion course. We all paired up and were given a map and compass. We were transported at night by deuce-and-a-half to different locations and dropped off to find our way back to the company base camp.

This was cross-country, through woods and a swamp, with several streams to ford. That day and night was overcast and rain fell from time to time. As my partner and I started, we decided to join up with another pair. The clouds broke from time to time, and there was a full moon to give us some light. We had pen light flashlights to illuminate our maps and compass. We had to watch out for the *enemy* who were looking for us and salivating at the thought of capturing and torturing anyone they could.

We came up to the first road that crossed our path. I crawled to the side of the road and looked up and down for any sign of the enemy. None. We decided to check the map and got out a poncho to cover us when we used our penlights. We all were under the poncho looking at the map. I looked out, checking for any sounds, and saw lights approaching from the trail we had just come from.

I alerted the others, and we ran across the road and hid under a grove of pine trees. The lights turned out to be fireflies dancing on the breeze. While lying under the trees we heard a truck approaching. The truck stopped several meters past us and several enemy soldiers got out.

One enemy yelled, "Ok we've got you, come out with your hands up."

Everyone froze, and I wondered how they had seen us from that distance. Then a dark figure stood up next to the road and gave up. We didn't even know he was there. The enemy took him and left. His partner slowly crawled in our direction. We said the password as he got to us, and he replied the correct answer. Turns out the man who was captured was one of my friends, and the enemy hadn't known he was there either. They just stopped from time to time and called to anyone who might be there to see if they would surrender. Later when I asked him of his ordeal, he said he wished he had stayed in the ditch.

We now had five in the team and continued on. Here the woods became very dark, and we had to move very close. Each of us behind the leader had to hold on to the pack ahead to stay up. As we moved we could hear a stream of water running; the sound got louder and louder. I was number two in line, suddenly the man I was holding onto just vanished. It was pitch black, and I had to turn on my penlight to see. Our point man had stepped off a six- foot bank and fallen into the stream. Luckily the stream wasn't too deep or wide, and he was ok.

At dawn, we finally made it back to the base camp. Several of our candidates had been caught. Only one had surrendered and was unmercifully ribbed for it. Several of the men had suffered broken bones trying to evade the enemy. They spent several weeks in the hospital and were recycled. My team made it through without injury or detection. We cleaned up the area and left for the regiment that morning.

We returned to an empty company. Our upperclassmen had graduated the day we left for AP Hill. Our next duty was the bayonet sheets. Only one man was unanimously bayoneted out of the regiment, our fearless leader at AP Hill. The following week we were promoted to the junior level phase of the cycle and issued white tabs to go under the brass OCS on our collars.

Now it was our turn to be the upperclassmen. We were given one week to prepare for the under class. Our job here was to thoroughly clean the first and second platoons barracks and decide how we were to train the new candidates. I had already decided how I was going to treat them and left the more vindictive ones to the harassment. When we turned junior, we were given pass privileges on the weekends. Unfortunately for me, I was always working off demerits from the tactical officers and very seldom got a pass. When I did it was great to be with my wife, even if only for a few hours.

When I was assigned to the underclass second platoon as their platoon leader for a week I instructed them on learning the nomenclature of their rifles and map reading. I didn't harass anyone. We were now being assigned to higher levels in the company and battalion levels. This gave us a broader sense of the normal duties of being an officer.

We were going on more field exercises now. After a grueling run one morning we were standing in formation outside our barracks waiting to be dismissed. The tactical officers had been on the run, and the second lieutenant decided we didn't have enough exercise, so we were to do a little uniform change drill. We were ordered to fall out and change into our class "A" uniforms, complete with brass and medals. This we had to accomplish in five minutes. Everyone ran into the barracks and amid much cussing got changed.

Several candidates were too slow, so we all had to go back in and change into clean fatigues with our field gear and packs. Again we were to do this in five minutes. The last man out the door was met with a barrage of harassment from the second lieutenant. He picked up a rolled up poncho from the ground and threw it at the candidate to show his disgust for his slowness. Murphy's Law intervened. The roll hit the candidate square in the head and knocked him cold.

The atmosphere suddenly changed, and the second lieutenant was transformed into a caring person. The first lieutenant called the orderly room and sent for a medic. We helped carry the candidate into the barracks. That was the end of the drill and that kind of harassment ended. The candidate finally regained consciousness and was ok.

During a night mission, we were to surround our sister platoon, who was protecting a hill. During our approach we were walking in single file, five meters apart on a dirt road; we were circling the hill. Our first lieutenant decided to hide in the ditch to the left behind brush. If we all passed him without detecting him, he was going to set off a ground flare to mark our approach. I was the last in line, and as I approached his position, I happened to look in his direction.

He must have thought I saw him, so he began to move toward me. I ordered him to halt and when he didn't, I fired my rifle in his direction. We were using blank shells, and I didn't think there was any danger. I didn't realize how close he was due to the darkness. I fired several rounds before he yelled for me to cease firing. I thought he was the enemy from our sister platoon. We were all wearing fatigues with the sleeves down. The first lieutenant was wearing a black tee shirt. The powder from the blanks shot out and burned him on the face and arms. He was taken to the base hospital.

My firing had started a chain reaction, and several of our platoon members began firing toward the hill. This caused the sister platoon to shift their position toward us and enabled our other squads to walk right into their camp and capture the hill. When we got back to the barracks, I figured I was going to be punished for shooting our tactical officer. Instead, he was there and praised me for being alert and seeing him before he had a chance to trip the flare. (A similar thing happened to a captain in Viet Nam while on a night patrol that nearly cost him his life.)

I was very lucky not to become a casualty during our training. During another patrol, I nearly broke my leg. I was walking point, the daylight was fading fast, and we stopped at the side of a road. I asked the squad leader which way he wanted to go, and he pointed across the road to a thick wooded area. I looked for enemy up and down the road and made a quick crossing. The far side of the road appeared to slope down and was covered by vines. When I got to the side of the road I stepped into the vines and went down butt first into a road culvert. I landed on a corner of a large timber, hitting on my right hip. I ended hanging upside down in the stream with my legs caught on the timbers.

The squad rushed to my aid and got me down. The leader called for a medic and ambulance. I told him to wait and let me try to walk it off. After several minutes, the pain subsided, and I was able to stay. Lucky! Lucky! Lucky! I had several more close calls before our graduation day.

We graduated on November 3rd, 1967 on a brilliant, bright autumn day. Ellen and I left for home on our thirty-day leave and then it was on to my first assigned duty at Fort Leonard Wood. It was cold, and snow was threatening the day we arrived at the fort. Similar to my first arrival except this time I was on the ground in a car. I reported to the First Brigade as ordered and was assigned to the Third Battalion. I reported to the Commanding Officer, Lieutenant Colonel Kenneth McLey. He looked over my records and decided to send me to Alpha Company where I had gone through training earlier in the year. I reported to the Commanding Officer, Captain Bruce Hartshorn. He assigned me to the second platoon to be their platoon leader.

Second Lieutenant Gary W. Suffern in dress blues at Fort Leonard Wood, Missouri, 1967.

The first sergeant called for the platoon sergeant to come to the orderly room to meet his new lieutenant. When the sergeant entered the room, I was surprised to see Sergeant First Class Troxell. He was still here and was to be my platoon sergeant. I asked him if he remembered me. He did. I asked if he was ok with me now being his platoon leader and having to take orders from a former trainee. He said he was ok with that, and he hoped we had got along when I was here before. I said I had no problems with him being my platoon sergeant. During my time here, we became friends.

Ellen and I were housed in the NCO area because of a shortage of officer housing. We weren't the only ones and had many fun nights with our neighbors, also a second lieutenant and his wife. We played cards almost every night and made up our own rules. Shortly after our arrival, we found out Ellen was pregnant with our first daughter who was born in August of 1968 just before I left for Viet Nam.

Soon after arriving in Alpha Company the commander and executive officer were ordered to Viet Nam. The new company commander was a first lieutenant who had a very acute problem with his nerves around senior officers. This caused some problems when the battalion commander would drop by for reveille or other training sites and find he was not present. I ran into this same problem with a company commander in Viet Nam. The battalion commander would call the first lieutenant to the headquarters almost weekly for a chat about his shaky nerves and absence from the company when he should be there.

I was sent to a teaching class after a disastrous attempt to teach a class for the entire battalion staff about holiday safety. I learned much from the master sergeant who taught the class, which has helped me to this day. After finishing the class, I was assigned to teach the map and compass course for Alpha Company and later the battalion. I learned much in the course myself, which helped me tremendously in Viet Nam. After seven months in Alpha Company, I was assigned to the brigade staff as a range officer for a new fire and movement Viet Nam Training Range.

I was assigned to Captain Teague, who was to start the program and build the ranges. I was the first to be assigned and was to run the only movement range where live ammunition was to be fired during the movement. Captain Teague and I flew to Fort Polk, Louisiana to observe the ranges they were using and get ideas on how to run ours.

This was the end of June and first week in July, so the weather was very hot and muggy. I was glad to get back to Fort Leonard Wood on the third of

July. The heat was hot here too but not as muggy. Ellen was eight months pregnant and in misery.

There were to be four ranges, and I had the fourth. When we got back, I went to my range and found it was nearly complete. I decided to make several posters of the range and how we would maneuver through it. One morning the post commander, a general, stopped by with our brigade commander for an inspection of the new training range. I showed him the posters and described how we were to run the range. The general declined to walk through the mile course, and left for the other ranges. Later Captain Teague told me the other range officers hadn't been at their ranges, causing an embarrassment to the colonel. They heard about it later and nearly lost their positions.

Here again I was in the right place, even though I should have been there, I might not have been. The range procedure was for two squads of men to start on line and walk through the woods until targets popped up. They would then fire at the targets until all were hit; a machine gun simulator was fired when targets were activated by a sergeant in the control tower to the right rear. A safety officer was required to go through the course with each group. This meant I had to go every other time. I lost a lot of weight.

After the first targets were shot up, the squads would move through more woods and finally come to a hill. Targets would pop up along the crest of the hill, and the squad was supposed to assault the hill and end up on the top. This took too long, and we ended up just shooting at the targets from a distance of several hundred meters. One morning we had reached the hill and began to fire when a plane suddenly flew up over the hill coming right at us. Before I could get the troops to stop firing, I could hear bullets hitting the plane.

I called the sergeant in the range tower and gave him the identification number of the plane. I had the sergeant call the post airport to find out if that's where the plane came from, and check on the occupants' condition. We always had a large red flag flying when we were live firing and also notified the airport terminal to warn anyone from flying in the area. Later Captain Teague told me the plane was being flown by a congressman's pilot and he and the post commander had been in the plane sight seeing that morning.

The plane had been hit several times. But not seriously and none of the passengers had been hit. It did shake them up a bit. Shortly after that, Ellen gave birth to our daughter. We named her Revallee Ann. The next week I received orders to move to the officers' quarters across the post. A day or two later, I received orders for Viet Nam. The brigade commander rescinded the orders to relocate on the post, as I was to leave in only two weeks.

CHAPTER 3
VIET NAM

Ellen and I packed our meager belongings and along with Revallee and Jack the cat, we left Fort Leonard Wood and headed home to southern California. We stopped for several days in Las Cruces, New Mexico, so my parents could enjoy their new granddaughter, and then we went on to Anaheim. I had thirty days leave and spent as much time with the family as I could before flying to Travis Air Force Base in northern California.

It was very hard to leave, and when the day came, tears flowed. I flew commercial jet to Oakland and met up with Dave Escarcega, who was just back from Nam, and working for the Graves Registration. He said to keep my head down and good luck. I left Travis at night, and after a stop in Hawaii and Guam, we landed in Ben Hoa Air Base in mid afternoon.

When the door of the plane was opened, the heat hit us like a blast furnace. Sweat instantly developed and the smell of human waste hung heavy in the air. We were told to exit the plane as fast as possible as Charlie (Viet Cong) had lobbed a few mortars earlier, and he liked to use the commercial jets as target practice. We scampered down the ladder and across the tarmac to the terminal. The heat made it difficult to move.

The Air Force sergeant at the terminal welcomed us to Viet Nam and said a bus would be here shortly to take us to the Army relocation camp at Long Bien. I was still a second lieutenant and had been told by my brigade commander I was being promoted to first lieutenant, and the orders would follow me to Nam. I was anxious to take off the gold bar and replace it with a silver bar. A captain was close by with many ribbons on his chest including the Viet Nam Service Medal and several Purple Hearts. He had been here before. I introduced myself and asked for some advice on staying alive.

He said to keep my eyes open and rely on my sergeants to help get me through the first few months. By then I should have enough experience to get me through, if I didn't get shot before then. The captain had been here two other tours, one as a sergeant and the other as a second lieutenant. He was with the Special Forces working with the mountain tribes on the Laotian and Cambodia borders. He was just returning from a thirty day leave after his promotion to captain. He invited me to tag along, and he would show me the ropes at the relocation center.

Several hours later, a blue Air Force bus drove up to the terminal, and we were advised to board for the trip to Long Bien. The windows of the bus were covered with heavy chain link fencing. The captain told me this kept the local Charlies from lobbing grenades through the windows, which they had done in the past. That would sure be a hell of a welcome on your first day in country. We rode on dirt roads through a maze of shanty buildings, some tin, some part stucco. Vietnamese were everywhere along the road, and I constantly watched in anticipation of a grenade flying through the air. I suspect the captain was reading my mind as he had a big grin on his face. He told me to relax. This was going to be a piece of cake.

We finally drove through a gate and stopped at the relocation center barracks and orientation buildings. We were assigned a barracks and after dropping off our bags and changing into state side fatigues (the captain already had his jungle fatigues) we headed to the Officers Club to get some cool beers and supper. It was 1800 hours (6 PM), and we didn't have any meetings until the next morning.

That night I had a very disturbing dream. I was being chased by a bright light in a very dark forest. I was finally trapped, and as the light drew near, I yelled, "NOOOOOO!" I woke up. I was sitting up, looking around and didn't know where I was for several minutes. Finally, the smells and heat reminded me I was in Nam; several minutes later, I drifted off to sleep. The next morning at morning mess, I heard several officers talking about the guy who was yelling in his sleep. I didn't fess up. The captain knew and said not to worry. Nam had that kind of effect on everyone, and their turn would come soon enough.

The captain already had his orders and was to leave for the Central Highlands that morning. Before he left, he told me to stay calm under fire, use my common sense, and keep my head down. He wished me good luck and then was gone.

All us FNGs (fuckin' new guys) were trucked to the supply depot to get our Viet Nam uniforms. These were fatigues, boots, sox and hats. No weapons or other field gear was issued here. That would come at our final duty station. So here we were to travel inside Nam from place to place without personal protection. We went to a tailor shop to have our rank insignia sewn on. I told the Vietnamese I was a first lieutenant and had black bars sewn on the collar instead of a brown bar. I caught a little flack from my first commander when I finally was promoted.

That afternoon was an orientation where our ration cards were issued along with a short explanation of some of the Viet Nam culture. We were introduced to several words and their meanings:
"lie da"—"come here" (to be used with the wave of the hand not a finger which was an insult)
"di di mau"—"let's get out of here" (used with rapid feet movement during a fire fight) "Beaucoup"—"many" (used like many VC, by the locals)
"dinky dau"—"crazy" (used like you're crazy for disarming mines)
"Chieu Hoi"—government program that encouraged enemy soldiers to come over to the South Vietnam side. (Sometimes yelled at the enemy during a firefight.)

We were told to be wary of Vietnamese who approached unless we knew or had worked with them. The VC liked to send children packed with explosives into a crowd of GIs and blow everyone to bits. Another favorite was to pack explosives into the tubing of a bicycle and have a child or women ride up to a formation and leave the bike. The fragmentation from the thin metal tubing caused an awful wound.

Finally, the next morning my name was on the assignment manifest to fly to Cam Rahn Bay for my first duty station. Several of us left by mid morning and took the bus ride back to Ben Hoa. As we arrived, explosions started to hit the runway toward the far end. The terminal sergeant yelled not to worry.

Charlie was just probing with his mortars and didn't usually get close to the terminal. The Army perimeter guards kept him moving. Sure enough after several mortars hit, all was quiet.

A C140 transport plane was taxiing in about this time, and the sergeant said that was our ride to Cam Rhan Bay. The back end of the plane lowered, and several men walked off and we walked on. The flight was short and gave us a look at the country. The day was clear and hot. As we landed, the heat waves caused the plane to bounce several times. One of the FNGs with us got sick. We were trucked to an Engineer base camp on the north side of the bay.

We were told to relax for a while, as it would probably be several days before we would be assigned to the next stop. I dumped my gear and looked for the Officers' Club. I spent most of my time drinking cheap mix drinks and talking to the veterans in the club. That night one of the veterans invited me to another club at another base camp.

We hopped a ride with a supply truck heading in that direction. At the gates of the different camps were guards who just waved everyone through. The perimeters here had lights shining out. At the gates were Vietnamese holding what looked like birds on a string. The birds turned out to be large moths the size of parakeets. The veteran told me the Vietnamese sold the moths for food. I watched one being sold, and the buyer pulled the wings off the moth and ate it as is.

Each night a movie was shown, *Hang 'Em High* with Clint Eastwood. This must have been the only movie in country as we saw this movie everywhere. I watched the movie every night I was there, as there wasn't anything else to do. By the third day, I was beginning to wonder if I would get an assignment. I was finally called to the personnel office. The major who assigned the duty said I was the ranking officer of the three there that day and had my choice of assignment. Only catch was he wouldn't say where the unit was located or what type of duty. All he would say was the number of the Command Group.

When I was a training officer at Fort Leonard Wood, the veteran sergeants from Nam told me if I had a choice to pick the highest number Command Group for the best duty. So I picked the 395th. I was assigned to Plieku to their headquarters for further assignment. After I left the building, a veteran at the Officers Club asked what unit I was going to. I told him, and he just shook his head, and said Beaucoup VC there. Great! The other two officers were assigned to units here at Cam Rahn Bay. Well at least I wasn't going to be referred to as a REMF (rear echelon mother fucker).

I hopped on a plane the next day and headed for the Central Highlands. Maybe I would see the captain I met the first day, as that was where he was going. Never did! We landed on a runway cut into the jungle. The thick trees were right up against the runway on the south side. The north side was clearer and had bare red earth hills. I could see infantry base camps on several hills surrounded by wire. The infantry were in their foxholes, some covered with ponchos.

When I walked to the terminal, a small-framed building, the sergeant there told me a truck from the main base camp would be along shortly. The deuce-and-a-half arrived, and the driver told me and the other replacements we would be heading back to the main camp as soon as a convoy came along. Here in this area no one dared to go on the road without an escort. This was a free fire zone, and Charlie was very active. Great, here we were with no weapons or field gear for protection. The driver said not to worry, if we did get into an ambush, just hug the floor in the back and pray.

I noticed there were sand bags on the floorboards in the cab. I asked why and he said for protection from land mines. No sand bags were on the floor of the back deck of the truck. Wonderful! Finally a convoy approached, and the driver started the truck and yelled for us all to get on. We climbed into the back and got settled.

The convoy was escorted by Military Police in jeeps at the front and rear. They had a machine gun mounted on a post and a gun operator standing on the back deck. Also here and there were Armor Personnel Carriers with three machine guns and several "deuce-and-a-halves" with quad fifties mounted in an open bed turret in the back. The signs on the trucks said *Have Guns Will Travel* and *Traveling Guns*.

Traveling Guns, also known as Have Guns Will Travel. Quad 50-caliber machineguns mounted on a turret on the back of a deuce-and-a-half truck bed, 1968.

When there was a gap in the line our driver quickly took the space. The road was dusty, and everyone was quickly covered with red dust. As the convoy moved along, there were the fast times and slow times. I kept watching out to see as much of the terrain as I could. Daylight was fading, and

I was getting more and more tense as the captain had told me dusk was Charlie's favorite time for an ambush on a convoy. As we approached the main base camp, suddenly I could heard gunfire up ahead. The driver yelled back to us to get down and hang on.

We all dropped to the floor. The firing got louder, and as we entered the kill zone, several bullets hit the sides of the truck and passed through. No one was hit, and we made it to the gate. As we stopped at the Group Headquarters, I watched as several helicopters flew over the area we just passed and hosed down the jungled hills with their machine guns and rockets. Several MPs had been hit and were being medevaced out. A medevac helicopter had no machine guns, only a big red cross of a target on the nose of the ship and on the sides; the pilots of the medevac were very courageous.

The duty officer at the headquarters told me to get settled in one of the barracks bunkers and showed me an underground bunker near the headquarters bunker to go to in case of a mortar or rocket attack. That night a rocket attack came, and everyone in the living bunker I was in ran to the underground bunker nearby. We all stayed there until an all-clear siren sounded. I noticed no perimeter lights were at this base camp. That kept the guards on their toes.

The next morning a personnel officer assigned several of the FNGs, me included, to a helicopter-repelling course. I had no idea what was coming and didn't ask. I was thinking, as we made our way to the helicopter pad, *this must be to show us how to get off the chopper at the landing zones* (LZs). We all gathered around the instructor sergeant. He was wearing a leg harness, and I hadn't seen that on anyone jumping off a chopper on the ground.

He explained that we were being trained to repel from the height of one to three hundred feet. We would slide down a rope, through the thick jungle canopy, cut and secure a landing zone for the infantry. As an officer, my job was to go down first to check the area before the rest of the platoon were lowered. He explained I wouldn't be going alone. A squad of men would be there with me, but I was required to go first. GREAT!

We worked on the proper technique for the drop and did so several times to get cleared by him for the job. I really didn't want the job but had no choice. The next day I was assigned to a platoon. The platoon leader, a first lieutenant, said this would be a piece of cake, a walk in the park. He would go down first with me close behind.

We harnessed up on the way in. We were riding in a Chinook helicopter and had the entire platoon aboard, about 30 men. By this time I had been

32

issued my field gear and an M16 rifle. We finally arrived at a site above a triple canopy jungle. I couldn't see through to the ground. The lieutenant said it would take me a while to get use to the drop through the trees. Later, he told me Charlie doesn't shoot at us while we're on the ropes. He waits until the infantry are on the ground and then tries to drop a chopper on the zone by rocket fire.

We dropped down into the trees. As we lowered, the lieutenant looked around below for a suitable site for the cut. Sometimes the LZ has to be moved from the original drop. This time we were able to cut here. After enough trees were cleared, I could hear many choppers circling over the area. Soon a yellow smoke was popped, and the choppers began to lower to the LZ; a company of infantry (grunts) were brought in. The engineer platoon had been placed around the LZ for security.

After the grunts were down and the last chopper left, a Chinook chopper landed to drop off supplies. I was getting ready to board the Chinook. The lieutenant said no, we would drop our tools off on the chopper and then move to another LZ site the grunts marked on the map. We would secure that site for the grunts and be around for them as a back up if they got into trouble. After the Chinook left, the infantry moved out. We stayed for a while and then moved in another direction.

I thought it was odd that we were to move in a set direction given by the infantry captain. I found out later we were to move through a known stronghold of the enemy as bait. If we were hit, then the infantry, who were waiting on either side of the valley, would come to our rescue. No one in the engineer platoon was happy about this arrangement. I asked the lieutenant how many times the company commander, a captain, went on these hikes. NEVER!

We moved slowly and were called several times by the infantry commander to pick up the pace. Everyone felt like they were mere cannon fodder, and the tension was high. We made it to the pickup point without any contact with Charlie. After we got back to the base camp, I went to the captain to have a little chat about the situation. He told me to obey my orders and keep my mouth shut, and I would get along fine here.

I was assigned to another drop in the morning with a different platoon. I turned to the captain and said, "See you in the field tomorrow?" I got no reply.

The next day we dropped into a previously cut LZ and secured the area. The infantry dropped two companies. Two Chinook choppers came in to drop supplies. The first came in and off loaded quickly. The second dropped in and as the pilot flared to land a rocket streaked across the LZ and hit the chopper in the belly. The chopper dropped to the ground and hit the trees on one side throwing wood and metal all over.

All hell broke loose, and Charlie seemed to be everywhere.

POP, POP, POP, SWISH BANG, POP, POP, POP.

Rifles were firing in every direction, and rockets were crossing from several spots around the LZ. Red tracers from our rifles and green tracers from Charlies' flew through the air in every direction including up. Smoke from the chopper and rifles and rockets drifted over the LZ. The chopper smoldered at first and then broke into a burst of flame. The supplies of ammunition began to cook off.

The flying shrapnel hit quite a few grunts and engineers. The grunt commanders called in artillery on the outer perimeter of the LZ. The lieutenant I was with told me we might have to call in artillery on the LZ and to get ready. Sure I know what to do, don't I? Suddenly Charlie broke off the attack and left. Quiet dropped on the LZ like a fog. Only the last snaps of the burning chopper were heard. I finally regained my hearing enough to hear the sound of moaning and whimpering. Looking over the LZ, I saw body after body.

Near me I saw the back of the lieutenant I was with. He was lying face down. Blotchy blood was all over the uniform. I grabbed his flack vest and rolled him over. His head separated from his body. His eyes were half open and dull, no shine or sparkle; he was dead. Close by was the platoon sergeant with bloody holes all over his front. He was on his back and his head was tilted back, his mouth open. I went to him and saw no head above his eyes. Looking around other bodies appeared similar in butchering.

I thought to myself this must have been what my family's friends and relatives went through the first time they were in bloody combat in World War Two. No wonder they didn't talk about it. Several had invited my wife and I to dinner before I left and wished me all the luck. The engineer platoon had been pulled back into the LZ to drop off their tools on the last chopper before continuing the mission. We were gathered all around the outer fringes in the LZ when the chopper went down. There was nowhere to go to get away from the chopper.

The wounds on the men didn't look like bullets. Large gashes cut across the uniforms; some were nearly decapitated. The men died in grotesque positions. Some still had jagged pieces of chopper lodged in their skin. I noticed the captain yelling to his platoons to regroup and make ready for a counter attack. I helped the medics check the rest of the men on the perimeter. Most were dead or dying. I was amazed that six of us were still standing without a scratch. Many had been hit by the chopper and burned. The crew was nearly burned to nothing. Burnt flesh smell was heavy near the chopper. I would smell this often in my tour. I still can!

One of the engineers came over to help, and I noticed blood splattered on his uniform. He looked at me and pointed to pieces of flesh and bone on mine. I looked down at the front of my flack vest and saw blotches of blood, bone, flesh and pieces of the chopper stuck in the fiber.

Then I noticed the smell of blood everywhere. Blood, smoke, gunpowder and dirt. Most of the engineer platoon had been hit. The rest of the day was spent getting the wounded and dead out of the LZ. I was ordered to remain with what was left of the engineer platoon and support the infantry for the night. The infantry captain assigned me to one of his platoons.

We dug in for the night. The platoon leader, a second lieutenant, motioned me over to his foxhole and asked how long I had been in country. When I told him, he grinned and said lowly, FNG. I asked him if this happened often. He said about once a month. I asked if he had ever seen the engineer company commander out here.

He said, "Not *Tommy Two Bars*." He explained that was the designation of any captain who sent his men out in the field but wouldn't join them.

He said he hadn't seen too many *Tommy Two Bars* yet, but he had been here only two months. I asked him about the set plan of movement, and he said we were the designated bait by order of the division commander. I didn't get much sleep that night. My ears were ringing, and the smell of death hung heavy in the air. Just when I thought my nose had got used to it a slight breeze would blow through, and new smells would emerge.

At dawn, we were ordered to move to another LZ where my platoon (all six of us) would be picked up and return to Plieku. The move through the jungle was slow and hot. Wait-a-minute vines were everywhere, going in all directions, and men stumbled with every step. Many cursed with each grab as loud as they dare. Several fell and had to be helped to their feet. Some were getting close to exhaustion. We were assigned to the rear guard squad of the platoon we were attached to the night before.

Finally, we hit an incline and entered a clearing on a hill. The hilltop was clear of trees and brush from continuous shelling and *Agent Orange* (a defoliant chemical). We settled in by mid afternoon. The infantry formed a perimeter, and the captain called Plieku command to request a supply chopper be sent. Several hours later, a chopper arrived with hot food for the infantry and ammunition. We were to hop a ride back to Plieku.

After we landed, I walked over to the training office to have a little chat with the captain. When I walked in, he looked up and with grin on his face said, "Finally baptized I hear."

I told him as a commander of a training company I felt he should have been the one to be there with a FNG on the first few missions. And I wasn't too thrilled with the bait position. He lost his grin and turned red. After slamming his office door, he proceeded to whittle me down to the status of a private. When he seemed to be pausing for breath, I started to argue my position. He stopped me with a raised hand and threatened to punish me if I didn't shut up and obey orders.

All I could say then was, "Yes, sir, Captain."

He told me to get to my bunker and be ready for another patrol with a new platoon in the morning. I walked to my bunker and was met by several FNG officers. They wanted to hear all about the ambush and get as much advice as they could, as none of them had been in an ambush yet. I told them what I could, but most of the time was a confusing mess, and I had a hard time knowing exactly where all the bullets were coming from. My ears were still ringing, and I had a headache. I had several beers and tried to sleep.

The next morning I was assigned to another drop. I walked out to the choppers and met a lieutenant who had been in country for two months. He said he had never been in an ambush, crossing himself and his fingers, and wanted to know what it was like. I asked him what he thought of the captain. He said I should just keep my thoughts to myself and do my job. The lieutenant looked like he was a nervous wreck. I shrugged and got on the slick chopper (troop carrier) for the ride to the new LZ.

I was riding on the left side of the chopper with my back to the pilots. I looked at the crew chief manning a M60 machine gun. A door gunner was on the other side manning his. As we dropped to approach the landing zone tracers began rising up to meet us. These were from 51 caliber anti-aircraft guns of the NVA. The tracers were coming from both sides of the aircraft, from guns located in the jungle.

The door gunners started a stream of their own tracers down at the gun sights. *TAP, TAP, TAP.*

Bullets hit the chopper. Everyone's eyes were wide open in fear. The chopper shuttered and began swinging, tail to the left. The stabilizer rotor had been hit, and the chopper started to rotate under the torque of the main rotor.

We were about 100 feet above the hill we were landing on. We completed one 360 degree turn before the pilot auto rotated us into the ground. We hit hard and broke the landing struts. The door gunner on the right side yelled, "shit, shit, shit" all the way down.

The crew chief yelled for us to get off NOW. Everyone jumped from the deck. My side was on the down side of the hill, and I slid half way down before stopping. No one was injured, except for a sore butt and spine from the sudden stop. The other three choppers behind us landed ok as the anti-aircraft guns quit firing when we went down. After the last chopper took off, all noise quieted down. The company commander had sent two platoons looking for the guns.

I looked around and discovered I was back to the same company I had left the day before. The company commander came over and welcomed me back and checked on our casualties. The lieutenant I was with turned white as a sheet. After everything calmed down and the two platoons returned empty handed, we were ordered to move in a specific direction, through several valleys. The infantry left in two different directions, and we were to wait for the chopper crane to lift the downed chopper out, back to Plieku.

While wasting time, I asked the platoon sergeant what he thought of the bait orders.

He looked at me, "Orders is orders, Lieutenant," and turned to his men.

The sergeant didn't look any older than me. So I asked him how long he had been in the army.

He said, "Four years, sir." That was more than me, and he was probably looking to spend his career in the Army, so he wasn't going to jeopardize it by bucking the upper brass.

The crane arrived and dropped a sling to the crew below. After attaching the sling to the top of the chopper, away they went. Before starting, I checked the map with the platoon leader and pointed out an alternative route that might save us some time and casualties. I did out rank the lieutenant by a few weeks, but he was in charge.

He looked at me and said, "Orders are orders."

We formed up and began making our way through the jungle. The valley we were to traverse was heavy with bamboo thickets. Here we had to watch for bamboo vipers that hung in the upper branches and dropped down when the stalks were disturbed. My back was getting sore as was the other lieutenant and the men who had been on the downed chopper. The medic gave us pain pills to help. I wasn't in a very good mood to have to watch for Charlie and snakes. The bamboo viper was also known as the *Two Step Snake*. Meaning, that's about how far you got after being bit. The snake venom was a nerve attacking type. They were a dark shiny green color, very difficult to see in the branches and dark of the jungle.

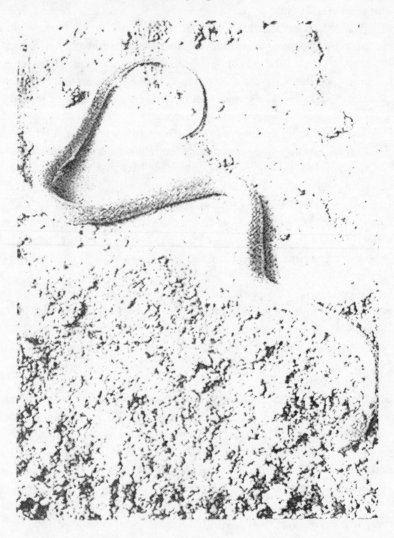

Deadly Bamboo Viper also known as the two- step snake. This one was run over by a tank. No more snake!

Several snakes did drop down, hitting men on the backs or bouncing off their helmets, but no one was bit. The men who were hit didn't see the snake, and the man behind usually jumped back to avoid it. So the enemy snakes escaped as well as Charlie with his 51 caliber machine guns. While making our way the lieutenant checked his map constantly and asked me for my opinion on our movement. I finally took the compass from him and after checking several azimuths gave him my opinion on the direction. He concurred, and we were moving again. I didn't know if he was checking my ability or was having a hard time with his navigation.

While walking I began thinking of how Charlie knew where we were landing yesterday before we got there. Thirty years later, I found out how he knew. The spy system in Viet Nam was quite complete. Through declassified documents, I found Charlie knew almost as fast as the junior commanders when and where the drops were going to be made. Vietnamese employees at the main base camps, bartenders in the Officers and NCO clubs, bar maids, equal ranking higher echelon brass, etc. In some cases, the corps commanders in the Army of the Republic of Viet Nam were the ones who spilled the beans to the NVA. Our own upper brass were usually back at the base camp or several thousand feet up in the air while the junior grade officers, non-commissioned officers and men had to slug it out on the ground.

No contact was made with Charlie that afternoon, and we made it to another hill several klicks (one klick was 1000 meters on the map) away. The infantry joined us later. A supply chopper landed just before dark to drop hot chow. The crew chief walked over to the company commander and handed him a message. The captain waved me over. He said I was to go back to Plieku on the chopper and report to the training captain.

I gathered my gear and said goodbye to the lieutenant. We rode back in the dark and after landing I walked to the training captains bunker office. He told me now that my training period was over I was being assigned to the 19th Battalion at LZ North English and good luck. I was to drop off my rifle and keep the rest of my gear. I was to catch a ride to the airfield in the morning and head over to Qui Nhon where the 19ths rear command base was located. I saluted the captain and turned away. After the supply drop, I went to my living bunker and had a few beers and slept. The walk in the jungle the past two days really wore me out.

I must say the tension of the ambush and downing of the chopper lifted when I knew I was going to be off for a couple of days. Little did I know! That morning I rode a supply truck to the airstrip. Now I was dirty and blood splattered and didn't feel like a FNG. The men at the airstrip looked at me differently. I suppose because I felt more confident and now had on combat field gear.

After waiting several hours, a C130 cargo plane landed. The sergeant at the terminal let me know that was my flight to Qui Nhon. The weather was clear at Plieku, but as we took off, I could see dark clouds to the east where we were heading.

We took off to the west and circled east. We crossed the mountains, and I could see the South China Sea as we crossed the foothills. Rain was falling hard as we landed. A jeep and driver were waiting at the terminal for me and after a short drive through the city of stucco buildings we arrived at the Division Headquarters.

A major in the personnel section greeted me and asked how long I had been in the unit. I told him, and he looked surprised. I explained the last few days, and he just went about his business of getting me out of the building and on my way north. I suppose it was the dirt of the uniform and the smell of the dried blood. I went outside to get some air. The rain was falling steady, and I stood in it to help cover the smell. It seemed to make it worse. A warrant officer came by and offered to have me shower and clean up before I left. I declined his offer.

Several minutes later a specialist came by and asked if I was the lieutenant going to LZ North English. I said yes, and we were off to the jeep. We waited for a convoy to form up.

CHAPTER 4
BONG SON

The convoy was set up with a military police jeep at the front and back and several armored personnel carriers positioned at certain intervals along the line. The rest of the convoy consisted of supply truck trailer rigs, jeeps, three quarter ton trucks, and many deuce-and-a-half trucks. One of the deuce-and-a halfs had steel sides around the bed with a quad fifty machine-gun, a gunner and several loaders. This machine-gun consisted of four fifty caliber guns mounted together, set in a base that rotates three hundred sixty degrees; quite a nasty weapon. The logo on the front of the truck was *Traveling Guns*, just like the ones seen in Plieku.

As we moved north out of Qui Nhon, we entered open hills and flat rice paddy terrain. The first bridge I saw was lying one end down into a river. It had been blown several years earlier. The bridge was next to a railroad bridge that was not operating and hadn't been for years.

Blown bridge on highway QL-1 north of Qui Nhon near Phu Cat.

41

We were riding on what I later found out was the main coastal roadway QL-1. The road was paved for a while until we got to Phu Cat, about five miles north of Qui Nhon. From here north to LZ North English, the road varied from paved to dirt with bypasses at nearly every bridge.

As we passed the road to Phu Cat, the driver pointed out that it was one of the air force base camps and had a good PX, if I ever got the chance to get down this way. Most of the vegetation had been cleared from the edge of the roadway out several hundred meters, to cut down on the accuracy of Charlies' ambushes. On the right there was a shanty-town. In the midst of the shacks was a bare hilltop covered by a Buddhist temple. The vegetation had been cut down by hand in lieu of being sprayed by Agent Orange.

While riding through the rice paddy areas, I was struck by the many different colors of each paddy. Workers, wearing conical hats, were planting each paddy with one sprig of rice plant at a time with different stages of growth. The colors varied from light green, to dark green, to brown on the rice about to be harvested.

Everything is done by hand. Men and women work in the fields bent over all day. The plowing is done by water buffalo and crude wooden plows. Water was being moved from one paddy to another manually. Men and women swing a woven basket between themselves from one ditch to another or a ditch to a paddy. Once in awhile, I saw a paddle wheel with wood like buckets attached at intervals doing the same work.

I took out my camera and started to photograph as much of this as I could. We passed two men on bicycles carrying twelve baskets each. The baskets were about four feet in diameter and two to three inches deep. These were for the separation of rice and chafe.

Several miles north, near An Nhon, I saw a base camp on our left where a Chinook helicopter was landing. The driver said that was the ROK (Republic of Korea) base camp. They were the fiercest fighters, and the NVA and VC didn't care to take them on.

Several miles farther, about half way to Bong Son, was a valley surrounded by high hills guarded by M60 tanks. These were positioned on both sides of the road throughout the length of the valley. The driver said to keep my eyes open. Charlie hadn't heard of the pacification here. Nothing happened as we passed, and I did have occasion to work here several months later.

I asked about the lack of helicopter cover for the convoy, and the driver said, "Sir, we are in a *Pacified Zone* and don't need one as bad as the convoys that run on the inland roadways."

That didn't make me feel any more relaxed. The day was getting darker, and we finally approached the Bong Son Bridge. As we passed over, I could see the bridge had been burnt in the past. There were large blisters on the painted surface. The driver said the bridge had been set on fire several times in the past years.

We crossed the bridge and turned right into the heart of the city of Bong Son. Here again there were white stucco buildings, with sheet metal sided buildings intermingled. As the convoy moved through, it had to slow to a crawl, to avoid running over all the kids gathering around the trucks.

"You want boom boom, GI?" they cried.

"I got number one sister for you."

"You got candy for me, GI?"

They had all the come ons down to a tee. The driver warned me to keep my camera inside the jeep and to watch out for the kids that tried to touch me. They would take off a watch at a blink of the eye.

He also said to watch the big crowds as we passed. Sometimes grenades would fly in from the group and land in open trucks or jeeps. There were so many crowds of people it was hard to watch everyone. The driver pointed out a Catholic run hospital in the middle of town. A ten-foot wall enclosed it.

He said after dark the gates closed, and no one was allowed in. Too many times innocent looking Vietnamese came to the gate only to toss a satchel charge or grenade inside.

As we left the city, the vegetation was getting closer to the road. Bamboo hedges and banana trees lined the road as close as five feet away.

The railroad berm was on our right; about fifty meters away, and there were water buffalo herds grazing amongst the trees. On the left were the remains of a large Catholic church, shot full of holes, both large and small. Around the church, a company of ARVN infantry was camped. There were pup tents erected over foxholes, and outside the perimeter was apron and concertina wire.

We came to a junction in the road. To the left ran a road the driver said went to the unit we were attached to, the 173rd Airborne Division, at LZ English. About half the convoy turned off here. We kept going north, without the MP jeeps.

At the LZ English junction was another shantytown. The driver pointed out, "This is were the boom boom action is located, be very careful around here and never let your weapon out of your sight if you stop to get a beer."

He also warned of buying beer and cokes from the coke girls that followed the troops around QL-1. The commanders allowed the buying, but warned of taking any can or bottle that wasn't opened in your presence; several soldiers had been killed by drinking from a bottle or can containing ground glass. Later in my tour, a supply sergeant had this very thing happen to him in Bong Son. He died on the way to the 173rd base camp medical evac station.

The coke girls, outside the cities and towns, were driven around on a motorcycle and pestered soldiers who were stopped on the road. We continued up QL-1. Several miles north, we came to an opening on our left. I could see a base camp across a large rice paddy. This was LZ North English, my home for about six months.

We turned left onto an access road, several hundred meters long. The camp was built on an old cemetery. I found out years later it was first called LZ Dog by the first infantry unit who used it. It was bordered on the north by a rice paddy and river, on the east by the access road, which had rice paddies on both sides, on the south by more paddies, and on the west by jungle.

In the base camp was the 19th Battalion Headquarters, Headquarters Company, Alpha Company, Heavy Equipment Company, 80 MM Mortar Company, one platoon of M60 tanks (four) and a platoon of Duster tanks (four). The tankers came to our aid many times during my tour. The M60 tanks were normal looking tanks, huge, with a closed turret. The duster tanks were about half the size of the M60 and had an open turret, with twin barrel 40mm cannons.

The camp was surrounded by a high dirt berm, with living-fighting bunkers built in. We drove through the gate and to the left, toward the center of the camp. The driver dropped me at the Battalion Command Center, where I was met by a chief warrant officer the head of battalion personnel. He introduced me to the battalion executive officer, a major, who told me to report to Headquarters Company to be issued my combat equipment (rifle, pack, ammunition, etc) and to report back to him.

He and another officer were going to LZ Lowboy that afternoon, to check on the quarry company. I was to tag along to see the terrain where I would be working.

The chief warrant officer took me to a bunker where I dumped my duffel bag. He showed me where Headquarters Company was located. My bunker was at the south end of the helicopter pad. The pad was in the middle of the base with the Battalion Headquarters on the east side, the mess hall building on the north side, the 80mm Mortar company on the west side and the Battalion Surgical Medical Evac Hospital and my bunker on the south side. I shared the bunker with the chief warrant officer, from personnel.

I walked over to Headquarters Company, on the far side of the Battalion HQ. I entered a tent surrounded by 55 gallon barrels full of sand. These were for protection against incoming mortar and artillery shell shrapnel.

The first sergeant took my orders and introduced me to the company commander. The captain welcomed me to Viet Nam and directed me to the supply sergeant for my equipment. I was issued a used, old model M15 and five cartridge magazines. At leased the rest of the equipment was new. The rifle damn near got me killed the first ambush. (I took it back and got an old M-14 rifle.)

By the time I got back to the Battalion Headquarters, the major had left, and I was to return to HQ Company for my assignment. By this time, it was late afternoon. The captain assigned me to the heavy equipment platoon. After shuffling paper at the command center, the captain offered to give me a tour of the camp.

I told him I was supposed to have gone with the major to LZ Lowboy but missed the jeep ride. He said, "It's kinda late for going up there, unless the major intended to stay over night." He explained once the day got to dusk, the road was unsafe for travel. The ARVN guards closed the bridges, and the road was blocked by barricades of wire at both bridge approaches.

He showed me where our company was responsible for berm protection. Day light was fading, and when we walked north to the main gate, I noticed it was shut. The captain said if anyone should come down the access road now it would be very dangerous.

Just then I heard a loud, swishing sound, and *KABANG* up to the north at the river crossing. Small arms firing, sounding like popcorn poping could be heard, and bullets were whizzing in all directions. Red and green tracers were flying in all directions through the palm trees and jungle.

The sounds were loud and crazy. I could hear men screaming for help. We ran to the northeast bunkers and couldn't see exactly what was going on but listened to the deaths of a platoon of heavy equipment operators and the battalion major and his driver.

The tank platoon, with their four M60 tanks, roared out of the base camp and turned north up QL-1. As the lead tank approached the roadblocks, the gunner fired a canister round to blow away the barricade, because the Army of the Republic of Viet Nam personnel (ARVN) wouldn't move it.

The captain said that was par for the course for the ARVN. They just sat in their bunkers at night and refused to come out. We watched as all four tanks moved out of sight up the road. Several loud bangs from the tank cannons, and the ambush started to slow. The pops of the rifle firing were a few here and there, and then nothing.

I could hear a guard at the north berm, to our left, yelling, "I can see them; I can see them; they're running west along the river. Can we shoot, can we shoot?"

We ran to the berm and could see about twenty NVA running through the jungle along the river. They were dressed in tan uniforms and were very identifiable with their distinct looking pith helmets.

The captain said, "Yes, open fire on those bastards."

The range was 400 to 500 meters, and the chance of hitting anyone was slim with the light fading.

Several platoons from Alpha Company were moving out the access road to assist in the rescue. The first sergeant of HQ Company ran up to us and gave the captain the bad news. All but two of the men in the convoy were killed. The battalion commander ordered the captain to send a recovery team out for the bodies.

A team from HQ Company was organized and went to the convoy, along with the captain and myself. The convoy was a mess. Every truck and jeep had been hit by rocket fire and disabled. The two surviving drivers told their horrifying account.

Most of the week the Heavy Equipment Company had several pieces of equipment working along QL-1 north and south of LZ Lowboy and were ready to move back to LZ North English. All the equipment, except a compacting roller, had been loaded and ready to go. The flat bed truck for the roller had become disabled, so it was to be left at LZ Lowboy.

The battalion executive officer (the major I was supposed to be with) arrived just as the convoy was to pull out at around 1500 hours (3 PM). The major didn't want the roller left behind. The platoon leader (a second lieutenant) tried to tell the major why the roller shouldn't be run with the convoy. (A compacting roller only travels at about 3 miles per hour). It would take the convoy almost 2 hours to make the five- mile distance.

The major ordered the lieutenant to get going with the roller in the front. So off they went. Slowly driving down the road, with everyone getting more and more tense as the time quickly passed. After they passed the ARVN White Horse Mechanized Base Camp (at Tam Quan), the lieutenant asked the major to have our battalion send the tank platoon to meet the convoy north of the bridge, as the light was fading fast. The major refused to call.

Tam Quan was about the half way junction between the two LZ s. As the lead roller, and lieutenant's truck were winding their way along the S curves,

46

one mile south of Tam Quan, a streak of orange was seen shooting past the roller and into the driver of the truck. *BANG!!!*

A second streak of orange came from the opposite direction and hit the lieutenant in the chest. *BANG!* (These were B-40 rockets fired from the shoulder) More rockets were fired at the rear trucks. The truck drivers were hit and killed. This blocked the road and AK 47 rifle fire opened up on the convoy in the middle. The two surviving drivers had jumped from their trucks and hid under their trucks, between the rear dual wheel axles of their flat bed trailers.

The men in the convoy didn't have a chance. They were hit from both sides of the road. After a few minutes, the NVA approached the road and shot anyone who was still alive. The ARVN White Horse Mechanized Unit arrived from the north; about the same time the tank platoon was hitting the bridge to the south. This caused the NVA to break off their killing and run to the west.

Bodies were on both sides of the road, and the battalion surgeon and his medics checked everyone for signs of life. All were dead. There was a heavy odor of blood in the air, along with gunpowder and cordite from the rockets. Several trucks were still burning.

All the bodies were lifted into deuce-and-a-halfs and taken back to the battalion medevac bunker, where they would wait for transport to Graves Registration. The two platoons from Alpha Company were ordered to set up a perimeter around the convoy that night.

I returned to the base camp in a numb state. The look of the dead soldiers and the smells were forever imbedded in my brain. I went to my bunker to sleep, drenched by a downpour, I hadn't even noticed.

The next day, after little sleep, I was assigned to go with my platoon sergeant to check on my platoon members, who were detached from the base camp, and located up and down QL-1 at the many outlying LZs. My platoon consisted of heavy equipment operators of dozers, road graders, front loaders and lowboy truck trailer transport rigs.

My platoon sergeant led me to our transportation, a three quarter ton soft roof truck. Mounted in the back of the truck was a M60 machine-gun on a steel swivel post. Between the driver and the right seat passenger was the radio.

On the floor were sand bags to ward off the effects of a land mine. We mounted the truck, and I began my first full day on my new job. The many LZs of the battalion were separated by about 200 miles, so we had a lot of traveling to do each day.

This day we drove north. We drove through the palm trees, where I had been the night before, and could see the effect of the ambush on the vehicles waiting to be removed, I felt a cold chill run up and down my back.

As we continued north, we passed the ARVN White Horse Mechanized units base camp, in the town of Tam Quan. The base camp was surrounded by a wall about ten feet high. We continued up QL-1, out of the palm trees, to an open slope up to coastal hills that reminded me of the scrub brush hills of southern California. As we continued up, off to the right, I could see the South China Sea about one mile away.

At the top of the climb was a base camp on our right. This was LZ Lowboy. Charlie Company, a line company (one which works in the field clearing booby traps, mine sweeping roads, patrolling, checking tunnels, demolition of tunnels or enemy camps, etc.) is located here as well as the quarry company. They crush the boulders down to a size to be used in the construction of the roadway.

One of our battalions' jobs was to continue the paving of QL-1 from Qui Nhon up to Da Nang. At this time, the paving was being concentrated on the airstrip at LZ English, for the 173 rd Airborne.

From here north, we were not to continue without an escort or convoy. So we had to wait for the next convoy heading north. We were still in a *Pacified Zone*, but there was no feeling of safety here. North was a free fire zone. In other words, we could shoot back if fired upon. Dust from a convoy could be seen, to the south, so we got ready.

As the convoy approached, they slowed, and as each truck and escort vehicle passed, the men carrying weapons test fired them into the hillside to the west. We did the same. I was carrying my M15 and a 45-caliber pistol. The machine gunner in the back test fired the platoons M60 machine gun.

We slid into the convoy and again headed north. The roadway dropped down to a long straight stretch, and at the bottom, about 1500 meters north, made several S curves into dense palm trees. This is the location where a Lieutenant from Bravo Company, who didn't wait for a convoy, was ambushed while riding in a jeep with only his driver. Thirty days later I replaced that officer in Bravo Company.

Even though the morning was sunny, in this area under the thick trees, it was very dark and eerie. As we continued, I kept looking for good spots for an ambush and always had my finger on the trigger. As we came out of the trees, several miles from LZ Lowboy, we passed an access road. The sergeant said it was to a Navy Supply Base called LZ Charlie Brown. (About five months later, this was my first stop on a dustoff medevac the first time I was wounded.)

We continued north with the convoy into *Death Canyon*. This was several S curves through a boulder choked canyon with, what was later found to be, many tunnels that ran under the road from the west hills to the coastal beaches. Several tunnels opened in the hills on both sides of the road, giving Charlie a good spot to fire his rockets and AK 47 rifles, with little or no fear of getting hit by return fire.

At the north end of the canyon, the road turned left, running along a beautiful shallow bay. Many times, later in my tour while on patrol here, we would watch the mud skipper fish, at low tide, as they skipped across the flats.

The convoy headed west about a mile and then swung to the right, heading north again. Now we were between hills, about 300 to 400 feet high. Terraces had been built along the sides of the hills from the bottom to the top. Between the cleared terraces were hedgerows of brush about five feet high. Different crops were planted on the terraces including marijuana and opium poppies.

As we continued, the hills on the right, to the east, gave way to coastal jungle. The brush had been cleared from QL-1, out to about 100 meters. We were going to Delta Company, LZ Thunder. They were located on a mountain that looked like it was a volcano in the middle of a sea of rice paddies. The LZ was about half way up the side of the mountain. The access road continued up to the top, where the American Division Headquarters was located. This was LZ Thunder Mountain.

We left the convoy, turning right, onto the access road to LZ Thunder Mountain. We entered LZ Thunder and stopped to talk to the company commander. He said my equipment operator was working on the road north of the mountain. We stayed for lunch. At Delta Company, the everyday chow at noon was dehydrated fish. At LZ, North English it was dehydrated beef. This diet never changed as long as I was there.

After lunch we again headed north to *Dead Man's Pass*, where the front loader operator was working with Delta Company's dozer operators. After checking on his needs, we continued north to Bravo Company at LZ Max. From LZ Thunder north to Chu Lia the road was considered safe enough to travel without escort. It wasn't!

Land mines were a constant threat, along with ambushes. Just because the terrain was more flat and open most of the way, didn't make it any more safe. At the north end of the pass, we crossed a bridge and passed the entrance to Duc Pho. This was the base camp for the main headquarters for the Americal

Division. I don't remember their LZ name. This is where our main helicopter support group was stationed, and we could always get fresh ammo at their ammo dump if we used any on the way here.

We continued north, several more miles, to LZ Max. The base camp was on the left, west side of QL-1. We checked on the welfare of our operator, and inspected a five- ton dump truck that had run over a mine that morning.

During mine sweep, the trucks are loaded with sand and driven backwards up the road. Several trucks are driven this way, staggered, and several meters apart so they might set off any large mines the mine detectors miss. Sometimes this works, sometimes it doesn't. The theory is the back dual wheels will set off the mine, not the front. This way the driver doesn't get injured.

Charlie decided he didn't like this ploy, so he started placing his detonators about 10 feet away from the mine. This caused the drivers of the trucks to get an awful head- ache. The mine would go off under the driver or engine. This particular mine went off under the left front wheel and took off the left side of the truck cab.

The driver, who was standing on the running board looking back, was ejected up into the head- ache pan over the cab. He was killed. Sand bags on the floor board couldn't save him in this case.

By this time it was mid afternoon, so we left to head south. We got to LZ Thunder and waited for a convoy. The late afternoon convoy arrived, and we headed back home. As we pulled out of the convoy at LZ North English, I realized how tense I had been all day. I was drained and ready for sleep.

Not so fast FNG. Your time had come for night guard commander for the company. Ok, I did get to snooze at the command bunker but had to check on the perimeter bunkers every two hours to ensure all the guards were awake and alert. I was warned not to enter a living-fighting bunker on the berm if we were under attack. This precaution was due to the problem of sappers getting into the base camp and throwing satchel charges into the bunkers at night. We never had that happen at LZ North English while I was there.

Perimeter lights that I had seen at other base camps were non- existent here. To me this kept everyone very alert during the night. Later in my tour, when we were transferred down to LZ Smith, near Bao Loc, we had perimeter light, and many of the duty guards slept during their tour.

The nights were dark here even with starlight. Moonlit nights where good but caused many spooky shadows as time passed. Many a night a guard would fire on a shadow figure moved by the wind. During the darkest nights, in very still air, you could hear things moving in the brush, outside and inside the perimeter wire. Most of the time your imagination would play tricks on you. Other times there was something there. Most of the time it turned out to be an animal. Sometimes it was the enemy crawling up on the positions.

If one guard fired, this would set off everyone on that side of the perimeter and for several minutes all hell broke loose. Red tracers would fly out in all directions away from the perimeter, and in all directions ricocheting off objects. Some times this would set off the entire base camp. Then the firing would resemble a mad minute. The mad minute was a weapons test firing we did every week at night up at LZ Debbie.

Many a time at daybreak, we would spot a dead animal such as a water buffalo or monkey. Many times during the day large groups of man sized monkeys, rock apes, were seen moving from one jungle area, across open rice paddies, to another. When on patrol, these times would often spook new members of the platoons especially during a night patrol.

I was warned about other animals and snakes in the area. Tigers lived in the hills west of our base camp and many were later seen in the Central Highlands. Several dangerous snakes lived here as well, the cobra and the bamboo viper. I saw several snakes during the year and only heard of a few men being bitten.

At LZ North English, there was a large starlight scope mounted up in the high tower. This was used to scan the perimeter at night. The tower was located on the southern half of the base camp, and mostly directed toward the south jungle, which was where we drew the most sniper activity. It took me awhile to get used to walking the perimeter at night and knowing all the shadows outside the perimeter.

I spent my first month at LZ North English with Headquarters Company. My days were spent traveling up and down QL-1, from Qui Nhon to Duc Pho. My platoon sergeant liked the ladies, and had several favorite boom boom hootches he liked to visit, while checking on our operators. I didn't see any reason to restrict his activities and waited for him with the driver and gunner. This was in the *Pacified Zone*, right?

Anyway, one day we drove up to one of his favorite places, just as a VC tossed a grenade into the midst of several soldiers cooling their heels inside. The grenade exploded, and the VC dressed as an ARVN (probably was one) ran off through the village. We ran after him. He cut between buildings and ran down alleys. We came around a corner behind a maze of turns, and there he was, standing with two others dressed in ARVN uniforms. They all raised their rifles, and we began shooting.

We were only ten to fifteen feet apart, and seven rifles were blasting at full automatic. Somehow the three ARVNs were hit and we weren't. The grenade thrower was killed. The other two were seriously wounded, and after all the excitement died down, were medevaced out to the Qui Nhon Military Hospital.

MACV advisers, who were stationed in the village and assigned to the ARVN unit near there, identified the ARVNs and demanded to know what happened. The wounded ARVNs claimed to have captured the VC, and were in the process of bringing him back, when we showed up. They were all laughing as we turned the corner and appeared to be friends of the VC.

The MACV advisors accepted our explanation and said they had suspected the three as being VC sympathizers. We left the area, and never mentioned our encounter back at the base camp.

Lieutenant Suffern on the beach at Qui Nhon, 1968.

One day, while heading down to the 35th Group headquarters to pick up the battalion mail, we decided to stop in at the Phu Cat Airforce Base PX. I couldn't believe the difference in base camps. The Air Force housing inside the perimeter was two story framed barracks, like state side, with concrete walls around the lower level. They had baseball fields, tennis courts, swimming pools, all state side base living conditions. We were envious, even though we didn't sleep on the ground.

When I first arrived in Long Bien, I was introduced to the anti-malaria pills I would be taking every day. They consisted of one a week orange pills the size of a nickel and about 1/4 inch thick, and a daily dose of a white pill, about 1/4 inch in diameter and 1/8 inch thick. The orange pill gave you a dose of diarrhea for three days. Many of the troops developed dehydration from the pills and never got over the trots to the latrine. Which made conditions worse when out on patrol.

I had many a scramble in the night to the latrine in my skivvies, only to come up short on the distance and discard my skivvies in the dump. Several officers and enlisted men ended up in the base hospital for several weeks to get over the dehydration.

I should describe the latrine facilities at our base camp. Because of the high water table at the coastal areas the human waste had to be gather in containers and burned. The containers were slid under the latrine holes. They consisted of 55 gallon steel barrels cut in half at the middle making two cylindrical receivers. The contents were dragged a short distance from the latrine by soldiers on shit detail, and dosed in diesel fuel, then ignited; such a lovely smell. I hope I never smell it again.

During the month I was with the "Heavy Junk Platoon," several events took place. The Bravo Company commander went out on a night patrol and was accidentally shot by his own men. He was at the lead of the team and suspected they were being followed. He stepped off the trail and motioned the next man in line to continue. He then slipped down into a clump of brush to conceal his location. As the rest of the team passed no one noticed him, until the last man approached.

The rear guard soldier thought the captain was a North Viet Nam Army (NVA) soldier and began firing. The captain was hit in the groin before he could identify himself. He wasn't killed and was medevaced to the Qui Nhon base hospital. The soldier who shot him was devastated because everyone in the company liked the captain. The captain told the executive officer of the company to let the men know the shooting was his (the captain's) fault, not

53

the rear guard. (This same thing happened to me while on night patrol in OCS.) Later after recovering, the captain returned to the battalion and was assigned to the battalion staff.

Also, a first lieutenant with Bravo Company was riding in his jeep with only his driver. They decided to chance a run up QL-1, from LZ Lowboy to LZ Max, without the protection of an escort or convoy. As they were heading north, descending down QL-1 from LZ Lowboy, they were ambushed from behind at the first curve.

The lieutenant was killed immediately, and the jeep engine was shot up. The jeep came to a sudden stop, and the driver managed to get the lieutenant out of the jeep and behind cover. A convoy heading south showed up about then and apparently scared off the enemy. The lieutenant's body was flown out by Dust Off medevac, and the driver was taken back to LZ Lowboy.

A few days later the executive officer of Bravo Company was wounded while riding in his jeep up near LZ Max. While returning from the morning mine sweep, the jeep was driven up to the approach of a bridge. As the front wheels neared the wood trestles, the left front tire hit a mine, and the jeep was flipped up and over backwards. The driver and machine gunner were killed, and the lieutenant was injured. He was treated for shock and a cut on his chin. After a week in the hospital in Qui Nhon, he returned to the company.

A captain, who was on the battalion staff, was transferred to Bravo Company to be the new company commander. I was transferred to Bravo Company to replace the dead officer in the second platoon. A week after my transfer, I also became the executive officer, second in command.

CHAPTER 5
BRAVO COMPANY

I assembled my belongings and was trucked over to Bravo Companies command post. Bravo Company had recently been switched with Alpha Company and was now located at LZ North English. Alpha Company was up north at LZ Max. Being at LZ North English, where I was somewhat familiar, was a relief to me. My first day at Bravo Company was dark, with heavy rain.

I reported to the captain, and he assigned me to the second platoon. I had heard rumors concerning this officer while at Battalion HQ. I had no way of confirming anything about his past, but who was I to question his ability to lead a company. I had heard that after he graduated from West Point, he was assigned to a special atomic demolition platoon in Germany, and his only command experience was pushing paper for high level NCOs.

The captain said our mission here was to keep QL-1 passable and patrol around LZ North English from LZ Lowboy south to Bong Son. He also reminded me we were in a *Pacified Zone* and were not to shoot back if fired upon unless we had specific orders to do so. I asked him if he had been here last month when the heavy equipment platoon had been wiped out just north of the base camp.

He said, "Yes. Our orders from MACV and the battalion commander are not to shoot back unless we have clearance from higher authority. Is that clear, Lieutenant?"

"Yes, sir."

When I left to go to my new living bunker I thought, *My responsibility here as I see it is to take care of my men and myself and common sense tells me to defend myself while out in enemy territory*. Every time we leave the base camp we lock and load our weapons (load up with live ammunition) that to me means shoot if shot at. While inside a base camp a safety factor was to unload and safe our weapons. Meaning no live rounds are to be in the rifle chamber to prevent accidental firing.

55

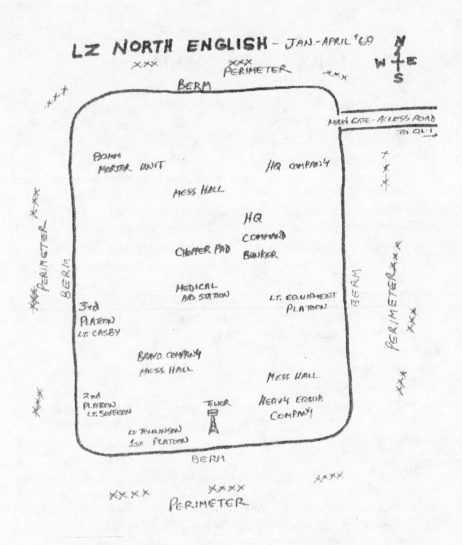

Land Zone North English perimeter drawing, 1968.

The current executive officer felt the same and wasn't going to change his mind during the last week he was here. He showed me my bunker and said my platoon was out on mine sweep and would be back around noon. My bunker was a two room stick frame building surrounded by 55 gallon steel barrels full of sand. The roof was covered with several layers of sand bags on top of pierced steel planking. Above this was a tin roof. This was to set off any incoming mortars before they got to the inner bunker.

Short timer party for Lieutenant Haney. Left to right: Lt. Haney, SFC Concepcion and SST Horton, 1968.

The bunker had a front screened in area and behind were two separate rooms; one for the platoon sergeant and the other for me, the platoon leader. On my side was a single wide metal cot and nothing more. The floor and walls were plywood and the entry had no door. I organized my footlocker and gear and settled in. I noticed my class-A khaki colored uniform was taking on a shade of green and my class-A black shoes were also covered with fuzzy green velvet mold.

I left the bunker to walk around my new company to get my bearings. Looking east, I could see the base camp tower looming above our shower and latrine building. This building looked like a tin shed as the sides and roof were covered by corrugated tin. There was no protection around this building or on top. Not a good place to be during a mortar attack. (This I found out later.)

To the south was the first platoon's area. They were responsible for the southwest corner of the battalion base camp. My platoon was responsible for half of the west side, and the third platoon was responsible for the northwest section of the perimeter. North of the shower shack was the mess hall and communication bunker. Behind them was the command center. To the west was my platoon's living fighting bunkers, and to the north was my supply tent.

Trucks began coming into the company area. First and second platoons were coming back from mine sweep. Lieutenant Haney, the Executive Officer, came out of the command post and motioned me over to meet the first platoon leader and his and my platoon sergeants. The first platoon leader was First Lieutenant Steve Tomlinson, who I had known at Fort Leonard Wood, and was only a few weeks my junior in grade from OCS. It was good to see a familiar face. He and I became very close during the rest of our tours. His Platoon Sergeant was Sergeant First Class Concepcion. My Platoon Sergeant was Staff Sergeant Meddars, also known as *sergeant cous* (because he was from a small town in Louisiana).

Lieutenant Steve Tomlinson in Bong Son, 1968.

SST Meddars and I went back to our bunker, and I asked him to assemble the squad leaders so I could meet them, and we could discuss our afternoon mission. We were to patrol north to Tam Quan then west about a mile (about two klicks on the map) then south to a village located southwest of our base camp and then back to QL-1 and our camp.

After lunch at the mess hall (which consisted of dried beef and dehydrated potato), we assembled our combat gear (helmet, combat web strap gear, ammunition, rifle, canteen, etc.) and walked to the front gate entry. There I ordered the platoon to move out in a column formation on either side of the access road with a six- meter distance between each man.

The front of the column (the point men) were out about twenty meters ahead. I took up a position close to the front about thirty meters behind the point. I always walked up at the point or close to it to maintain my awareness over the patrols. I was constantly being told by others not to do this as it was putting myself in a vulnerable position. I always felt I couldn't ask anyone to do something I was not willing to do and felt my attention was always alert at the front.

We walked down the access road and turned left at QL-1. Vietnamese vehicles were moving up and down QL-1 by this time and kicking up dust. The sky had cleared by this time and with it came almost instant drying. The temperature was in the nineties, and everyone was covered in sweat. I was the worst not being used to the heat and humidity.

This was my first time entering into the area, on foot, where the killing was done the first day I arrived. We approached the ARVN held bridge south of the ambush zone. I told my men to be alert, and if they were shot at, to return fire. My platoon sergeant asked if we had been given clearance to do that, and I said you just did. (I must say I did get into trouble several times for this and stood my ground each time I had to report to the captain or battalion commander.)

QL-1 at this point was a two-lane dirt road, and the bridge was a wood trestle structure. At either end, on one side, was a sand bag bunker the ARVNs were supposed to occupy during the night and have a sentry at the bridge during the day. Barbed wire fencing was placed down across the river from one end to the other and a barbed wire and wood barricade was off to the side of the road that blocked the entries at night.

No one was in sight as we crossed the bridge. This gave me a chill and made me leery about continuing up the curved palm tree covered road. I was warned to watch out when the locals ran from their rice paddys or suddenly vanished from their posts. A shot rang out several hundred meters to our right.

I looked over in that direction and could see, through the trees, ARVNs standing on the top of the railroad berm. The platoon sergeant said that was normal, that the ARVNs and Regular Forces (ruff puffs) regularly fired their rifles in the air as the troops passed. My thought was they were warning their VC buddies of our location. As my tour progressed, I noticed they always had a big grin on their faces as they fired; our wonderful allies.

I changed the column formation to a diamond formation with the first squad to lead on the road. The second and third squads moved off the road to the left and right as the flank guard and the forth squad took up the rear guard on the road about fifty meters back. I stayed up front with the point and had my radio telephone operator (RTO) stay back with the first squad.

I allowed the platoon sergeant to be where ever he felt he should be. I never felt a need to order him to a different position. How could I? He had over twenty years in the army, he should know where to go, he was an infantry sergeant. I never asked why he was assigned to an engineer unit.

We had to move off the road, as a convoy was moving north. We all waved at the drivers and their escorts, giving them the V sign and others in return. Several Vietnamese motorcycles and lambretas were traveling along. The lambretas were a three- wheel motorcycle with the driver up front and a flat bed covered platform behind.

Some of these vehicles were so packed that they could hardly move. When starting, passengers in the back would get out and push until the lambreta got momentum and then they would jump on.

On one mission while we were repairing a blown bridge, a lambreta came by, carrying a water buffalo and many humans. They had to travel on the by pass which had steep entries and exits. Going down the slope off QL-1 was no problem. Coming back up the other side was very difficult. All the Vietnamese passengers got off and pushed. As the front wheel of the lambreta got higher, the back end got heavier, and finally the front wheel lifted off the ground.

I went over to the driver and tried to get him to off load the water buffalo but he refused. After watching them back the lambreta down the ramp and try several times to run up to QL-1, the traffic behind was getting impatient. A convoy was coming, so we moved a five-ton dump truck to the front of the lambreta and hooked him up to the tow bar. In a few seconds he was up and heading down the road.

After the convoy passed and the dust settled, we pushed off again moving along the S curves toward Tam Qhan. When we could see the beginnings of the village, we were at the turning point. Through the palm tree trunks and brush I could see bamboo- framed hootches with palm fronds for walls and roofs. Not a very good structure to hide behind during a firefight or grenade throwing contest as many soldiers found out.

I stopped the formation and ordered a left flanking turn. Now we would be moving through thick under growth of *wait a minute* vines and bamboo. Here we had to be very alert for booby traps and snakes, not to mention ambushes. The ground here was very sandy. As we continued west, I noticed it was difficult keeping the flank squads in sight. We had to keep our noise down to a minimum, so I stopped the formation and had the squad leaders assemble with me behind the first squad. I told them to tighten up the formation while we were in the thickets and spread out when we entered a more open area.

They adjusted their positions and we moved out. About mid day, we came to a clearing near some French style houses shot full of large and small holes. The terrain was void of the *wait a minute* vines and other lower vegetation. Just many palm trees and clumps of bamboo thickets.

I decided this was a good place to turn south, so we did. After making the turn, I stopped the formation for a break. I talked with the platoon sergeant and squad leaders to get input on our patrol. The squad leaders said they had never been on a patrol this far out from the base camp before and wanted to do more. Charlie seemed to have the idea that we combat engineers were stay at home kinda soldiers, and he didn't have much to worry about. I remembered what the colonel and captain said about this being a *Pacified Zone* and wondered if they meant we were the pacified soldiers not Charlie. The afternoon shadows were starting to lengthen to the east, so we pushed off south.

I checked my map and decided to swing to the left in a southeasterly direction, so we would be closer to the base camp at dusk. After the platoon moved about three hundred meters, shots rang out to our left front.

Pop, pop, pop—the familiar sound of an AK-47 Russian rifle.

The first and second squads fired in return and dove for cover. At first, I felt we were being sniped at, but the amount of incoming rounds increased after several minutes, and it appeared we had walked into an ambush.

As I was signaling my right flank and rear guard to circle to the left and right, the soldier in front of me got hit and jerked back into me. His helmet flew off backwards and hit me square in the face stunning me for a few seconds. Our medic immediately came up from the center of the formation and began attending to the hit man. He asked if I was shot as blood was running down my face from a cut on my head. I hadn't even realized I was bleeding.

I got to the RTO and told him to call for a medevac and inform the base camp we were under fire, and it appeared to be a small force. Suddenly, all incoming fire stopped, and the enemy broke off the ambush and slipped into the jungle. The squads I sent to circle the enemy must have caused them to break off the attack.

The soldier hit had a sucking chest wound. He was conscious and kept saying he was ok and could walk back to the base camp. Quite a lot of blood was spread over his green fatigue jacket and I told him to just stay put until the chopper got there. Several minutes later the medevac chopper, with its red cross on the nose, began circling.

Medevac chopper flying low and fast over river and jungle terrain north of Bong Son.

We popped green smoke, and the pilot confirmed the color before landing. (Charlie had a habit of popping smoke grenades he had borrowed from us to get the choppers to land in the wrong spot.) So we on the ground would pop smoke, the pilots would call the color, and we would confirm or deny it.

Two gunship helicopters were also circling, and I called them to direct them to the escaping enemy. They remained to our southeast circling while the medevac chopper landed. Several platoon members carried the wounded man to the chopper, and he was placed on a stretcher. The chopper took off in a cloud of dust and was gone.

The gunship pilots raked the jungle ahead of us as we moved out toward our base camp. An hour later as the light in the sky was dimming we broke out of the jungle southwest of the base camp. I called the chopper pilots and thanked them for the escort. They broke off and headed back to LZ English saying, "Any time ground pounders need assistance, just call."

I had the RTO call our company command post and let them know where we were and get clearance to come into the base camp. After several minutes, we were cleared to approach the front gate. Even if you could see the guards on the berm, it was better to warn them of your approach as some of the FNGs could fire before really knowing what they're shooting at. Especially in a dusky light situation as this was.

We skirted around the north perimeter wire obstacles and made our way to the front gate. I waited on the access road until all my men were through the gate. While waiting I checked out the several shacks along the road. This is where the mamasans washed the laundry for the base camp. Several mamasans were getting ready to leave for the day, preparing to ride on the backs of motorcycles driven by papasans (Probably the local VC.) They rode off in a cloud of dust.

As we straggled back to Bravo Company, I noticed the men were not in very good shape for long marches even though they were in good spirits and eager to go after the VC or NVA. The wind had begun to pick up, and clouds were forming for what smelled like another rainy night. Tonight I wasn't on guard duty for our section of perimeter. The night bugs were starting to make noise, and the mosquitoes were buzzing about.

Sergeant Meddars told the men to dump their gear and get some chow before guard duty. The executive officer caught up with me before I got to my bunker and said I was to report to the captain immediately. I walked over to the command post and reported to the captain. He said to close the door to his office and stand at attention.

After doing so, he wanted to know if he hadn't been clear on the firing back procedure. I told him he had been very clear and was he aware that one of my men had been shot and as far as I knew we had only wasted some government ammunition and had not hit any of the enemy. But if we had had the opportunity, "My platoon would have killed every one of them, sir."

My blood pressure was beginning to rise, and I was coming to a very definite opinion of the character of this captain. He was also getting very red in the face at my "insubordination," and before he could respond, I invited him to come along on the next patrol in the morning.

The captain just sat down hard behind his desk and told me not to let it happen again, and I was dismissed. As I turned to leave, he demanded I salute before I go.

This I did as smartly as I could and said, "See you tomorrow morning on the patrol!"

"Get out," was his reply.

As I closed the door, I looked up and there was the executive officer and first sergeant standing in the orderly room with a slight smirk of a smile on their faces. I decided then and there this was a *Tommy Two Bars* kind of captain.

I went back to my bunker and Lieutenant Tomlinson was waiting with some chow and several cold beers. He had already heard what had just been discussed with *Tommy Two Bars* and said, "Welcome to the *Pacified Zone*."

I lit the two 36 inch tall, three inch diameter red candles I had bought in Bong Son, and Lieutenant Tomlinson and I drank our beers and reminisced about our days in OCS. Thus ended my first full day in a line company.

CHAPTER 6
MAGICAL MYSTERY TOUR

The next morning we were up before dawn and getting ready for a mine sweep to the south on QL-1. As the platoon prepared to exit the base camp, my RTO called the company communication operator to give him our personnel status. So many Echo Mikes (enlisted men), so many November Charlie Oscars (non-commissioned officers), and one Oscar (officer). These mine sweeps were what the RTOs referred to as the "Magical Mystery Tour," I suppose from the Beatles song at that time.

We were given clearance to leave and thanked them profusely. I had the RTO confirm we should wait for the Lead Oscar before leaving but was advised that wouldn't be necessary. I was again to stand in front of *Tommy Two Bars* for that remark. I won't bother you with the details only to say I was very submissive and kept my thoughts to myself.

As we left the gate I ordered everyone to lock and load, and we started down the access road. Lieutenant Tomlinson and his platoon were behind us and would be heading north to LZ Lowboy. The mine sweep formation was made up like this.

At the front were the point men, usually two. Then came the mine detectors staggered diagonally across the road. There were two teams of four so as to thoroughly sweep the road. Next came a Duster Tank with their 40 MM twin guns as escort protection. Why we needed the protection was beyond me because, "Weren't we in a *Pacified Zone*?" (Sorry, just couldn't resist the dig on *Tommy Two Bars.*)

Next came several five-ton dump trucks loaded with dirt. These were driven backwards and also staggered across the road to set off any large mines that the detectors might have missed. The drivers would set the throttle low and set the gear, so they could stand on the running board and watch how the sweep was progressing and steer accordingly.

Next came my three quarter ton truck with a fifty caliber machine gun mounted in the back bed and then another escort vehicle, either another Duster Tank or an Armored Personnel Carrier which had one fifty caliber machine gun at the front, and two M 60 machine guns on each side. No,

Tommy Two Bars did not accompany this sweep nor did he ever accompany any sweep his entire tour.

As we got to QL-1, the sun was just coming up over the railroad berm to the east and looked so golden and serene through a light wisp of ground fog. The vehicle engines blocked out the sound of the bugs out in the jungle. I could still hear them from the night just as I had remembered them from the *Victory At Sea* records I would listen to when I was younger.

When I looked south, I could see, several hundred meters down the road, a blockade of stones and tree trunks. We approached with caution. I told the flanking guard squads to get into a line formation and sweep south beyond the blockades looking for any sign of an ambush or detonation wires leading up to the road to a mine.

Mine sweep known as the Magical Mystery Tour. Dawn on QL-1 south of LZ North English. Boobie traps where placed amongst rocks and other objects on the road to slow down the sweep.

The squads were off the road on the right and left and about fifty meters out when in a line formation. Nothing was found, and I had them stop and stay in their positions until the road sweep team cleared the blockades. They were our protection if we were hit by an ambush here in the *Pacified Zone*. (However, remember I would have to call back to the command center for permission to fire back if they were hit by an ambush. So what was their protection?)

To our left, through the palm trees and jungle vegetation, we could see the old railroad berm. The berm was elevated eight to ten feet above the jungle floor to protect the tracks from flooding. At this time, there were no tracks or railroad timbers. How long they had been gone I had no idea. The berm did offer a good shield for an ambush. I constantly watched in that direction for any movement. At each stream bridge were located Local Reactionary Forces (ruff puffs) who would fire one shot as we passed.

Several times I asked our company interpreter and MACV interpreters why the RFs did this but got no explanation. Several times RFs would throw grenades into the stream pools below the bridges to kill fish for their breakfast. Of course, they would wait until we were almost past and cause everyone to jump. I'm sure they got a big kick out of watching us.

As we continued down the road, my platoon sergeant came up to my side and said as long as there were Vietnamese out in their rice fields or walking in that direction there probably was no ambush or direct detonation mine along the route. If we saw no one along the route or the locals running away from an area, then we should get ready for a firefight. This was a clue to watch out for; many times when this was observed, the first convoy coming through would get hit.

We continued south and finally came to the outskirts of the town of Bong Son. Here the road was paved to the bridge on the south end of town, and the sweep teams were allowed to mount the trucks to the bridge. There we would take a break and talk to the tank platoon leader and his tankers who were protecting the bridge at night.

After thirty minutes, the road was declared open, and we would head back to the base camp. After mine sweep, we would go on whatever mission was assigned. If we weren't on a patrol then we would get to work on clearing a drainage ditch in Bong Son, or rebuild a blown bridge or culvert, or defuse a booby trap or land mine, etc.

One day while the platoon was working on the drainage near the Bong Son Bridge, I noticed the local workers diving into the brown muddy water at the blocked culvert. The water was topped by a green slimy algae. When they would surface, they would have small fish, about three to five inches long. They would hold the squirming fish by the tail and with the other hand would make one cleaning swipe and then pop it into their mouths and swallow it whole, muddy slime and all. Yum Yum!

While working in and around the larger cities, our battalion was allowed to hire local workers to do the main labor while most of the platoon was used to set up a perimeter guard. We always had to contend with the coke girls, popcycle boys, and boot shine boys. Most of the time they didn't bother us while we were working but did know to show up just before break time and lunch.

In the late afternoon ,when we were convoying back to the base camp from Bong Son, we would see a large herd of water buffalo at the north end of town. The herd would be grazing between the road and the railroad berm. Small boys would be herding the buffalo usually riding on the back of one of the animals. These were the plow pullers of the local farmers and a very prized possession. If a water buffalo was killed during an ambush, the local province chief would have to be compensated immediately. Usually 500 Piasters (Vietnamese money), which was about $26 U. S. dollars.

One afternoon while we were returning from a job south of Bong Son, the convoy we were traveling with was ambushed right at the spot where the herd was grazing. The Traveling Guns quad fifty machine gun truck was just approaching that spot when the shooting began. Most of the herd was killed along with several of the boys with the herd.

By the time we got to the spot, the ambush was all over and only the dead bodies of the herd and herders lay along the road. The owners of the water buffalo were paid the usual and the families of the boys were given much less. MACV advisers and their ARVNs had responded from Bong Son and were securing the area.

Each day started with a mine sweep. Each platoon was alternated to go north, south, or stay at the base camp to pull perimeter duty until the sweep was done, and to be available for a response team if one of the platoons got into an ambush too hot to shoot their way out.

When heading north to LZ Lowboy, we passed through the villages of Tam Quan and An Thai. Tam Quan was the home of the ARVN Mechanized Infantry known as the White Horse unit. There were quite a few bamboo-framed buildings and some French style stucco white buildings. The village of An Thai was a few bamboo- framed hootches scattered along the west side of the road.

In each small village were small, bamboo-framed structures covering a dugout trench about three to four feet deep. This was the place for their water buffalo at night to protect the buffalo from firefights and mortars. The villagers all had underground dugouts they could hide in if danger came near. We had to check out these holes each day to look for weapons caches. Very seldom did we find anything along this stretch of QL-1.

CHAPTER 7
JUST RECRUITING BODIES

One morning when returning from LZ Lowboy my RTO received a call from the command post; an ARVN convoy heading north had been ambushed across from our battalion base camp, and several ARVNs had been captured. Our mission was to get to the ambush sight and follow the enemy if possible and try to help MACV recover the captured ARVNs.

We found the convoy stopped south of our access road. Apparently, there were only about twenty ARVNs in the convoy, and they were very reluctant to follow the enemy into the jungle. The ambush had been sprung from the east side of the road in thick vegetation that came close to the roadside. When the lead driver of the front truck had been killed and the convoy stopped, several NVA troops had run out of the brush and grabbed several of the closest ARVNs. (Probably just recruiting new bodies.)

MACV advisers from Bong Son were already there and had a local farmer off to the side of the road interrogating him. The advisers had a Vietnamese interpreter who would ask the farmer a question, and all he got back was a shaking of his head, "NO." The farmer was not giving the right answers. I found out later in my tour that the ARVN supplied interpreters were usually from wealthy families down in Saigon and didn't speak the same dialect as the poor dirt farmers north of Saigon.

After several "NO" answers, the interpreter was getting angry. Out came his side arm, a U.S. 45- caliber pistol. This he placed against the side of the farmers' head. I yelled, "STOP" and approached the MACV advisers. I asked if this was necessary and was told to mind my own business and let the ARVN do his job. The MACV advisers were a major and captain so what could I do?

About that time several ARVNs who were milling around the village hootches began setting them on fire. As one of the thatched roofs lit up in orange flame, shots rang out from the railroad berm; bullets whizzed by like angry bees and the ARVNs *di di maued* (ran like hell was after them) to the other side of the road.

I don't know where the MACV advisers went. My platoon spread out along the village and returned fire. I ran toward the berm to get a better firing position behind the trunk of a large palm tree. My RTO was with me, and I had him call our company to give them a situation report and request the duster tanks for support. They were always itching for a fight and would respond at the drop of a hat.

The company radio operator acknowledged our transmission and said to standby. I took the handset from the RTO and added we requested permission to shoot back (we already were) and requested *Tommy Two Bars* respond with the tankers. I received no reply on the second request. I was advised I had a free fire clearance and to proceed against the enemy.

I called to the platoon to get on line and move forward to the berm. We made our way under automatic rifle fire from tree to tree until we were at the west side of the railroad berm. Whatever size NVA force was there was right on the other side of the berm. My platoon was strung out along the berm, and several men would pop up and fire a burst over the berm, and the NVA would do the same. After several minutes, this was getting us nowhere, so I yelled for grenades. I pulled the pin on a fragmentation grenade, let the spring loaded spoon fly, counted to three and tossed the grenade over.

Several of the squad members did the same.

Boom, boom, boom, boom.

Dirt and shrapnel went flying. Just as the sound began to fade, I looked up and saw several Chinese communist grenades coming over towards us. Several of us in the platoon shouted a warning, and everyone got down.

Boom, boom, boom, on our side.

Luckily, they were only concussion grenades. Several platoon members were hit by shrapnel but not seriously wounded.

I looked up and saw an M60 tank coming up the berm from the south. We were still receiving rifle fire but not as heavy. The tank stopped in front of our position and swung its big gun over to the east away from us. The tank commander, a sergeant, opened a hatch on the back of the turret and yelled for us to get down, so he could fire a canister round.

A canister round was a shell loaded with hundreds of small steel arrows called flechetes. I yelled for my men to get down as the first shell was fired. *KABANG*, there was a tremendous back blast concussion and dust flew everywhere. *KABANG*, again more dust. I looked up just as the second round was fired and watched vegetation fly up into the air forty or fifty meters. *KABANG*, the tank turret swung a little to the left and right as the cannon was fired. *KABANG*, more brush and small trees went flying. My ears were ringing, and I had a headache. Everything got very quiet.

I saw the hatch open again, and the sergeant popped up to say, "That should've got em, Lieutenant."

Looking to my right and left my men were still hugging the ground covered with dust. I told my sergeant to stay put, and I would move up the slope to check for any sign of the NVA.

I moved to my left toward our left flank. I slowly climbed the eight feet up to the top to take a quick peek. I popped up long enough to look right and left. I didn't see anyone. I moved farther to my left, to the end of our left flank, and told the men there to move up with me for cover. I motioned the rest of the platoon to stay put. We eased our way up, and I popped up again this time taking a longer look. No one.

I motioned to the other two we were going to cross over to the other side and to be ready. We spread out several meters apart and ran up and over the top. Once on the top, I could see the enemy had vacated the area. We dropped down to the other side, and I looked into the jungle for any movement. Vegetation was lying down in a wide arc from the tank out; the smell of cannon powder and cut brush hung thick in the air. A green mist hung several meters above the ground in the hot, humid, dead calm silence.

Only the tanks motors could be heard. Of course with everyone's ears ringing, no wonder. I called for the rest of the platoon to follow over. I ordered everyone to be alert and to move out in a line formation about twenty to thirty meters into the jungle looking for dead bodies, equipment or blood trails. Everyone spread out and began looking through the downed vegetation. The only plant life that didn't get cut down were the palm, bread- fruit and similar type large trees.

I looked back toward the berm and saw our battalion commander, a lieutenant colonel and the battalion command sergeant major, all decked out in full battle gear. I went over to the lieutenant colonel to report. I didn't salute. When in the field of combat, no one with any sense acknowledged rank. This the enemy was always looking for to snipe at the leaders. We did it, and they did it. I probably would have saluted *Tommy Two Bars* just to increase his anxiety, if nothing else. I never got the chance during my tour to find out his reaction.

I briefed the lieutenant colonel on the situation, and he first wanted to know where my company commander was. I told him I would check with the company communication sergeant on the disposition of the re-enforcement's and the whereabouts of their leader. I told my RTO to call and make the request but not to identify the lieutenant colonel as being here. Several

73

minutes later, the reply was we were on our own with no *Tommy Two Bars* to respond.

About this time, the duster tank commander called to say he was on our right flank about a quarter mile to the south and just saw a large NVA unit leave the jungle to our front, cross the open rice fields, and enter another island of jungle to our southeast. In this area of coastal plain, there were islands of jungle disbursed throughout the large rice fields. The jungled islands were any where from several hundred meters in diameter to several thousand meters in diameter.

The lieutenant colonel ordered me to sweep this jungled island to the rice fields, and he would call the 173rd to send an infantry unit to our southeast to try an intercept. We were to hold on the far side of the jungle to block any crossing to the north. The duster tanks were to hold on our right flank to warn us of any movement toward us from the southeast. The M60 tanks moved up to our left flank to cover us on the north side of the jungle.

I gave my platoon sergeant the orders, and he pointed out what the men found. No bodies or equipment. Only a few blood trails, which could have been the ARVN captives. I called the duster tank commander and asked if he had seen any captives.

He said, "No, they were too far away and moving through tall grass to see clearly."

I told him we were moving out into the jungle and would stay in touch.

My platoon sergeant pointed out why we had no kills. There were slit trenches running parallel to the berm about twenty meters inside the jungles edge with short trenches running diagonal and intersecting the longer trenches. These afforded the enemy the cover from the tank cannons and any grenades landing near the trenches. Probably after the tank commander said he was done the NVA ran (*di di maued*) back through the jungle while we were getting organized to cross the berm.

The NVA had a habit of picking up all their gear and wounded or dead and taking them out of the area. If they couldn't take the dead because of distance they would quickly dig a shallow grave and cover them and their equipment. We didn't have time to look for possible graves. I ordered the platoon into a line formation and to sweep through the jungle slowly towards the east. The lieutenant colonel and command sergeant major remained with the tanks and monitored the radio traffic.

Once into the uncut jungle, one could only see several meters in any direction. It was very hard to keep track of the men. After about thirty minutes shots rang out to my left, then several more to the right.

I yelled, "What are you shooting at?"

Several voices yelled NVA were running to the left and right in front of us. My right flank had pushed faster than the left and caught the two NVA who were running from the left flank.

The NVA soldiers were out of ammunition and surrendered when they rounded a hedgerow of bamboo right into the right flank. My men yelled they had two down, and I ordered the line to halt where they were until I moved over to the enemy position. I had to call several times to locate where my men had the prisoners. I finally found them. The NVA were bunched on the ground on their knees being prodded by my men's gun barrels. I ordered that stopped and told my men to take the NVAs' equipment and tie their hands behind their backs and to blind fold their eyes.

My RTO reported the capture to the lieutenant colonel. I ordered two men to stay put with the NVA and keep watch for more. The rest of the platoon pushed off into the jungle, and we finally came to the east side of the jungle island. Several men located openings to tunnels where the NVA had been first sighted. I had the RTO call for demolition to be brought out to us. I also suggested *Tommy Two Bars* come out for a peek, knowing the lieutenant colonel was listening.

This might have been close to insubordination, as *Tommy Two Bars* later commented, but I was getting very frustrated by his lack of participation with the rest of the company out in the field. After all we were expected to be out here, in the *Pacified Zone*, getting shot at and so was the lieutenant colonel. At this time, I had no idea how far up the chain of command the frustration was going concerning *Tommy Two Bars* behavior. But in time I was to find out!

My platoon set up on the southeast corner of the jungled island, watching for any movement from the jungle island across the rice fields to our southeast. We could see the tracks the NVA made as they crossed from one island to the other. There were three definite ARVN boot tracks along with the NVA tracks. We watched the infantry choppers circling farther southeast and drop down behind the jungle cover.

About an hour later, we saw movement near the edge of the far island. The 173rd had swept through the jungle and found nothing. My RTO call the lieutenant colonel to report our sighting, and he called the 173rd. About that time, the first platoon arrived with the demolition to close the tunnels. The lieutenant colonel ordered me to secure from the blocking position and bring the NVA prisoners to him.

I had several men escort the prisoners back and met up with the first platoon. The first platoon brought the explosives to the tunnels. Before I set the charges, I decided I wanted to take a look inside the tunnels. The entries were covered with vegetation and would never have been seen if the NVA had not popped up and run. I moved the vegetation aside and looked down into the hole.

It was about two feet in rough diameter and dropped down about four feet. At the bottom was a ninety- degree turn. This is where a booby trap could be located. Either a grenade attached to a trip wire, a buried small anti-personnel mine, or a two- step snake (bamboo viper) hanging up at the roofline ready to bite.

I dropped down to the bottom and, using a flashlight, peeked down the passage- way. The tunnel continued about ten meters straight to another turn. The more I looked at the turn I could see there was a "T" intersection. Sometimes with this kind of intersection, one side would make another ninety degree turn shortly up the tunnel and double- back parallel to the stretch I was looking down. That tunnel would stop and there would be a small hole about half way up the wall between the two. That gave Charlie the opportunity to drop a grenade behind anyone crawling in after him.

I could see no snake but couldn't tell if there was any booby trap waiting for me. I decided to toss a grenade into the tunnel to set off any booby traps. I backed out and pulled out a grenade. I told the men near the hole to spread out in case there was a big booby trap down below designed to get more than the tunnel rat coming in. Sometimes Charlie would set a fifty pound mine as a surprise for the unfortunate tunnel rat and his buddies.

I pulled the pin and tossed the grenade down into the tunnel. I ran to the others who were twenty to thirty meters away. *BUMP*. The grenade sound was muffled and black smoke belched from the ground.

Several minutes later several platoon members called,"Hey Lieutenant, look at the smoke coming up out of the ground."

I went over and saw smoke coming up from several other holes around the area.

The lieutenant colonel radioed and inquired on our progress. I told him of the discovery of many connected tunnels. He said to mark the tunnels and return to QL-1 as the daylight was fading, and we could bring mitymite gas out tomorrow to close the system. I ordered the first platoon to form up on line and sweep back to QL-1 with my platoon following their rear. We moved quickly while looking for any sign of more NVA.

When back at QL-1, the platoons were sent back to our base camp with the lieutenant colonel, command sergeant major, the first platoon, and myself being the last to enter the camp. I was told by the lieutenant colonel not to mention to *Tommy Two Bars* (not his choice of reference) of his presence during the mission.

"Yes sir, Colonel," I replied and left him at the entrance to the Battalion Command Center. Lt. Steve (Tomlinson) and I walked back to the company area and a few much needed cold beers.

Upon arriving, I reported to *Tommy Two Bars*, on the events of the afternoon and mentioned the mitymite for the next day.

Tommy Two Bars comment, "I'll make the decision on your mission for tomorrow, Lieutenant, *is that clear?*"

"Yes sir, very clear, sir, is that all, sir?" I was dismissed. I turned to leave and was again stopped for a courtesy salute to the captain. I must say I was looking forward to the next day after the colonel requested a report from *Tommy Two Bars* on the tunnels if we didn't finish the job.

Left to right: Sgt. Delagarza and Sgt. MacCarthy with captured NVA flag after ARVN ambush across from LZ North English, January 1969. Note sand filled 55 gallon drums in the back ground.

I went back to my bunker, and as I was dropping off my gear, a shot rang out from Lieutenant Steve's bunker. I ran over with several others. Lieutenant Steve was lying on his cot with a shocked look. He had his 45-caliber automatic in his right hand and a beer in his left. The tip of his right boot had been shot off.

When Lieutenant Steve regained himself, he said, "I was lying here having a cool beer waiting for you when a rat the size of a large cat jumped up on the end of the cot and slowly walked across. I slowly got my pistol and took aim. I must've aimed too low, and when I pulled the trigger, the bullet went under the rat and hit my boot."

He took off his boot and luckily hadn't hit his foot. That would have been a court martial offense even if an accident.

"God damn it, Steve," I hollered, "Are you nuts, you can't get wounded and leave me here all alone with *Tommy Two Bars*!"

He just sat there looking at his boot and then his pistol.

Finally I said, "Where's my beer?" We both broke out laughing and that was that.

CHAPTER 8
WHAT A MISTAKE!

The next morning when we got our missions, Lieutenant Steve was sent to blow the tunnels, and I was going on another helicopter ride. The first platoon and third platoon went on mine sweep at daybreak. My platoon sergeant and I were picked up at the battalion pad by a troop transport helicopter and flown south about forty miles to the sight of a blown culvert. This happened to be in the pass being protected by the tank battalion I had seen when I first rode up QL-1 several months earlier.

M-60 tank on QL-1 protecting road working crew. Note the search light over the cannon.

As we circled the blown culvert, I could see a large hole covering half the road. This was blown by a fifty- pound mine or larger. I looked out, up and down the pass, and saw the same tanks every two to three hundred meters along both sides of the road. The pilot landed on the road. The hole was even bigger up close. This culvert was at least six feet in diameter and down eight to ten feet below the road grade. This was going to take more than a few men and a shovel.

A lieutenant from the tankers walked over from the nearest tank and introduced himself. He said that during the night old Charlie must have snuck by the infantry in the surrounding foothills and planted the mine. The tanks are pulled back to their base camp at night and redeployed every morning to guard the pass. Several companies of infantry are deployed along both sides of the pass in the foothills to discourage this type of behavior.

I pointed out to the lieutenant that we are in a *Pacified Zone* and this type on behavior is frowned upon. I would bring it up with my lieutenant colonel and company commander when I returned to the battalion.

We jumped back in the helicopter and took off. The air at fifteen hundred feet was cool and refreshing. The ride back to the battalion was much too short. As we passed LZ North English I looked up north on the east side of the railroad berm trying to get sight of Lieutenant Steve and his platoon in the jungle, too thick to see much of anything. No wonder our pilots and door gunners had such a hard time seeing their targets and landing in safe landing zones. Charlie could have been taking aim right in front of me, and I wouldn't see him until it was all over. This happened all too often on the ground too.

After landing, I thanked the pilots for a ride, this always made them happy, and I went to report to *Tommy Two Bars*. He told me to get the necessary equipment and men together and take care of the mission. I suppose I was expecting him to at least handle some of the base camp logistics, but I guess he was training me to be self-sufficient.

Either sink or swim was how he trained his junior officers. I suppose I deserved some of this type of training for my testy way of trying to help him get to know his men better by consorting with them in a combat setting. At least he was getting to know the men in his headquarters platoon.

I walked over to the Heavy Equipment Company and told the company first sergeant what I needed. His company commander, a first lieutenant, was out in the field checking on his men and should be back by noon. He said he would get the necessary equipment ready. All he needed was a mission number to authorize the men and equipment. As I was giving him the number, a loud bang was heard coming from the east. The first sergeant looked up and commented, "Must be another ambush."

"No," I said, "just Lieutenant Steve and his platoon blowing a tunnel complex we had found yesterday while tracking the NVA platoons that ambushed the ARVNs."

I was sure disappointed at not getting the opportunity to use mitymite to blow those tunnels. Not that blowing the tunnels was going to slow Charlie down but seeing how many openings where involved gives an idea how big the complex was. I would have to wait for Lieutenant Steve's report.

I walked back to my platoon area and saw that my platoon sergeant was getting the equipment ready. Everyone in the platoon was cleaning weapons and checking the gear we would be taking. We also drew extra C rations incase we would be out for several days. Several hours later Lieutenant Steve returned with his platoon and reported his mission to me in his version not the one he related to *Tommy Two Bars*.

After a normal, dull, mine sweep to the south, the platoon stopped across from our access road and lugged the mitymite gas equipment into the jungle. The lead squad swept the area of the tunnels before the rest of the platoon set up the gas. Mitymite gas is acetylene vapor pumped into the tunnels by fan, run by a small six hundred watt generator. First a smoke grenade, either yellow or red, (a color easily seen drifting up through the thick vegetation), is tossed into the tunnel and a plastic poncho is used to cover the entrance. This forces a draft and the smoke drifts throughout the tunnels and rises to the exits. Once the exit holes are found they are covered by several men at a distance in case there are any Charlies down below trying to escape.

Then the gas is pumped into the tunnel. After twenty to thirty minutes, the pump is removed, and a TNT charge is set in the tunnel entrance to be detonated by an electrical blasting cap charged by a small hand cranked generator, called a *clacker*. These were also used to detonate the claymore mines set out for perimeter protection at night in the field and in the perimeter wire around the base camp.

Lieutenant Steve discovered a much bigger area, than had been thought, and had to spread his platoon out a wider perimeter. He decided to use a fragmentation grenade to set off the charge. He checked the pattern of the holes and decided he had enough room to run directly to the west after tossing in the grenade. Could have been a big mistake. When the blast occurred, the ground under Lieutenant Steve heaved up as he was running and threw him back the way he had come.

Due to the largeness of the complex and the amount of vegetation, no one was hurt. Only ringing ears and headaches. Lieutenant Steve decided to withhold this description of events from *Tommy Two Bars*. I told Lieutenant Steve as the executive officer of the company it was my duty to report this incident to the commander at once. We both had a good laugh over that one and went to eat lunch.

I thought, *I'm glad he's ok, and everything turned out with no injuries.*

Many times while on my tour, I made decisions contrary to procedure or took chances and lucked out with no injury to my men or myself. I tried to use common sense as much as I could and if it was contrary to military procedure so be it. It was my decision.

The next morning, after mine sweep was completed, I gathered the heavy equipment operators and my platoon and told them where we were going and what our next secret mission consisted of. We set up the convoy and after notifying the company communications operator of our status (number of EM, NCOs and Officers) the convoy left the base camp.

The drive south went well, and when we arrived, I showed the heavy equipment NCO in charge what needed to be done, and he organized his men to start. My platoon sergeant set up a perimeter out about fifty meters to protect the operators while they worked. A D9 dozer was off loaded from its lowboy trailer and began uncovering the asphalt from the undamaged part of the road. Another dozer quickly cut a road out in the jungle around the culvert, so convoys could pass us without holding up our work.

After exposing the top of the culvert, the first dozer dropped off to the damaged side of the culvert to remove mud and debris around the entry. The mud in the streambed was deeper than expected, and the dozer quickly dug itself deep into the stream. The mud came up to the base of the drivers seat with the dozer blade up at about a twenty- degree angle.

The heavy equipment NCO motioned the other dozer operator to come over to help get the first dozer out. The second dozer operator maneuvered his dozer to the front of the first, blade to blade. Heavy steel cables were attached between the two and as the first tried to move forward the second tried to backup. Neither moved, and the second began digging down into the soft dirt.

The tank commander was watching and came over to offer his tank for the pull, saying, "I'll get him out of that little mess, we do this all the time with our tanks."

He motioned for his tank driver to bring over the M60 tank. The second dozer uncoupled and went back to work. The big tank backed up to the dozer blade and was cabled up.

Again both tried to move forward. The big tank shuddered and the treads began to slip and slide the tank to the left off the asphalt onto the shoulder of the road. The tank was uncoupled and moved to a different angle to the right front of the dozer so as to be completely on the asphalt. Both were again cabled up and had the same result. The mud was sucking the dozer so hard, there was no moving forward, and every time the dozer track moved, the deeper the dozer dug itself in.

I remembered an OCS instructor, an old NCO at heavy equipment orientation, saying the way to unstuck a stuck dozer was to use explosives. I told the lieutenant, and he laughed saying we would have to send for a tank retriever up at his base camp several miles north. I said only if the explosive didn't work.

I had several men dig down behind the dozer to create an open pocket to place the explosives. I decided to go light on the charge as to minimize any damage to the dozer. I set four blocks of quarter pound TNT across the lower back of the dozer, with an electric blasting cap detonator, so I could fire them at the right time. When ready, I motioned everyone back and told the driver of the dozer to leave the dozer in neutral and get off. Then I motioned the tanker to begin a slow tug on the cables. When the cable was tight and straining, I blew the charge and the tank pulled forward with the dozer like it was a light-weight car. The tank driver thought the cable had broke and dragged the dozer forty or fifty meters down the road.

Boy was I glad that I remembered what that NCO had told us. At least I did get something out of my training in OCS besides how to harass my lower ranking men and lack of sleep. By this time it was mid day, and we were running out of time to get the job done today.

I had a hole dug on the south side of the undamaged section of the culvert, down to the bottom, so I could pack enough C4 explosive under it to lift it up and out to the east side of the road. This, I figured, would clear the blown culvert out of the way, so the new one could be lowered in its place.

I decided sixty pounds of C4 should do the trick. I packed the white rectangular shaped blocks of C4 side by side under the culvert. The C4 explosive came in blocks two inches square by about eight inches long. C4 was of a soft doughy consistency and easy to work with. I also decided to use timed detonation fuse instead of detonation by electric charge. *What a mistake!*

I had the men move the equipment and themselves away from the culvert about seventy-five meters. Then I cut a twenty-minute section of fuse and stuck it in the end of a blasting cap. I carefully crimped the end of the cap down on the fuse. Then it was gently forced into the mass of explosive. Once I was satisfied all was ready I lit the fuse and walked the seventy-five meters to the trucks and men. We waited. I watched the wisps of blue smoke rise from the pit and glanced at my watch. We had set guards north and south on the road to stop any traffic that might come along. None did.

As the twentieth minute approached, I called out for one more minute. By then, I wasn't paying much attention to the smoke.

Five, four, three, two, one. *Silence*.

I looked up at the culvert. Nothing. By this time of the day, there were long shadows blanketing the canyon. I got my binoculars out of the truck and took a closer look. As time marched on my heart pounded harder by the minute. The procedure now was to let an additional fifteen minutes go by before approaching the explosives, in the event of a miss cut on the time fuse, or damp fuse which could still be slowly burning.

In this humid area, damp fuses occurred often. I scanned the culvert praying for a sudden blast. I didn't want to have to walk up there. At plus five minutes, I saw a definite puff of blue smoke rise from the pit.

HOPE, HOPE, HOPE!!! Nothing.

The smoke drifted on the air like it was laughing at me. Plus ten and I began sweating, more than just from the hot humid air. The more I looked through the binoculars, the more I either didn't see anything, or I thought I saw wisps of blue smoke. The light was fading fast, and I had to go in.

Plus fifteen came and went and my platoon sergeant suggested we give it another fifteen. I said, "No, we've gone through the procedure, now I have to walk out there to check the charge."

My legs were beginning to shake, and I was having difficulty breathing. My skin felt like it was on fire. I had to go. That was my job as the officer in charge. I couldn't send anyone else. If I did, I would lose any respect I demanded from my men, and my own self-respect. I sure didn't want to be branded like *Tommy Two Bars*. I would rather die than get that hung on my head.

Slowly, I stepped around the trucks and started off to the culvert, my legs didn't want to move in that direction. I kept looking at the pit for any sign of blue smoke to indicate I could stop and wait. Several times I thought I saw smoke, but my mind was racing, and the dim light was causing everything to look blue. I stopped about half way and looked through my binoculars. Nothing. The sweat was running down my face, and I felt like my life was at an end. My mouth and throat felt like a desert.

My heart was pounding so hard I could hardly get my legs to start up. Fear will do strange things to a man. I looked back at the men and so wanted to turn and run back to safety. I took a deep breath and started off to the culvert and possible death. I walked faster as I got close, as no matter what happened, I had passed the point of no return. I got to the lip of the pit and look down. I could see the fuse had stopped about six inches from the explosive. Just then a puff of smoke popped up from the fuse.

I jumped down in the pit and grabbed the fuse, ahead of the smoking end, and jerked it out of the explosive. I took a deep breath and pulled the fuse out of the blasting cap. I tossed the fuse out of the pit and sat down hard on the dirt. Suddenly, I felt awash with relief and had to urinate, I stood and relieved myself then and there. I felt so alive and alert by the adrenaline running through my veins. A few moments later, my breathing was calm, and I rose to the top of the pit. I tried to yell to the sergeant to bring an electric blasting cap and electric zip cord. My mouth was so dry I couldn't talk. I walked toward the others and motioned my sergeant to come to me.

The men came running to get the story on the fuse and say how they were glad I was ok. I was so relieved as the adrenaline began to fade I felt like crying. But I was their tough leader and couldn't show any emotion, just another day of an officer in Uncle Sam's Army.

I let the sergeant and his demolition team set the electric blasting-cap while I watched and then let them blow the culvert. What a relief to watch that steel culvert fly through the air to the east side of the road. Of course, it went twice as far as I had wanted, but I didn't care.

The crane operator quickly had the new culvert hooked up and set into the hole. I must say I wasn't paying to much attention, as I was winding down from my ordeal. The tankers would stay out here, with us, for the night and began to move into a perimeter formation around our position. Light was fading fast, and I brought in the two squads who had been on guard around the area.

My platoon sergeant assigned the night guard duty, C rations were eaten and we settled in for the night. Didn't get much sleep though. Hand flares were popping all up and down the canyon, along the hills around our position. Sudden fire fights would erupt here and there lasting only seconds with lots of tracers, both red and green, flying in all directions. Then all would be quite, except for a pop now and again in the same general direction of the ambush. This was the reality of the *Pacified Zone*.

Activity slowed down as the night wore on and by dawn all was quiet. Several medevac helicopters flew over and landed at different spots on the ridge to the east. The tank crews spread out down the canyon, and I had our security squads set up a wide perimeter again with orders to stay alert. The heavy equipment NCO got his men going, and the abutments at either end of the culvert were finished by noon.

Work was stopped for chow, and coke girls showed up with a large convoy heading north. As the military convoy was passing our area, mortars started hitting in the jungle to the east, about fifty meters off the road. Apparently, Charlie was still up in the hills. The tanks quickly started returning fire to the top of a ridge- line about half a mile northeast of us. Five tanks, north and south of us, fired and several moved from their fixed position up QL-1 to get a better angle. I noticed an L-19 spotter plane over the ridge. That would explain how the tanks knew where to direct their cannon fire. The small aircraft continued to circle and, every few minutes, dove toward the ridge and fired a smoke rocket into the jungle, marking a spot for the tanks to target. The mortar rounds stopped hitting quickly once the tanks opened up.

I told my platoon sergeant we should get our job done and gather up our troops for the trip back. He agreed and checked the concrete on the abutment for curing to determine if it was ready for pressure from the back fill of crushed rock. It appeared to be, so the dump trucks were brought up and the filling began. By mid-afternoon the job was complete, and we had our own convoy ready to go. I called the tank commander and thanked him for his protection, and we were off.

By the time we were back at LZ North English, the sun was behind the west mountains, and we were all ready for a shower and a beer. Lieutenant Steve was just coming from his platoon mission, and we both were highly agitated when we found out our shower water tanks hadn't been filled this day. This was the Battalion Headquarters Company responsibility and had not been done. Of course they and the battalion staff had water.

So Lieutenant Steve and I decided to sneak over to their shower tent on the other side of the base camp. We didn't really sneak; we rode in Lieutenant Steve's platoon truck. We just didn't tell anyone where we were going since we weren't needed at that time, and we didn't think *Tommy Two Bars* had a need to know. By the time we got there, the shower tent was empty. The tent was OD green, about ten feet wide and twenty feet long. Kinda like the one in the movie M.A.S.H.

I was just lathering up when I heard an odd sound. Kinda like an arrow flying overhead. I stopped to listen and *KWAAAAM*. Shrapnel hit the top of the tent.

Lieutenant Steve said, "I think we just got hit."

Swwwiissssh, swwwiisssh, *KWAAAAM, KWAAAAM.*

We both went flying for the floor. Here we were stark naked, with no protection around the tent, and neither of us brought our helmets or flack vests. Just then all went quiet. No more incoming, and no perimeter shooting, which was the normal response.

We both quickly dressed and drove over to our company area in the direction of the explosions. I was shocked to see the damage to my platoon buildings. The second platoon supply tent had a direct hit and was scattered all around the inside of the perimeter. Shrapnel had struck my bunker, penetrating from four feet high to the roof. Many pieces entered on the north side and exited on the south side. My platoon sergeant had been lying on his bunk. He was protected by the fifty five gallon steel barrels full of sand, which stopped the shrapnel from the ground up to four feet.

The shower tin sided building looked like a strainer, with hundreds of jagged holes from the ground to the top. If anyone had been in there, they would've been killed. I later called the headquarters company commander and asked him to personally thank his water tanker operators for not filling our tank.

The shrapnel also hit my platoon living-fighting bunker, and several men had been seriously wounded. These men had been standing when the shells came in. Our medics took care of the men, and they were taken to the battalion medical station a few meters to our north. Some shrapnel flew all over the battalion base camp, but the only casualties were in my platoon.

Later, *Tommy Two Bars* advised me the incoming shells had been friendly fire from an artillery unit based at LZ English. Apparently an FNG artillery officer had decided to test fire his battery and used an old pre set grid co-ordinate for his target. The shells that came whistling in were 155mm sized rounds. These are big buggers; only one hit inside our base camp. The others hit in our outer perimeter. One landed in front of an occupied perimeter guard bunker and was a dud. If it had blown, it would have taken the two perimeter guards to their graves.

A medevac chopper came in and picked up my two men before I could get over to the medical station. Our battalion surgeon said they were seriously wounded but should recover. I realized fate had again stepped in to remove me from harms way. I began thinking I was immune from injury.

WRONG!

CHAPTER 9
U SHAPED AMBUSH

Several days later, my platoon and the first platoon were assigned to mine sweep QL-1. First platoon and my platoon point men headed up the access road together. The first platoon was on the left, and the second platoon was on the right in columns separated by five meters. The first was going to head up QL-1 to the north, and we to the south. This particular day I decided not to walk point and was riding in my platoon command truck until we got to QL-1 and were heading south. Both groups of men reached the entry of our access road and split to the left and right. As the mine detector operators reached the intersection and began turning ...*KABANG!*

A claymore mine was activated; directed right down our access road. The mine had been tied to a large tree just north of the intersection. Thankfully the mine had been placed too high to hit the men up close and most of the buck shot sized pellets (all 400 of them) went up and over our heads. Only one man in the first platoon was hit. He was at the rear of the column and had not zipped up his flack vest. One pellet hit him square in the heart and killed him on the spot. It went perfectly between the unzipped zipper on the vest.

Shots began coming from all around our access road. We were caught in a horseshoe ambush and were receiving rifle fire from three different directions. I jumped out of the truck and at first was confused as to the direction the incoming fire was coming; it wasn't a continuous rapid fire from only one direction. Several bullets flew close to my head, sounding like bees zipping by from front, right and left.

I directed my fifty caliber machine gunner to fire to the right, because to the front were the bulk of our own troops, still on the road. As he began to direct his fire toward the rice paddies to the right, a lot of bullets hit the side of the truck and forced him to bail out to the road. I directed my grenadier to launch grenades to the rice fields out about one hundred meters. I could see the movement of the rifle fire and the green tracers coming from below the tops of the green rice stalks in several different places, to the right and left of our position. I wasn't concerned with the front at that time. Lieutenant Steve was up there.

A single lambreta suddenly appeared on QL-1 heading north. He was on our right moving to our left. The driver was caught in a cross fire and like slow motion I watched as bullets hit all around the lambreta and it's passengers. Not once did a bullet hit the vehicle as he sped up passing through the killing zone. I yelled at my right and left flank squads to swing out into the paddies and overrun the enemy positions. They began to move, and with the help of the grenadier and his well placed launched grenades, the incoming fire diminished.

The flank squads spotted the VC as they came on line with them in the rice paddies. A quick shootout killed or wounded them. No one from my platoon was hit. When all was finally quiet, I went out to check on the VC and their positions. They were all dressed in black silk clothing and were armed with the latest AK-47 rifles. The VC had dug pits in the rice paddies, so they would be below ground during the ambush.

This was probably why no one was shot and only one of our men had been hit by the mine. It looked like the VC were relying on the mine to take most of us out and then they would have the opportunity to pick off wounded or stranded troops up and down the road. I had heard of this type of ambush before.

Both platoons swept the jungle to the east of QL-1 and found only spent shell casings. After our adrenaline rush was over, we regrouped and continued on our original mission of mine sweep. I guess you could say we definitely missed that mine on the sweep. I talked to the point men in the first platoon, asking them if they noticed the mine on the tree trunk, or anything out of the ordinary. They said they were looking out past the tree, because it was so close to the road. A lesson learned by all. The man killed by the pellet was just outside our base camp gate and was carried back to the base camp medical station by medics who came running during the fire fight. He was kept there until a medevac helicopter came to take him to Qui Nhon for graves registration and his final trip home.

The rest of our mine sweep was uneventful. When we returned to the base camp, I was ordered to take my platoon north to assist Delta Company in a security position along QL-1, north of *Death Canyon*. I assembled my platoon members and told them where we were going and to bring extra ammunition. We rode in several trucks to LZ Lowboy and waited for the midday convoy. A large supply convoy arrived, and we fell in amongst them. There was a definite feeling of security in large numbers. I wasn't too concerned about another ambush this day.

As we continued north, I watched all the good spots for an ambush, but we drove by with no activity. We passed through *Death Canyon* and as we turned left, heading west, a feeling of dread came over me and I could smell death in the air. I asked my driver if he could smell it, and he said yes. It was a sharp smell of fresh blood and flesh that seemed to hang heavy on the humid air.

Up the road we turned north, and there was the platoon from Delta Company we were to assist in a sweep along both sides of QL-1. A large crater was in the center of the dirt road. After stopping to the side of the road, I walked over to the platoon leader and asked what caused the smell of death. The lieutenant said that earlier, while on mine sweep, a mine was located over there where the hole was. One of his sergeants, a short timer who was to return to the world at the end of the week, wanted to disarm the mine and lift it from the road, so he would have the experience to tell about.

He had been in the company all his tour and the platoon sergeant said the buck sergeant had the experience to lift the mine instead of blowing it in place. As he dug around the plastic explosive he determined it was about the size of a fifty- pound mine. A blasting cap had been inserted into the side and led to a bamboo trip device. The sergeant slowly pulled the blasting cap out of the explosive and cut the two wires leading to it, one at a time, which is correct procedure. Then he dug deeper around the sides to free the mine from the dirt. He started rocking the mine back and forth while he lifted the mine up. *KABOOOOOM*.

The mine detonated, and the sergeant *disappeared*. Nothing remained to be identified as human. Even his steel helmet and rifle were gone. Only the strong smell of vaporized human flesh hung in the air; tough luck for such a short time soldier.

I was assigned to sweep the west side of the road, from this point to the closest bridge north, which was about a mile up the road. I told my men to keep their eyes open for boobie traps and trip wires. I had my platoon sergeant set the platoon into a diamond formation and we pushed off, along the road and west about one hundred meters. Here, there was scrub brush and hills on both sides.

Once we arrived at the bridge, guarded by ARVNs, Delta Company's commander arrived, and ordered me to take my platoon to a position at the north end of *Death Canyon* and hold any north bound traffic there, while the Air Force made runs on a suspected NVA-VC supply camp, west of the spot of the Sergeant's killing. We rode back to that location. I spread my platoon out on either side of the road and waited for the Air Force to arrive.

The day was hot and humid, nothing new, with a pale blue sky and scattered clouds. The first jets came screaming from the east, heading to the west, up a valley between the hills and mountains on the west side of the road.

The planes dropped large bombs. A plume of black smoke would shoot up before we heard the sharp report of the explosion. After twenty or thirty minutes of bombing, the planes streaked down low and strafed the valley with their wing cannons. The cannons sounded like a moaning rumble, and then many reports of lesser explosions, as the rounds hit the targets or ground.

Bombing of NVA caught in coastal village.

This went on for several passes, and we were cheering them on. Suddenly, a streak of orange light shot up at a slow moving jet (at least from our point of view, it wasn't moving as fast as the others) and hit the jet in the belly.

The jet began to move up and down, and from side to side, and then went straight up a ways, until it stopped dead in the air, and fell tail first into the valley below trailing bursts of black smoke and orange flame. When the jet hit the ground, it burst into a large ball of red orange flame and loud bang.

I was called by one of the pilots to confirm any sighting of an ejection by the pilot of the crashed plane. We hadn't seen any ejection or parachute. The remaining planes continued their passes from different angles this time for several more minutes before breaking off and leaving for their home base. I was called by the Delta Company commander and told to hold my position while the troops of the Americal Division were sent into the valley to make a sweep.

I watched as twelve helicopters made their way along the coast, about half a mile east of us, and turned west as they came even with our location. They flew over us and entered the smoking valley. The choppers dropped into the trees, out of our sight. They went in to drop off the troops, one or two at a time. The door gunners started firing just before we lost sight of each one. After being on the ground a few seconds, the choppers would again lift into the air and circle back in our direction.

Gunship helicopters were circling as the troops were dropped off and continually fired their guns and rockets into the tree lines and jungle brush, at possible enemy positions. I listened to the infantry commanders as they pushed throughout the valley. Their battalion commander was in a helicopter several thousand feet above them. They came across the burning wreckage of the plane and confirmed the pilot was killed. Once the infantry were on the ground and moving, very little was heard coming from the valley. Many NVA bodies were found in and around a bunker complex tucked into the sides of a streambed flowing through the valley.

Several hours later the Delta Company commander called to release us . from the position and thanked us for our help. We married up with the next convoy heading south and made it back to LZ North English before darkness set in.

CHAPTER 10
WEST POINT, RANGER

Several days later, our battalion commander decided he had enough of *Tommy Two Bars* lack of command ability. He ordered him to personally take a patrol out at night. Battalion intelligence had been warned that a regimental size force of NVA were going to be moving through our area toward LZ English. *Tommy Two Bars* ordered Lieutenant Steve to get his platoon ready to go out that night.

Lieutenant Steve asked, "Sir, you don't mean the entire platoon to go out on a night patrol, do you, sir?"

Tommy Two Bars turned bright red. "You, Lieutenant, do not question my orders."

I broke in at this point and pointed out to the captain that it wasn't good procedure to take out an entire platoon at night. For this, I was blasted in the best *Tommy Two Bars* manner and given a lesson on his authority and training as a *West Point* graduate. Not to mention, but we will mention, his training in the *Ranger* program. Didn't I see the *Ranger* patch on his shoulder? This was taking place in the captain's office, with the company senior NCOs present.

I felt like a green schoolboy getting chewed out by a teacher in front of the class. I decided my loyalty to Lieutenant Steve and the company men was worth more than a possible court-martial from *Tommy Two Bars*. I felt I needed to try to talk some sense into the captain to avert a potential disaster.

Unfortunately, in the military, the person who has the rank prevails, and the lowly junior officers have little or no say, even though we may have more actual experience. As far as *Tommy Two Bars* was concerned, Lieutenant Steve and I were babes in the woods, regardless of the fact he had not been out in the field with his company from day one. He was under pressure from the battalion commander to personally take out a patrol.

This conversation was taking place late in the afternoon and by the time the platoon would be ready to go night would have been upon us; not only that, six new men had been assigned to the first platoon, and had little or no time out in the hostile world of Viet Nam. I requested a word with the captain after everyone left the office.

I asked, "Sir, can I go along on the patrol?"

"No you can't, Lieutenant, and that's final," he replied.

I then tried to get him to at least leave the new men back at the base camp. Not an option, the more men on the patrol the better, was his feeling. I tried again to explain to him the danger of moving out at night with that many men, and trying to set up an ambush point in the dark. Again I got a threat of court-martial for insubordination toward him, and was told to go to my platoon area and not one more word.

I turned to leave and was again stopped by *Tommy Two Bars* for the complimentary salute. Boy, did I not like this man! The light was fading fast. I walked over to the first platoon (off limits to me now) to have a talk with Lieutenant Steve. I told him he should leave the FNGs back at the base camp for their sake.

I knew he couldn't, even if he wanted to, *Tommy Two Bars* would have a fit if he tried. The sun was down now, and darkness was upon us. *Tommy Two Bars* walked up to us and ordered Lieutenant Steve to get his platoon moving to the base camp gate for departure.

Lieutenant Steve again questioned the sanity of going out after dark with this many, and *Tommy Two Bars* lost his patience with us. He ordered the first platoon sergeant to move out and ordered Lieutenant Steve to take up a position at the back of the column. I wished them well and told Lieutenant Steve I would keep my platoon and the third ready to come out if they should get into trouble. I watched as they walked away to the gate and their fate.

The platoon left the base camp and circled to the left. They passed around the north and west sides of the camp to finally head south into the jungle. I climbed up the fifty foot tower to watch their progress through the large starlight scope and listen to the radio. (*No*, not the arm forces radio with the tunes of the day. The platoon RTO talking to the communications sergeant as they moved through the jungle.)

Everything was moving smoothly for the first thirty minutes. *Tommy Two Bars* was several meters behind the point men followed by the platoon sergeant. I don't know the conversation if any between them. Lieutenant Steve was in the back of the column about six up from the rear. Luckily, Lieutenant Steve had talked *Tommy Two Bars* into letting him take the rifle starlight scope. At least he could check the surroundings as they moved.

After thirty minutes of several turns in the jungle *Tommy Two Bars* was completely lost. He decided to stop for a break. (Probably to try to get hold of himself some how. My thoughts on the subject.) *Tommy Two Bars* called to talk to me. (He knew I was in the tower.) I answered. He asked if I could see their position. No, I had lost sight of them after they entered the jungle, and couldn't keep track of the many turns they made. I was *no* help!

At that time, it dawned on me I didn't recall the captain giving his men permission to shoot back if they were hit. It crossed my mind to ask over the radio that particular point but decided *Tommy Two Bars* was probably on the verge of panic, and I didn't want to make the situation worse by antagonizing him.

About that time, Lieutenant Steve called from his position to the RTO up front of the column and asked what the delay was, why hadn't they been moving? The RTO said the column had been moving for about *ten minutes*.

Not the one Lieutenant Steve was in. He moved up the line and came to the end. One of the FNGs had panicked when the column stopped for a rest, and froze in place when the man in front of him took off. Now there were two groups out in the jungle, not knowing where each was located, and the first was making turns. At least they were now both about the correct size for a night patrol.

As time moved on, Lieutenant Steve had to decide to either try to marry up with the rest of his platoon, or work his way back to the base camp and hope they didn't cross *Tommy Two Bars* patrol and possible disaster. I decided to make the decision for him. I ordered him to return to the base camp as best he could.

About that time his patrol began being hit by rocks. He checked his surroundings, by the starlight scope, and was shocked to see villagers near his location throwing rocks. They were probably trying to get them to move before the NVA passed by and caught them (the villagers) in a cross- fire.

I called Lieutenant Steve and told him to watch for a hand flare I would have the west perimeter guard fire so he could get his bearings and move in that direction. Of course, if Charlie was listening to this, he would get a pretty good idea of their location too. The flare went up and drifted off to the north for a few minutes. Lieutenant Steve acknowledged the flare and began his move. Several minutes passed, and suddenly shots rang out about a half-mile south of the base camp.

The first platoon RTO, with *Tommy Two Bars*, called to report they had been hit by sniper fire and two of their men had been shot and they needed help. I called the battalion command center for permission to respond and was told the tank platoon (who were always ready for a fight) would be sent down QL-1 to get them out of the jungle.

The four big tanks roared out of the gate and with their large search- lights on, (these were mounted above the cannon and the size of a twenty five inch TV), raced out to QL-1 and turned right to head south. They called for the platoon to let them know when the tanks were even with them in distance from the base camp, and they would turn into the jungle and get them out. The platoon RTO called the tank commander and advised he was approaching their position in relation to QL-1

The tanks turned off the road and headed west. So far so good! Keeping watch on the south perimeter, I called our medical station to confirm they knew we had injured coming in. They were aware and were ready.

Lieutenant Steve again was pelted with rocks, and considered shooting, but decided to crawl to the opening up ahead at the outer edge of our perimeter. Now that the shooting had started he wouldn't trust the perimeter guards to hold their fire.

A NCO in the tower motioned there was movement in the jungle outside the perimeter. I looked at the starlight scope and seeing Lieutenant Steve looking through the brush near the ground, radioed him, and had him wait until I called the perimeter guards and let them know where the patrol was and they would be coming in shortly. Once the guard commanders confirmed that information and everyone was ready, I called Lieutenant Steve and told him to come in. Even then, he later told me, he had reservations on just walking in without being shot by our own men.

The tanks finally got to *Tommy Two Bars* patrol and told them to get aboard for the ride back to the base camp. *Tommy Two Bars* only wanted the wounded to go back. The tank platoon leader told the captain the battalion commander had aborted the mission, and he was to return to the base camp and report to the commander *NOW!* This he agreed to do, and the tanks returned to camp without further incident.

I climbed down from the tower once Lieutenant Steve was approaching the front gate. I met him half way back to the company area. He was so relieved to get back in one piece with his men. He was also ready to plug *Tommy Two Bars*. I told him what I knew at this time, which wasn't much, and to get back to his platoon area and I would wait for the tankers to return.

When the tanks returned, they went to the medical station with the two wounded, and I had a talk with the platoon sergeant. He was fit to be tied and was threatening to shoot *Tommy Two Bars*.

This is his story.

When the platoon was leaving the front gate the platoon sergeant turned to *Tommy Two Bars* and suggested, for the sake of the men and platoon morale, the platoon leader should be brought to the front. *Tommy Two Bars* cut him off and reminded him of who was in command here. As the platoon moved out from the base camp, it was becoming more and more clear to the platoon sergeant that *Tommy Two Bars* was way over his head on this patrol.

As the platoon entered the realm of darkness, under the canopy of jungle, vision was getting worse by the minute. The point men stopped frequently to ask which way they should go. *Tommy Two Bars* left it up to them on the direction and told them not to look to the platoon sergeant for direction. After moving in a rather random way, *Tommy Two Bars* called for a halt, to take a breather, and try to get his bearings. Apparently he wasn't keeping track of how long they had been moving and making mental notes on the stars they could see through the trees. This, the platoon sergeant was doing, so he at least had an idea about where they were.

After five minutes, *Tommy Two Bars* ordered the point to move out. The platoon sergeant moved up to *Tommy Two Bars* and asked how far he intended to go before settling into an ambush point. *Tommy Two Bars* told the platoon sergeant he would be advised when and where the platoon was to settle in. Several minutes later, the RTO, received a call from Lieutenant Steve on the movement.

When the RTO told Lieutenant Steve the platoon had been moving for a while and found out they weren't, he advised *Tommy Two Bars* of their dilemma. *Tommy Two Bars* became very agitated, and swore he would get rid of Lieutenant Steve when they returned. He ordered the RTO to tell Lieutenant Steve to get moving and join them as soon as possible.

This is where I was heard by the RTO to call Lieutenant Steve and tell him to bring the rest of his group back to the base camp. The RTO whispered this to the platoon sergeant. The sergeant told the RTO not to mention this to *Tommy Two Bars* deciding to keep the information to himself. It was asinine for the captain to expect half the platoon to find them in the dark after he had been making so many turns. Hell, they might stumble across the others and get into a fire- fight with themselves anyway, and save Charlie the trouble. About this time the platoon dog started to growl slow and soft, which in the past has meant they were in danger.

At this point I should explain about the company dogs. Several small mutts were rescued at some time by each of the platoons and adopted as mascots. Usually dogs were the evening feast of the locals, and these were

97

saved from that fate. Anyway, each platoon had their dog mascot. The first platoon's was tan with a white star in its forehead, and for this it was named *Star*. The second platoon's dog was black and white, and its name was *Shit Head*. The third platoons dog was also tan with white feet, and I don't recall its name. These dogs earned their keep, as they went on mine sweep, patrols, and where ever their respective platoons went.

Star, the first platoon mascot. Earned a purple heart for a wound while on mine sweep. Lost at LZ Debbie, 1969.

Tommy Two Bars told the nearest man to keep that dog quiet, and why was that damn dog out here anyway.

BAM, BAM, BAM.

The platoon was hit by several sniper shots.

CRACK, CRACK, CRACK, CRACK.

Tommy Two Bars fired his M16 wildly to the front. The two point men went down and yelled out in pain. Everyone scattered to the right and left and went to ground. The platoon medic and sergeant went forward to the men shot. The platoon sergeant told the RTO to call battalion and tell them of the situation.

The platoon sergeant turned to *Tommy Two Bars*, and yelled, "You've just shot my men in the back!"

"No, they were hit by the incoming rounds," shrieked *Tommy Two Bars*.

The platoon sergeant got up into *Tommy Two Bars* face and told him, as respectfully as he could, under the circumstances, that everyone behind the captain had seen him shoot wildly forward, and watched, by the flash of his gun, as the two were hit from behind.

The RTO told the platoon sergeant that I had called and confirmed the tanks were on their way and to watch for their light to the east. Also that Lieutenant Steve and his group were ok and on their way back to the base camp. The two wounded men were being given first aid by the platoon medic and were moaning. *Tommy Two Bars* leaned down over them, ordering them to keep quiet. The platoon sergeant immediately saw red and pulled his 45-caliber pistol from its holster and stuck it in *Tommy Two Bars* face, telling him if he said one more word to anyone, he would be going home in a box tonight.

The tanks were sighted, and the RTO called to mark their location. Then they just prayed Charlie wasn't in a position near there to open up on the whole bunch as they were trying to get out of this mess. *Tommy Two Bars* went to the first tank and talked to the tank commander, a lieutenant, who told *Tommy Two Bars* everyone was ordered back to the base camp by the battalion commander. All four tanks made their way out to the platoon, and at the relief of the men, they climbed aboard and rode back to the base camp.

If *Tommy Two Bars* hadn't quickly walked off to the battalion command center, he might have been shot at the company area by any number of men from the first platoon. I asked Lieutenant Steve and the platoon sergeant to take their men back to the company area and try to calm down. I would stay at the medical station with the wounded until the medevac chopper arrived to take them to the hospital in Qui Nhon.

The company first sergeant also stayed but didn't have much to say on the situation, and I wasn't in much of a mood to prod him to give his opinion, as he was mostly behind the captain, no matter what. Must have been his way of keeping his stripes for so many years in the service. Why stick his neck out for a couple of insignificant men in the company and a lower ranking sergeant.

Captain Swan the Battalion Surgeon patched up the two men as best he could. After ten or fifteen minutes, I could hear a chopper coming fast and very low over the trees, south of the base camp. That's how the chopper pilots in the medevac choppers came in to get us out when we needed them. A bunch of very courageous pilots; I owe much to the chopper pilots who worked in our area. Not only for transporting us to and from LZs, but coming to our rescue when we were hit, pinned down, and needed our wounded out of harm's way, or resupply under terrific enemy fire.

The chopper landed on the battalion pad, illuminated by two jeeps at either end. The two wounded men were carried to the chopper and it was off in a flash, heading for the hospital; the men, if they lived, would hopefully go back to the world and not come back here.

I walked back to our company command center with the first sergeant. Not a word was said. I decided to wait for *Tommy Two Bars*. I don't really know why. I wasn't in the mood for his bullshit, but felt I had better find out what the battalion commander had to say; *as if the captain would tell.*

After several minutes, *Tommy Two Bars* came walking in. He looked shell shocked from the ordeal, and I noticed the smell of alcohol. Must have got that at the battalion to calm him down. When *Tommy Two Bars* saw me there, he just turned away and told me to get lost. I didn't even have to *salute* the rank that night.

CHAPTER 11
A DARK DAY

Life goes on. The next morning broke with a beautiful sunrise, the beams streaking through the jungle trees. A slight wisp of ground fog here and there. My platoon was given a mission of building a Bailey Bridge across the Bong Son River. Some civil engineer had decided that because the single lane French built bridge, crossing the river, had been burnt recently, the steel structure had become weakened and, with the amount of large trucks and tanks crossing daily, there was a real threat of the bridge collapsing.

I won't explain how a Bailey Bridge is made, only that it is like an erector set with many steel sections that fit together easily, to ford a river or span a short distance. The bridge is very sturdy and depending on the weight of traffic, more side panels can be added to increase its structural integrity. My platoon was to help prepare the approaches to the two bridges and then build them. A good presentation of the building of one has been shown in the movie *A Bridge Too Far*.

After several days in Bong Son, I was assigned to be a prosecutor in a summary court martial. This is an assignment given to anyone in a junior officer capacity. This particular court-martial was to take place at LZ Thunder, the home of Delta Company. I took my driver and machine gunner to head up to LZ Thunder. While waiting for a convoy at LZ Lowboy, several Vietnamese vehicles and motorcycles passed us and continued north. Five or six school teachers were riding in one of the lambretas. The female teachers in Viet Nam wore long flowing white garments and conical hats. You could always pick them out of a crowd.

Finally, a convoy came north, and we tagged along. On this day, I was to interview several enlisted personnel, at Delta Company, concerning an assault between an NCO and one of his squad members. We wound our way up QL-1, eating dust. We passed LZ Charlie Brown, tensely crossed through *Death Canyon*, and slowed as we approached the area where we had helped Delta Company several weeks earlier, when the jet aircraft had been shot down.

As we finally got to what was slowing the convoy down, I recognized the lambreta that had been carrying the teachers. It was in small pieces, spread all over both sides of the road. I had my driver pull over after I recognized the Delta Company commander. He and several of his platoons had been working in the area when the land mine exploded. He said he was looking in the direction when the lambreta struck the mine. It lifted up about twenty feet in the air intact. At that height the lambreta and its occupants were blown in every direction. Only four bodies were found out in the rice field to the west. The bodies were badly mangled and appeared to have gone through an auger twist, as there was a large gash running in a twist from bottom to top of what was left. Two of the bodies were of the teachers with no lower parts.

How the other two maintained most of their bodies is a mystery. Explosive forces move in many ways. The rest of the passengers were gone. Some of the local Vietnamese were helping recover the parts, scattered all around. A hand here, a foot there, a ear, a finger. The smell of death was heavy in the still air.

After a while we pushed on to Delta Company to do the interviews. While driving back to LZ North English, I kept thinking, *What a waste of life here*. There didn't seem to be any goal to ending this carnage.

Several days later while on a sweep patrol west of LZ North English, my RTO received a call from our company communications sergeant. I was to bring the patrol back to the base camp and report to *Tommy Two Bars*.

An hour later, I reported to the captain. He ordered me to the stockade at LZ English. I demanded to know his reason for sending me there. *Tommy Two Bars* told me to shut up. I was not being sent to the stockade as punishment, but to pick up Lieutenant Steve, who had been arrested in Qui Nhon by the Military Police.

Tommy Two Bars refused to go, and Lieutenant Steve had to be released to a superior officer, me, the executive officer of the company. *Tommy Two Bars* had let it be known how he felt about us OCS officers, and since he was reluctant to participate in any field exercises of any kind, I was to go.

I got my driver and machine gunner and left. We notified our company communication sergeant of our destination and number of personnel. *Tommy Two Bars* wouldn't tell me what Lieutenant Steve had done, so the speculation was running at a fevered pitch all the way to the stockade.

Since we were in the *Pacified Zone*, I didn't feel we needed an escort to LZ English, only a few miles south. We were about half way there when I saw a lone ARVN running from the tree line to our right. He was heading for QL-1. Twice, he jerked to one side then the other. As we approached, I could see bright red on his upper arms. He made it to QL-1 as we got to him. I told my machine gunner to hose down the tree line a few bursts to discourage whomever was after this guy.

We got him into the jeep and drove off to LZ English. Bullets had hit his upper arms from the back and caused large holes, three to four inches wide, where they exited. The NVA chasing him had killed the rest of his platoon in an ambush right here in the *Pacified Zone*, in broad daylight. We dropped him off at the field hospital on the base camp and went to the stockade.

A stockade is the army's prison. The largest was down in Long Bien, north of Saigon, where the military extended jail time personnel where kept. I walked in and asked the MP sergeant at the front desk were I might find Lieutenant Steve, and how I could get him out of here. He said the paper work was ready, and all I had to do was show my identification as his superior officer, and he would be released. They already knew I was coming; once I signed to take custody of him, they had me wait while one of the MPs went to get him.

As Lieutenant Steve came walking up the hallway, he had a down cast look, like a kid just caught with his hand in the cookie jar. Unfortunately, this was much more serious than that. We stepped outside before I asked what was going on. Lieutenant Steve turned to me and said he really fucked up this time. A few weeks ago he had bought a 38 caliber revolver from a tanker who was going home and couldn't take it out of the country. The tanker's father had sent it to him as a backup gun because of his tight position in the tank. This type of revolver is not an authorized weapon for anyone in the Engineer Battalion.

Lieutenant Steve bought the revolver and took the ammunition from the tanker. The revolver had been in the glove box of Lieutenant Steve's jeep until this morning, when he opened the box to show the pistol to his sergeant. They were in Qui Nhon to pick up the company payroll. When Lieutenant Steve pulled the pistol out of the box, several MPs were walking by and saw it.

The MP in charge was an E-6 sergeant who wasn't accepting any of Lieutenant Steve's explanations, but would have just taken the pistol, had Lieutenant Steve not objected. That's when things got ugly. When the MPs asked for any ammo Lieutenant Steve had, the shit really hit the fan. Some of the 38- caliber ammunition he was carrying was dumdum rounds which are forbidden in the military.

That's when things got uglier. The sergeant placed Lieutenant Steve under arrest, and a scuffle occurred. Lieutenant Steve was subdued by several MPs and carted off to the stockade. At that point, I understood why *Tommy Two Bars* refused to drive down to the stockade and be further embarrassed by one of his fine officers. We drove back to the base camp in silence.

I dropped Lieutenant Steve off at the company command center and went back to my platoon area. Lieutenant Steve reported to *Tommy Two Bars*. Before the captain had a chance to jump down his throat, the first sergeant jumped in, and began raking him for *ruining* the morale of his men.

This statement caused quite a scuffle in the command center, and when all was again quiet, Lieutenant Steve was restricted to his quarters for three weeks while off duty, pending the finding of the commanding general of the 173rd Airborne. Lieutenant Steve sure lost a lot of sleep and sweat waiting for the outcome. He could have been ordered to stand a general court-martial and possibly lose his rank and do jail time. Several weeks later, Lieutenant Steve was told he was to be fined $150 dollars, and a permanent letter of reprimand would be inserted into his file. This could jeopardize any long-term commitment in the U.S. Army for Lieutenant Steve Tomlinson.

CHAPTER 12
THEY'LL NEVER GET ME!

Early April, and I've been in country for five months, going into my sixth. I didn't feel like a FNG, hadn't since the first day in Bravo Company. Many things have changed since I arrived. Men died or left due to wounds or rotation home. The battalion commander position changed and would change again before I left. I was forced to play the position of leadership for the company that was expected of the captain.

A new first lieutenant arrived in the battalion during this time. The FNG lieutenant was to be assigned to Bravo Company. The day he arrived someone in the battalion brass decided the FNG should go on a supply run up north to get a feel for the country he would be working in. He drew his gear at Headquarters Company and was to ride shotgun in a deuce-and-a-half truck carrying supplies to Charlie, Delta, and Alpha Companies.

The ride up QL-1 was rather mundane, and the truck stopped at the three companys, allowing the FNG lieutenant to meet some of the officers and NCOs at the base camps. The following information I learned six months later from the battalion adjutant officer, who had been one of my upperclassmen in OCS. I probably never would've known any of this, if he hadn't.

On the ride back to the battalion, while moving with a convoy as it was passing through the treacherous road from LZ Charlie Brown to LZ Lowboy, the driver of the deuce-and-a-half did a very *bad* thing. As he was following the vehicle ahead, he noticed it had straddled an object lying on the road. He decided to run over the object with his driver side front tire.

As he passed over the object, *KABANG!*

A large mine blew up under the driver's side and disintegrated the driver and his side of the truck. Sand bags on the floorboard saved the FNG lieutenant from any physical harm, other than a headache.

When the FNG lieutenant returned to LZ North English, he went to his assigned bunker and refused to come out. I can understand how he felt. The shock of being so close to death so soon after arrival is un-nerving, to say the least. But that's why he is here and why he went through all the training.

However, you never know how you are going to react to being under combat until you are there.

When I was on my way over to Viet Nam, I had dreams of being a failure to my men and worried every day, the entire time I was there, about letting them down when I was needed in a crucial time.

This FNG lieutenant was to join us in Bravo Company, giving the battalion brass the option to relieve *Tommy Two Bars*, and place me into the role of company commander. The shortage of junior officers in the battalion was one of the reasons given for keeping *Tommy Two Bars* in command.

After trying several days to coax the FNG lieutenant out of his bunker, he was physically removed by several medics and flown down to Qui Nhon hospital to the psychiatric ward for further observation. He never returned to the battalion, and we had to endure *Tommy Two Bars* for another five months.

Rumor had it he spent several weeks in the psych ward at Qui Nhon and was finally reassigned to a staff job down in Saigon. What a way to get out of the field assignment. (Probably no truth to the rumor.)

During that time, a supply sergeant with Headquarters Company was selling company supplies on the black market down in Bong Son. He had been doing this for quite a while and knew many of the local merchants and their friends. He had a girlfriend in town and was at her home behind one of the shops, a French style stucco building. Apparently, he said something to offend her.

He asked for a bottle of Tiger Beer. She went out of the room, returning several minutes later with an opened bottle. From the first day I was in Viet Nam, I was warned several times not to drink from a bottle I didn't open, and better not to accept anything in a glass bottle. The sergeant took the bottle and drank down half the contents.

Almost immediately he had pain in his stomach and began to cough up blood. The bottle had been laced with ground glass. The glass was cutting his stomach to shreds. The sergeant managed to get to the front of the shop before collapsing on the street. Several MPs found the sergeant and tried to keep him alive on the ride back to LZ English. He died before they got to the gate. This was a real eye opener for most of the men in the battalion! The incident spread throughout the battalion like wild fire, and everyone was extra cautious about accepting drinks from the locals. (A deadly lesson, well taken.)

My platoon was assigned to pull security for a landfill location. A dozer and front loader were being used to cut a hillside, obtaining fill dirt for the runway at LZ English. The hill was several miles north of LZ English and several miles south of LZ North English.

I positioned the platoon around the hill and took up a position on the west side, looking out over the rice fields and jungled islands scattered below. After several hours, I decided to take a squad on a patrol check across several rice paddies and into a jungle island to our west, about 500 meters out.

We crossed the paddies, using the dikes, and entered the jungle. I was up front with the point man and told him to take it slow and easy. Even though we were in a *Pacified Zone,* I still wasn't taking any chances.

We circled around the interior of the jungle but didn't get close to the west side. After several hours, I decided to return to the hill. I told the point to go ahead and cross the paddies, I would stay at the rear with the last man to cover their movement. Once the point was half the way up the hill, I started with the last man.

About half way over the rice paddies, I saw my sergeant waving to us and pointing in a westerly direction. My RTO was up front and stopped to let me catch up. He said a large force of NVA were moving into the jungle we had just left. We ran up to the top of the hill. I looked west, across the top of the jungle trees, seeing several soldiers crossing the rice paddies on the other side. I used my binoculars to confirm they were NVA. From that distance, they could have been ARVNs. When I caught sight of the last two, before they got into the trees, I could clearly see the NVA uniforms and pith style helmets.

I called the battalion communications center and reported the sighting. I requested permission to call in artillery. I was asked if they had fired on me. I said no. I was told to stay put, watch their movement, and they would call the 173rd Infantry. Only if the NVA moved out of the trees and toward our position, could we engage in firing on them.

"We are in a *Pacified Zone,* remember."

A company of 173rd Infantry showed up about thirty minutes later. Their company commander asked what I had seen. After telling him, his reply was, "Why didn't you call in artillery?" I explained, and he just turned and led his company down into the jungle. All was quiet the rest of the day. Later I was told the infantry company had seen signs of a large enemy force in the jungle, but it had moved out of the area before their arrival.

Because of my luck during the first five months of my tour, I was beginning to feel immortal. I had made, what I felt, was the right decisions at the right time and had used my common sense to get through difficult times. Several times I was slow to respond to sniper fire, while in the base camp, and was told by my fellow officers I had better run for cover, or I was going to get shot. I would simply reply, *They'll never get me.*

Several days later, I had to return to Delta Company at LZ Thunder for the court-martial trial. I took my driver and machine gunner and decided to bring one more to help with the machine gun if we should get into trouble on the road up to LZ Thunder. The day was overcast and threatening to rain.

We made it to LZ Thunder before noon, and had time to eat a fine fish lunch, a welcome change from the dried beef or assortment of C rations. The court-martial lasted several hours. Once finished, I wanted to get back on the road and back down to LZ North English.

We waited about 30 minutes at the gate for a convoy. None came. A supply truck from the battalion was ready to return from Delta Company to LZ North English, so I decided two were better than one, and we probably wouldn't have any trouble anyway. The afternoon was waning, no rain yet, the road was dusty, not for us, but for the driver of the deuce-and-a-half behind us. As we rode south, we passed the location of the mined lambreta. There was no evidence of the killing now, only in my memory. We curved to the left and approached the blown railroad bridge that was the entrance to *Death Canyon.*

As we passed through the gap of the railroad berm, I could see dust spitting up from the road up ahead. My driver was moving at a fast speed, and as we drove through this phenomenon, bullets hit the vehicle, and I was hit in the left arm. My left arm flew up, and I was hit again.

I was thrown into the corner of the door and seat. Sound was no longer with me, all I saw was the floorboard of the truck. My rifle was there. A bright red stream, the diameter of a pencil, was shooting across my vision.

Everything was in slow motion as I gazed to my left, I could see my driver yelling and moving in a jerky motion. I couldn't hear anything. I slowly looked back to my side of the truck, and saw red blood everywhere.

Again, I saw the stream of red, shooting across and hitting the inside of the door. Slowly I watched my right hand cross over to my left, covering the inside of my left elbow, where the stream was coming from. I didn't feel any pain, only numbness in my left arm, the sensation of being hit very hard, as if by a baseball bat.

I started to hear ringing in my ears. Then the sound of the 50-caliber machine-gun, far, far away. Sound suddenly came flooding back, I could hear the driver yelling that the ambush was on the left, keep shooting to the left. He drove on through the canyon and came to a stop, several minutes later at the south end.

I told the gunner to watch our backs to the north and east. To our right (west) was a rock cliff and as long as Charlie wasn't up above, ready to toss down grenades, I felt we were secure where we were.

To our front was a large bay, which the road skirted on the west side to our right. While the driver looked at my bullet holes and began to apply bandages, I called for help. All I got back on the radio was static. I looked back up the road to the north, toward the ambush site, and again tried to raise our battalion communication net. I noticed something was missing, and realized the antenna was gone. It had been shot off. Also the deuce-and-a-half was no longer with us.

Just then the driver yelled, "Hey, Lieutenant, look what's coming up the road." I turned to the front, and there was a mechanized infantry unit coming north, with my battalion S-4 major, riding in the front Armored Personnel Carrier.

The APC stopped in front of our truck. The major said he had heard me calling as they were coming up the road. Several of the lead APCs passed and went looking for the ambushers. The major called for a medevac, and told his RTO to call our battalion to report my shooting. A loud exchange of gunfire erupted up the road. Red and green tracers flashed up over the rocks behind us.

Several more APCs raced up the road to help their buddies. The major said the lead APCs had run into a platoon of NVA coming up the road, probably looking for us. I told the major a supply truck had been behind us just before the ambush. I didn't known what happened to him or his shotgun passenger.

Later, I was told the driver was far enough back at the start of the ambush, and had stopped and turned around. High tailing it back to Delta Company, he and his passenger spent the night there.

The following information I was told months later.

Back at Bravo Company the phone rang in the command post. "Bravo Company command post, Specialist Monday here." "Yes, sir, do you want to speak to the first sergeant or company commander? I'll relay the message, yes sir, right away, sir." The clerk hung up the phone, went to the company commanders closed door and knocked. "Captain, a message just came in from the battalion communications officer. Lieutenant Suffern has been shot and killed in an ambush on QL-1 south of LZ Thunder. His body is being flown to LZ English, sir."

Tommy Two Bars acknowledged the message and dismissed the clerk. After the clerk closed the door, he heard *Tommy Two Bars* say, "One down, one to go. First Sergeant, go down to LZ English and identify the body, and let me know any information you can gather about the ambush."

The first sergeant came out of the office and told the clerk where he was going and to hold any information that came in about the ambush until he got back. This the clerk did.

Back at QL-1 the medevac chopper was heard coming, close to the treetops. Suddenly, there he was, crossing the bay and doing a 180 degree turn to our east, above the hill on our left. He slipped to his right, and lowered down to the side of the road parallel to us. I walked over to the open side and a medic on board helped me in. I was wearing my flack vest and helmet. The battalion major told me to leave the helmet and my rifle. I wouldn't need them any more. I settled on the floor of the chopper bay, my back against the back firewall. I began to feel tired and cold.

The medevac quickly lifted off, and we crossed the bay to LZ Charlie Brown, where the chopper landed. A navy doctor was at the LZ. I was walked to their evacuation hospital. The doctor checked the two bullet holes on my inner left arm and rebandaged them. I was then walked back to the chopper, and flown to LZ English, where I was taken into their evacuation field hospital for another look.

I was starting to feel very light headed. I was put on a stretcher. The doctors there looked at my arm, deciding I would have to go to the main hospital in Qui Nhon for an operation.

I was still wearing my combat fatigue clothing, and flack vest. As the medics carried me to the medevac chopper, Bravo Company first sergeant walked up. Looking relieved, he said he was so glad to see I wasn't dead, as had been reported.

He hoped I would be able to recover and come back to the company, as he really needed me there. I certainly didn't feel the same. At the side of the chopper, I told the medics I could get in and sit up while flying down to Qui Nhon. I got in and the medic on board placed a set of headphones over my ears.

Armed Forces Radio was on, and as we lifted off and swung south, the song, *It's the Time of the Season*, by the Zombies, started to play. Every time I hear that song, even today, I go back to looking out over the landscape we passed, on the way to Qui Nhon.

I felt colder and colder as we headed south. The medic asked how I was feeling, because I didn't look so good. I, being a macho, tough officer, said I was ok. He said, "Ok, if you say so, sir." They had just got a call about a wounded ARVN, who they would be picking up on the way, if I felt up to it. I said ok, go ahead.

We landed on LZ Rolling Thunder, the base camp of the tankers who guarded us when I was nearly blown to pieces by the wet time fuse. The ARVN was on a stretcher, had an oxygen mask over his face, and a bottle of fluid attached to his arm by a clear small tube.

He was much worse than me, I thought, full of small holes all over his body. Must have been hit by shrapnel from a mortar or several grenades. His clothing had been partially cut away, and the bigger holes had been bandaged. The smaller ones were mostly just open. Some jagged, not much blood flowing. He must have bled more, earlier, as his uniform was black with his own blood.

We took off and flew close to the dark clouds. Some rain blew in. I was getting very cold now. Figured it was because of the altitude and the rain, even though it was quite hot when we were ambushed. After twenty or thirty minutes, we were over Qui Nhon and landing at the triage center. Several American Army nurses, in green fatigues, ran to the side of the chopper. The ARVN was slid off the deck of the chopper and run into the swinging doors of the triage room.

A nurse came to me and asked how I was doing. I couldn't even answer. I was so weak and began to shiver. She yelled for the other medics to get another stretcher, and as I was laid back, they took off my flack vest and fatigue shirt. The left side of the shirt and the back of my pants were drenched with blood. I took one look and sank into darkness.

I had been hit three times. The third, which had gone un-noticed, had hit the side of my flack vest, penetrated it and hit me in the armpit, entering my chest. My sleeve had been rolled up. The blood from my chest wound had stopped there, and run down the inside of the shirt. No one had noticed. The nurses, I later talked to, said I was very close to the end of my life when I got to the triage center.

If the nurses there hadn't seen the signs I was showing, I probably would have bled out before I got to the operating table. I owe my life to the nurses at the Qui Nhon hospital. The only nurses I can remember are Pat and Mary. To them, and the others, I am eternally grateful.

I heard a vague screaming from a distance. Then I heard a voice saying, "It's ok, you'll be ok, Lieutenant; you are waking up from surgery." I opened my eyes and saw a beautiful blond woman looking down on me. She was upside down; I couldn't understand where I was. I asked her if I was in heaven and she said, "No, you're in the hospital. You're recovering from your surgery."

I asked about the yelling. She said not to worry, he was shot in the head, his brain was swelling. He would quiet down shortly. When he did, he was dead. Darkness enveloped me again, and according to the nurses, I was close to the same event.

CHAPTER 13
MEDEVAC MISSION

When I finally awoke, and realized where I was, I felt like I was draining away. The nurses said that was because of the morphine. That's when I began feeling the effects of the operation. The initial bullets impact only felt like a hard whack by a baseball bat and a sudden numbing. This was hell. The pain was searing and at times I felt I couldn't take it and had to have the morphine. At the beginning, the morphine was given to me every few hours. But after I finally was able to get around on my own to the latrine and around the ward, they began to lower my dose.

When I was coherent enough, a donut dolly from the Red Cross stopped at my bed, gave me paper and pen and encouraged me to write to my wife and folks back home, to let them know I was ok. Better getting it from me instead of from a telegram. That sounded reasonable to me, and she volunteered to help me if I needed it.

The nurses, Pat and Mary, who worked on the ward, told me the doctors said after I recovered enough I would be flown to Japan for further rehabilitation, then on back to the world (United States). This really improved my moral, and I wrote home to let everyone know the good news. Little did I know that *Tommy Two Bars* would be coming down to see the colonel of the hospital, getting him to keep me here longer, to see if I would recover enough to return to the battalion.

During the first week I was awake, the base camp at Qui Nhon was hit by a ground attack. First, mortars were lobbed into our area and then the perimeter was breached. This was around two or three AM. I could hear all the firing and yelling by the Americans and Vietnamese. I really perked up when I heard someone yell, "They're inside the wire."

Here we were with no means of defending ourselves, and the enemy was inside the wire, which usually meant Charlie had satchel charges and was going after the wounded.

KABANG, KABANG!

Several charges blew in the next building. The nurses in our ward yelled for us to get on the floor, and if we could, pull our mattress over ourselves. I

113

wasn't in any condition to move, and Pat came over and stayed with me until the danger passed. Several wounded men in the next building had been killed or additionally wounded. Thankfully, rockets weren't fired into the hospital wards.

I spent three weeks on this ward and on the last day, Mary came to me and said I was being discharged from the hospital. I said great, when do I get on the freedom bird to Japan. She looked away and said I wasn't going to Japan. Hadn't the doctors told me? I was going back to my battalion.

I was shocked and dismayed to hear the news. My wounds were still open and every day the nurses would scrub them with peroxide, keeping the beginning infections from spreading.

The wound on my inner bicep was partially closed by steel wires. She was going to remove them, and place butterfly sutures over the four inch opening to keep it closed. One of the men from my company, a mechanic from the motor pool, stopped by at this time to see how I was doing and say goodbye. His tour was up, and he was going home.

I asked him to stay while Mary took out the steel wires and closed the wound. She had to inject pain- killer into the wound to take out the wires. The injection hurt more than the recovery from the surgery. The mechanic passed out on the bed next to me just watching.

After he finally recovered, with some smelling salts, we said our goodbyes and he left. I was issued new fatigues, and boots and released from the hospital. I went down to the helicopter pad, where I had been brought in, to catch a ride back to LZ North English. After watching several choppers land and take off, I decided I wasn't ready to go back. I went back to the ward and asked Pat if I could stay one more night. She agreed, saying, if I didn't mention who I was, and as long as there was a bed available, I could stay. So I slept at the far end of the ward, away from all the other patients.

That night, while waiting to sleep, I thought about what happened to Charlie Company while I was here. A sergeant, from one of their platoons, came in with a badly shot up leg and told me this. During a mine sweep, from LZ Lowboy north, his platoon was ambushed, and they and the duster tank escorts lost ninety percent of their men. FNGs who had arrived in country a few days earlier made up half the platoon.

As the sweep moved up the darkened stretch of road, where the jungle comes to within ten meters of the road on either side, they were first hit on their left. The NVA ambushers had let the two point men get passed the ambush before firing on the main group. The men with the mine detectors were hit in the first few seconds of the attack. The duster tanks turned left, and began firing their 40 mm cannons into the jungle. After a few minutes, NVA troops on the right side of the road fired their B-40 rockets into the open turrets of the duster tanks, killing the gunners, loaders and platoon sergeant on both tanks. The only survivors were the drivers.

A B-40 rocket also hit the platoon leaders truck, behind the front seat into the radio. The driver and platoon leader, riding in the front, were killed. The platoon was not deployed for a mine sweep with flanking squads off the road. Most of the platoon was riding in the five- ton dump trucks. The sergeant and the platoon leader were FNGs who hadn't been in the company too long. All the trucks were hit by B-40 rockets from the right side of the road, this spooked most of the men, who dropped their rifles, jumped from the trucks, and ran down the road.

The NVA troops walked out from the jungle firing at the troops running, and captured some, who were shot then and there. The RTO, who was walking up with the point men, managed to get off a call for help, and about five minutes after the ambush hit, there were helicopter gunships from Duc Pho overhead. By then the RTO was dead, and no one was communicating. The road was littered with bodies, the NVA were running up and down the road shooting anyone who appeared to be alive.

The sergeant managed to crawl into the jungle, staying there until the rest of Charlie Company came running from the base camp. The choppers only fired at the enemy after they broke off from the ambush and ran into the west side jungle. Once the company commander and his troops arrived, it was all over.

The two point men had taken cover behind large palm trees, north of the kill zone, and managed to kill three NVA who were trying to get to them. The company medic, who hadn't gone on the sweep that morning, located the sergeant and stop the bleeding and secured his leg wounds.

That word *Pacified Zone* came looming up again. The sergeant was highly agitated, as I had been many times over that policy. Most of the FNGs get a sense of safety, when told they are in a *Pacified Zone*, and probably won't get shot at much while here in the battalion.

Little do they know, they are not only in a bastard unit, detached from their main division, to be used as seen fit by whom they are attached, but they are also in a country, whose citizens don't want them here, and don't know what the term *Pacified Zone* means. At least the sergeant, whose leg was shattered several places, was going home and was probably going to be retired, due to the extent of the injury. So were the others in the platoon who were going in a metal box for eternity.

I suppose no one explained to the FNG lieutenant, the *Pacified Zone* ended at their LZ, and everything north was a free fire zone, for *them and us*. LZ Lowboy was on the border of the I Corp, II Corps of Viet Nam. From the LZ, south to Qui Nhon, was the *Pacified Zone*, where only *Charlie* was allowed a free fire zone.

The sergeant said he hadn't been in any fire fights since he got here four weeks ago, and the only one he heard of was some company commander that shot his point men on a night patrol, and a week ago an officer was killed in an ambush on QL-1 in *Death Canyon*. I acknowledged I was that officer, and I was still alive and kicking. I didn't mention *Tommy Two Bars*.

He said everyone was afraid of that canyon. All the mine sweeps he had been on were slowed to a crawl; to let Delta Company, who was sweeping down from the north, pass through the canyon first. He said the point men from Delta Company often cussed them for not moving fast enough. (That bit of information came in handy later.)

The next morning I decided I had better get back to the company. The day was clear and bright with a slight breeze. It was already in the nineties and promised to be another humid scorcher. As I sat outside the triage building, I again thanked Pat and Mary for saving my life.

A medevac chopper arrived with their load. Several troopers were in pretty bad shape, and the chopper bay was covered with dark red blood. I asked the pilot if I could get a ride to LZ North English. He said he could take me to their chopper base where I could probably get a ride up north, if I didn't mind riding in the mess in the back.

I hopped on with the medics and away we flew. When we landed at their base, the medics got out a hose to clean up. I offered to help them for giving me a ride. So for a few minutes I cleaned up and shot the shit with them. The pilots walked over to their command post for a briefing. The medics said the pilots never helped clean up. They weren't pissed about it. These pilots were the bravest they had seen in their two tours. These guys would fly into a hot LZ and never look nervous. They saved many troopers from a bad situation.

Just as we were finishing, the pilots came running back with a new mission. The lead pilot told me he had told his commander I was looking for a flight to LZ North English, and he would keep a lookout for me. I asked if I could go with them on this mission. He said sure, if I wanted to take my life into my own hands. He wasn't taking the responsibility for my safety, and they could always use an extra hand in the back. The pilots wound up the chopper rotors, and we lifted off in a hurry.

Damn, what was I thinking? Here I was, just out of the hospital, and looking for another adrenaline rush. We headed west to the central highlands. Ahead I could see smoke rising from the jungle canopy below. I looked at the crew chief medic; he nodded yes that's it.

We were just over the trees now, and the medics were standing on the landing runners below the bay, leaning out to see what was ahead. I stayed put in the bay, against the back firewall. Several gunship choppers were circling around one spot, firing rockets into the tree line. Their door gunners were firing continuously with their M60 machine guns, down into the trees.

I could hear *TAP, TAP, TAP* as we circled the trees. The crew chief yelled we were taking hits and to stay put. I looked out and saw a gunship pass close to our right. The door gunner on our side was hanging outside his side, held there by his safety belt.

Blood was streaming down the side of the chopper as they passed us. A pair of Cobra Gunships arrived and began to spray the trees, as the other two gunships left. Cobra Gunships were newer style helicopters. They were very skinny and had a lot of armament. There was a pilot and gunner on board. They sat in line, in the fuselage, instead of across from each other like in a car.

Red and green tracers were streaking across the sky, from every tree line I saw. I began thinking, *What am I doing here*?

Too late now! More *TAP, TAP, TAP*.

Bullets were hitting the skin of the chopper; it isn't very thick. I kept looking at the bay floor of diamond plate aluminum, waiting to see bullets come flying through. I wasn't disappointed, they did, but I never saw them as they did.

We suddenly turned left and swooped down. The crew chief yelled to hang on; we're going into a hot LZ.

As the chopper neared the ground, the pilot suddenly did a 180-degree turn, and landed hard. Troopers came running with wounded, who were being carried in poncho liners. I grabbed the ends of the liners as they were passed into the bay. We stacked seven and quickly took off.

The medics did all they could for the men as we flew for Qui Nhon. When we landed in Qui Nhon, Pat and Mary came running over to the chopper to help get the wounded off. Pat looked at me and said, "What are you doing here?" I just shrugged, as she and the rest ran the wounded into the triage center.

The crew chief told me they were headed back to their base to refuel and go back out. The pilot told him I would have to stay behind to make room for more wounded, and thanked me for my help. We took off in a hurry and landed several minutes later.

I walked over to the command post to talk to their commander. I hadn't realized I had blood splattered on my new fatigues. At least I felt useful. The commander pointed to a chopper across the tarmac, and said I could get a ride to LZ English in a few minutes. He didn't comment on my appearance.

I walked over to the chopper and the crew chief asked if I was the lieutenant looking for a ride to LZ North English. I could barely get out, "Yes I am," my mouth was so dry from the other ride. He handed me a cold can of lemonade. I was grateful.

We sat there, and he asked how the ride was on the Dustoff. I said ok. He laughed. The pilots came walking up from the command center, and we took off for LZ English. This ride was nice and quiet. The pilot landed smoothly at LZ English, and the crew chief said this was as far north as they were going. I got out and looked for a ride to LZ North English.

I found a supply truck heading to LZ North English, so I hopped in the back. I noticed my bandages were soaked with sweat and blood. I figured the blood was from the troops I helped onto the Dustoff until I got to the base camp, and reported in to the field hospital to Captain Swan, our battalion surgeon.

He uncovered the bandages and found that the butterfly stitches had loosened with the sweat; the wound had opened. White, infection puss sacks had formed again, so he scrubbed the wound with peroxide and ordered me restricted to the base camp, until the wound sealed.

I walked over to Bravo Company command post and surprise, surprise, I found my favorite captain there. I reported in and told him of my restriction. He didn't have much to say, so I left for my platoon bunker. None of the platoons were in the base camp. It was about 1500 hours (3 PM).

I changed my fatigues and got a cool beer from my marimac can. I always had beer and lemonade in water, in a marimac can (an insulated can used to carry hot chow to the troops). I tried not to drink the water from the urtilator processing plant if I could avoid it. Later in my tour, doing so nearly killed me.

CHAPTER 14
WELCOME BACK LIEUTENANT!

Later that afternoon, I was in my platoon bunker tape recording a letter to my wife and parents, informing them of the change of events. I would not be coming home, as I had earlier written them, and was back in Bravo Company at LZ North English. A burst of gunfire was heard coming from the south, in the general direction of QL-1. I looked out the front of the bunker and saw the sun had set; we were in twilight. I noticed my platoon hadn't returned to the base camp.

I hurried over to the communication center while gunshots continued to pop in a ferocious firefight. When I got to the communication center, I heard my RTO calling in a high-pitched voice. The platoon had been ambushed about half a mile south, and there were casualties. The gunshots petered out. The RTO said the enemy had disengaged and were heading east into the jungle.

The RTO reported the platoon was regrouping and again heading to the base camp with the casualties. By this time, darkness had fallen like a blanket. I walked over to the Battalion Aid Station and saw they were already preparing for the incoming wounded.

The platoon trucks arrived a few minutes later, and a truck stopped at the hospital. One man was carried in on a litter: he was dead. The other man, Richard Hatten, was led in, walking. He had been riding shotgun on the dead man's five-ton dump truck and had glass shards in his eyes.

He was taken to a table where Dr Swan administered a liquid pain killer into his eyes. I walked over to the dead man on the stretcher to identify him. I couldn't. His face was swollen so badly, from two bullet holes in his face. One was under his right eye; the other was above his right eyebrow. Blood was gathering under his head. The back of his head was gone. It was plastered on the back of the truck cab, behind the drivers seat.

My men were glad to see me. My platoon sergeant arrived and told me what had happened. The platoon had finished the day's work on the bailey bridges in Bong Son and convoyed up QL-1. The light of day was waning fast, and they had to maintain their speed to accommodate the grader with

119

them. Suddenly, shots rang out from the railroad berm east of the road. He felt there might have been only two or three Charlies, because of the amount of incoming fire after the initial hits on the truck. The driver had been a new guy by the name of Yost. That's the reason I couldn't recognize him. He had been assigned to us while I was in the hospital in Qui Nhon.

I then sensed the presence of someone in the room. I turned and before I could acknowledge a lieutenant colonel was present, he said, "Be at ease men, this is no place for formality." He came over to me and introduced himself. He was Lieutenant Colonel Andrews the new Battalion Commander. Our previous commander, Lieutenant Colonel Burns, had moved on to his next assignment.

The lieutenant colonel said he had been monitoring the radio and came over to see the wounded men and thought I was *Tommy Two Bars*. I told him who I was. He said he wasn't aware I had been released from the hospital, and had been told I was going to Japan and back to the states. He also wanted to know where Bravo Company's commander was.

I told him not here. The lieutenant colonel briefly talked to Captain Swan about Hatten's wounds. He then came over to tell me to come over to the Battalion Command Center when I was done here. I told Sergeant Meddars of my restriction to the base camp, until my wounds were healed, and he was still in charge of the platoon. I heard a chopper coming in over the battalion. With two jeeps parked on the north and south of the pad with lights on, it landed in a cloud of dust. The two casualties were carried to the chopper and were gone just as quick as the chopper had arrived.

I walked over to the Battalion Command Center in the dark. The only noise was the distant hum of the base camp power generators. I went down the steps to the underground bunker. The light inside was blinding for a few seconds.

The colonel invited me into his office for a talk. He said he had heard of me from Colonel Burns and wanted an in person back ground of my tour so far. He also wanted to assure me of his complete support of all his officers who demonstrated their leadership for the men in their command. Nothing was said about *Tommy Two Bars*. I didn't feel it was my place to bring it up.

The colonel told me our battalion was being detached from the 173rd Airborne Division and attached to the Americal Division up north. He showed me the location of our new base camp, which was being built, as we spoke, by Lieutenant Steve's platoon. That's why no one from his platoon was around when I got back. The LZ was to be named *Debbie*, and located next to Delta Company, LZ Thunder. Also the third platoon, led by Lieutenant Casbey, had been transferred to the Quarry Company to increase their production.

The battalion staff had considered placing Bravo Company in *Death Canyon*, at the south end where I had been picked up by the medevac chopper. But that hill was reserved for an ARVN unit, being moved up here from their cushy camp in Qui Nhon. I was relieved to hear that. Our company would build their camp as soon as we built ours and moved up there.

The colonel said the battalion headquarters would be cut in half, with the colonel and part of his staff to be located at LZ Thunder, and the rest to be located at LZ Lowboy. So I was brought up to date by the battalion commander; instead of the company commander. I left the colonel, feeling more relaxed about being back in the battalion.

The next day *Tommy Two Bars* assigned me to the task of preparing concrete slabs for an artillery unit, who would be moving into the battalion base camp as soon as we left. So, for the next couple of weeks, while my wounds healed, I was in charge of the third platoon and the slab construction.

It felt good to be back on mine sweep with my own platoon, when I was off restriction. While at the Bong Son River, working on the Bailey bridges, a Chinook helicopter landed and dropped off a company of infantry. I went over to talk to the company commander.

He said a few days earlier, while the company was crossing the Bong Son River, closer to the ocean, he lost several men to sharks. They were crossing through the river at night and hadn't had any problems in the past. Didn't even know there were sharks venturing up the river. So, he warned me to keep my men out of the water. Even here, only a few miles inland, wasn't safe. The infantry were on a sweep through the jungle to the south, and the captain said there was suppose to be a large unit of NVA passing down from the north, next to our base camp and LZ English soon.

That night our base camp was put on 100 percent alert. I was walking up and down our perimeter, checking the guards, and making sure they stayed alert. The sky was clear, and the mosquitoes were out in force. No matter how much repellent you slathered on, they still dove in for a fill. All you got was a sticky stink.

Around midnight, several guards on the east side of the perimeter reported seeing green and red lights out in the jungle, in the direction of the railroad berm. I heard the reports and walked over to see for myself. This was the Heavy Equipment Companies area, and I had worked with their company commander, a first lieutenant, several times.

121

I found him at the center of his perimeter area checking the railroad berm with binoculars. There was no moon that night, and the jungle, at the railroad berm, was several hundred meters away. While we both scanned the area, I clearly saw a signal by a green light. I had my RTO notify our communication center to notify battalion of the sighting. Several minutes later, I could hear choppers coming from the south. The first chopper dropped parachute flares as it passed along QL-1, heading north.

Five flares lit up and began their slow descent to the ground. The flares swung back and forth under the parachutes, giving off an eerie, bright light, illuminating large areas, as long as they were up high. Each swing seemed to cause the trees and brush to sway as if they were in a fierce storm.

As the other choppers arrived, they lined up on the same direction as the first, and began firing rockets into the jungle below. I couldn't see what they were going after, but it must have been a large force, not only were choppers continually circling, but artillery from LZ English began crashing down as well.

This lasted well into the night and started fires in several different places. When the choppers had to leave to refuel and rearm, a fixed wing plane, known a snoopy, showed up to continue to hose down the area.

Snoopy was an AC-47 aircraft with the side door removed. Several mini-gattling guns were mounted in the door and as the plane circled, a red ribbon of death streamed down. Tracers were positioned every five rounds, and with the amount of firing per minute the gun could spit out, it appeared every round was a tracer. These planes saved our butts several times later in my tour up north.

When the aircrafts were finally done the sun was rising over the South China Sea. Several companies of infantry were dropped in at Tam Quan, and started their way south, on the east side of the railroad berm. Our battalion was to remain at our position, along the west side of QL-1, as they passed.

We were being used as a blocking unit, in case the NVA tried to break out to the west. As the infantry passed us, our company was ordered to continue south, on the west side of QL-1, as their right flank. Bravo Company consisted of the second and third platoons, of which I was in charge. *Tommy Two Bars* was tied up with administrative duties.

We moved south to Bong Son, with no sign of any live NVA. In the jungle east of the railroad berm, several bodies were found. The bodies were brought to QL-1 and left by the side of the road for the graves registration to dispose of. I was told if the bodies could be identified, notification was sent to Hanoi, in hopes of them doing the same for our troops killed by them. I found out years later, our graves registration units were sending notification to Hanoi through our negotiators in Paris.

CHAPTER 15
LZ DEBBIE

A week later I was ordered to head up north to our new base camp to check on the progress by Lieutenant Steve and his platoon. I rode up in *Tommy Two Bars* jeep, which had steel sides welded on to protect *all* the occupants. This was the chicken jeep. I tried to get him to let me go up in one of the duster tanks, since my jeep was down for repairs but was ordered to use his jeep. This jeep was seldom seen outside the base camp, as you can imagine. I still don't understand why the sides were put on if the jeep wasn't used on QL-1.

As our convoy approached *Death Canyon*, I began to get a sick, sinking feeling. I constantly looked back and forth watching for the first incoming bullets. We continued through the canyon with no event and made it to LZ Debbie in one piece.

Troops building a living-fighting bunker on the perimeter berm at LZ Debbie. In the back ground is the command post tent. May, 1969.

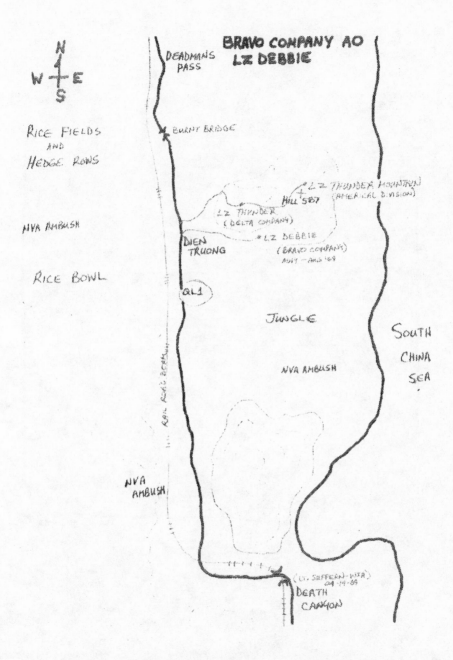

Bravo Company area of operation at LZ Debbie.

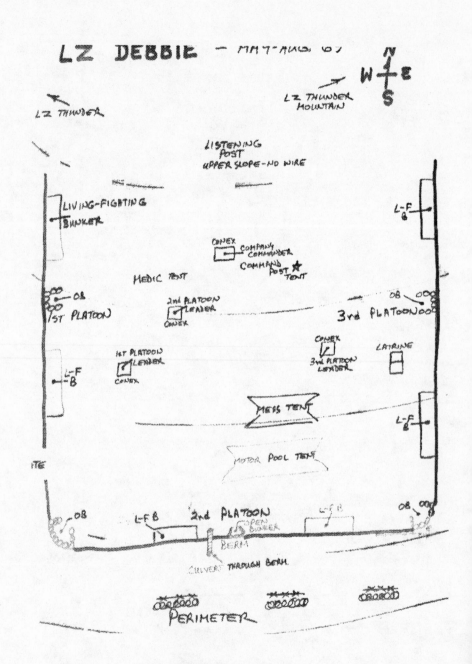

LZ Debbie perimeter.

126

The perimeter was in the shape of the letter D, with the curved portion facing south. The straight side was on a slope to the north and had no wire, as Delta Company was above and to the west, and the road to the Americal Division ran parallel up the mountain. Only one listening post bunker was placed here. Lieutenant Steve felt the terrain was too steep for any penetration.

Boy was that wrong! We were fortunate, on our side of the mountain, that we were never attacked this way, but the Americal Division, who thought the same on the north side, got their butts kicked one night by NVA who slipped up the side, under a smoke screen from a burning bridge, and killed every bunker guard there. These sides were almost straight up, and several thousand feet from the rice field valley floor below.

The rest of the perimeter was close to being finished, and the living fighting bunkers were being built. So in a few days, I got my platoon ready, and bid LZ North English goodbye. I moved up to LZ Debbie and took command. *Tommy Two Bars* decided to remain at LZ North English, until LZ Debbie was complete.

By the time we arrived at LZ Debbie, the daylight was going fast. As I was settling in my metal supply connex box, I was told by my RTO that either the battalion commander or a staff member, would be coming down from Delta Company shortly to inspect our defenses.

I asked Lieutenant Steve for a diagram of the perimeter defenses. He had none. I looked around and decided where we should place the machine guns and claymore mines. Then I ordered at least the mines to be placed and began to draw up a diagram of the perimeter showing our intentions to who ever showed-up. Several minutes later, the battalion commander did arrive, and luckily, I had the drawing done and some of the claymores had been set. He was satisfied with the defense of the perimeter and left.

Once we were settled in Bravo Company was ordered to start mine sweeps to the south, relieving Delta Company of that chore. They then had the north route, to marry up with Alpha Company coming down from LZ Max. We would marry up with Charlie Company coming up from LZ Lowboy.

Due to the nastiness of the area I decided that two platoons should run mine sweep. Each traded off with the headgear and mine detectors every other day. The men who used the mine detectors would get tone deaf after fifteen or twenty minutes. They were rotated with the flank guards or point as the sweep went on.

When I was walking sweep, I would walk close to the point and probe any suspicious potholes or marks on the dirt road. Down at LZ North English we never came across a mine in the road, only booby traps along the sides or inside culverts. I purchased a Bowie knife in Bong Son, with a fourteen-inch blade. The metal gave me a better feel for the texture of the ground than a bayonet. Lieutenant Haney, the officer I replaced as executive officer, clued me into that trick.

Up here, on this stretch of QL-1, Charlie liked to play his games. I'm sure they watched us on the sweeps and knew what the mine detectors were for. The mines we found were made from C-4 plastic explosive, taken from undetonated bombs. This way of retrieving explosives was very dangerous but did get them plenty.

The explosives were formed into a square, about ten to twelve inches, and about five to ten inches thick. An electric blasting cap was shoved into the side or top of the explosive. This was either run to a set of old discarded batteries and then a two or three foot section of two inch diameter bamboo, or run directly off the road into the jungle where it was attached to a clacker (hand detonating generator).

The two-inch bamboo was cut in two, length wise, and separated by pieces of bamboo, about a quarter inch square and two inches long. These were placed across the bamboo to keep it separated. On each inner side of the bamboo was placed a flattened steel can. Across the cans was placed a bare section of communication wire (como wire) to form a cross. These wires were connected to the batteries, and the blasting cap, in such a way as to cause the cap to detonate if the wires made contact. This type of detonator was used for heavy trucks.

Charlie would dig out a precise hole for the mine and run the wires and detonator about ten meters away. This would allow the trucks backing down the road, in a mine sweep, to run over the mine. When the back duels would hit the detonator, the mine would blow under the cab and get the driver and his shotgun rider. Or it would get any heavy truck running in a convoy. I think this is the type of mine that got the Lambreta I described earlier.

Charlie liked to play tricks on us. He would bury *C* ration cans in the road. Sometimes only one, other times several, one on top of the other. When I would find these, I had to be very careful in digging them up, as I did with all suspect mines. An anti-lift device could be rigged to these false mines, with a real one under or near by. I always took the responsibility of uncovering any mine or object we found. I felt it was my position as leader to do so, and even though I trained several men how to do it, I never let them. Most mines found were detonated in place, by using a quarter pound block of TNT placed on top, using a timed fuse and blasting cap.

Charlie was very good at camouflaging the locations of the mines. I felt I had changed after my stay at Qui Nhon hospital, and seemed to have an extra sense when I was out in the field. I would check every pothole, even if I had checked it the day before, and it didn't look like it had been disturbed during the day. Several times I would drag the knife blade through the pothole and find nothing. Then the next time I would feel the texture of plastic. Most of the plastic mines and detonators would be wrapped in green plastic poncho material. Which had a definite pattern in the plastic.

One morning, during a hot and humid period, we had gone to the north end of *Death Canyon* and found no mines. I decided to stop the sweep for a break and to change the men on the mine detectors. While this was being done, my RTO and I were standing in the middle of the gravel road.

He looked down and said, "Look, Lieutenant, isn't that a blasting cap?"

I looked down and saw a glint of sun light off a piece of metal. The sun had just come up to our front and was shining down the road. I stooped down and carefully moved several rocks, and sure enough, there was a cap, sticking straight up, with electric wires, covered with dirt, running to the side of the road. I walked over to the side and saw, what to me looked like a large rope, running into the jungle.

The rope turned out to be only regular como wire, about the size of a lamp cord, but when you think about what's on the other end of the cord getting ready to blow the mine, everything looks larger. I yelled at everyone to get off the road and directed the right flank to spread out and move into the jungle to locate Charlie. As the squad started to move into the trees, Charlie cranked the clacker, and the mine blew. I heard the definite signature sound of the device, just before the blast.

I started shooting in the direction of the disappearing como wire into the jungle. So did everyone on that side of the road. Pieces of gravel and dirt started falling all over. No incoming bullets or rockets came, so I stopped the shooting spree and had the flank squad make a sweep one hundred meters out. They found the end of the wire but nothing else. We regrouped and finished the sweep. Even with the delays of blowing a mine in place or being ambushed, Charlie Company never did get through *Death Canyon* before us. I constantly remembered what the Charlie Company NCO told me while in the hospital.

129

Every time we would meet Charlie Company on the south side I would chide them on their slow sweeps and vow to wait on the north side of the canyon the next day and make them come through. I never did. I just wanted to get the sweep over with as soon as possible. After *Tommy Two Bars* moved up to LZ Debbie, the two platoon sweeps came to an end, unless there was a warning from battalion of a possible ambush by a large force.

CHAPTER 16
CONNEX BOX

The entire time Bravo Company was at LZ Debbie, myself, Lieutenant Steve and *Tommy Two Bars* had to sleep in metal connex boxes. The base camp was built on a slope, and every night, Charlie would sneak down to the culvert under QL-1, to our south, and fire several shots into the company area. One of the first nights there I was sitting in front of my box (which faced south) talking to Sergeant Meddars and *POP, POP, POP*, here comes green tracers right at me. I hit the ground and watched the tracers come right at me. There was no place to go as the ground in front of me dropped away. I covered up my head and prayed I didn't get hit. The bullets entered the connex box and made a hell of a racket when they hit the back.

The next morning I ordered the start of steel planked walls to be built between all connexes and the south slope. These were eventually connected with a continuous wall and roof system. The roof was sand bagged two feet thick and a false roof was built over that to detonate any mortars that might hit. That would cause the explosive to dissipate onto the lower sand bags. All the bunkers were built this way. Unfortunately, there was no air movement in the steel connexes, and when the days were very hot, the connex became a cooker.

At night they stayed hot until almost daybreak. Even with the walls and roof, with the air dead still, the connex bunker was hard to live with. Especially when the rats decided to move in. Each platoon leader had basically the same setup. Two small connexes, each about five feet wide, seven feet high and seven feet long; one for the platoon leader and the other for the platoon sergeant. The connexes were placed side by side with the doors open. After the rats moved into the larger walled bunker, we started closing the doors while we were gone to keep the vermin out of the living quarters.

To kill the rats, some as big as cats, we shot them with our 45- caliber pistols. But because of the steel connex we had to be careful how and where we aimed. We also had to warn each other of a possible shooting, so the other could get earplugs.

CHAPTER 17
MAD MINUTES

After several weeks of settling in, *Tommy Two Bars* arrived to take over. A large boulder had been left in the outer perimeter on the eastside, between wire obstacles. *Tommy Two Bars* ordered that boulder removed. Lieutenant Steve and I went out to look at the boulder and decide how much C4 explosive we would need to remove it.

The granite boulder was half the size of a full size dump truck. We didn't know how deep it went into the earth. I had one of my men dig down under the west side so I could place the explosive. I don't remember how much we decided on, but after the blast, it was definitely *too* much. The boulder was no more, and the remains took out a good portion of the perimeter fencing on the east side. After the blast, *Tommy Two Bars* came out to inspect, and got so mad at both of us, he ordered us to *never* work together again.

Because we were laughing over the excess of explosives, he ordered us not to be seen together talking. He then turned and stomped back up to his command post.

There was a simultaneous salute of disgust from both Lieutenant Steve and myself as he left. I turned to Lieutenant Steve and ordered him to clean up this mess, and get that fence repaired before Charlie got wind of its damage. I then reminded Lieutenant Steve we were not to be seen together, so I turned and went to the other side of the perimeter.

That night was designated a *Mad Minute* night. A Mad Minute is a test firing of all perimeter weapons. Of course, this also gives Charlie, if he's watching, the exact position of our automatic weapons in the perimeter. We did move the position once a week, and the Mad Minute was only once or twice a month.

During the Mad Minute, a rain of bullets is directed out several hundred meters into the jungle. Of course, we didn't give forewarning, since we were in a free fire zone. Anything moving at night, other than our own, was fair game. With Delta Company above and to our right rear, we could see a wall of red raining down over our perimeter.

132

The perimeter here, as it was at LZ North English, had no perimeter lights. Many base camps did, and there, guards had a sense of security, to the point of sleeping at night. The element of darkness did tend to keep the fear level high enough to discourage sleeping. Dozing was happening, but usually when a guard realized he had closed his eyes, Charlie would appear right in front of his post, ready to kill. This really made for a sudden jolt of adrenaline. Charlie wasn't there, but the mind said he was, and rifles would pop at imagined objects inside and outside the wire. Many hand flares were fired during the nights at LZ Debbie more so than in the *Pacified Zone* at LZ North English.

A hand flare was an aluminum cylinder about one inch in diameter and twelve inches long. To fire it, you hit the charged end with your hand or any solid object. This fired the flare up about three hundred feet, where a parachute would open and the flare would ignite, giving a bright light for several minutes, depending on the weather and wind. When flares lit in foggy or rainy conditions the light was surreal, reflecting off raindrops or through different thickness of mist.

From now on mine sweeps were conducted by one platoon, unless other wise ordered. This day my platoon was on mine sweep. Afterward the drivers of the vehicles would return to LZ Debbie, and the rest of the platoon was to go on a search and destroy mission.

CHAPTER 18
SHIT HEAD TO THE RESCUE

Every road and path was dirt here, with no pavement anywhere. Charlie was a constant threat: from ambush, mines, and boobie traps. I walked up front with the point men, checking every pothole and suspicious marking on the road. Each culvert was checked before anyone crossed.

The bridges were supposedly protected by the local reactionary force (ruff puffs) with many at the bridge, but none out in the field. Several small villages lined the road here and there, down to *Death Canyon*. Usually no Vietnamese were seen on the road, before the sweep, or even in the villages as we passed. The American Division had an infantry unit working above *Death Canyon*, on the west side. We could see them moving around up in the hills while we were walking south approaching the canyon.

As we passed through the cut in the railroad berm, where I was shot, I became very focused on every thing around me. My sense of smell and hearing seemed to increase. We continued south looking for Charlie Company. Almost every sweep, our contact with them didn't come until south of *Death Canyon*, near or at the access road to LZ Charlie Brown. Pleasantries were exchanged, and we would head back to LZ Debbie.

This day, I had most of the platoon dropped off, north of the canyon. We would patrol through the jungle, to the coastal beach, then north to the mountain where our LZ was located. I sent the trucks back to LZ Debbie. I set up a diamond formation, with the first squad on point, second squad on left flank, third squad on right flank, and fourth squad in rear guard.

I had the RTO notify our communication center of the count of men and time we were stepping off into the jungle. We passed through a small village, checking around the hootches for signs of VC or NVA. None were seen, and we moved on. The jungle here was more open than in the central highlands but still confining. The trees were palm, breadfruit and what looked like macadamia. Thickets of bamboo were in clumps and banana trees were everywhere. Some elephant grass grew here in open spaces. This grass was six to ten feet tall and had razor sharp edges to the blades.

While moving through elephant grass, you had to expect cuts on your arms and face. Snakes were also a concern, especially cobras. I walked up front with the first squad; the platoon sergeant took up a position in the middle with the RTO. Our search was going fine until we reached the first large opening in the jungle. The point man stopped and motioned me up. I stepped to his side, and we whispered about our movement through. The trail in front of us led right through the center. The jungle opening was about 100 meters long and half as wide, roughly in an oval design.

Vision was limited here as well, due to elephant grass and clumps of bamboo and banana trees. The trail disappeared into the brush ahead. I listened for any sounds coming from the clearing, nothing, not even animal or birds. I smelled death on the air and motioned for the platoon dog, *Shit Head*, to be brought up. Shit Head sniffed the air, and the hair on her back began to rise up. Shit Head didn't growl, but that was enough to convince me we didn't want to pass through here.

I told the point man to stay put and motioned for all the squad leaders to meet me at the platoon sergeants location. I told them of the clearing and that I decided to skirt both sides. I assigned the third and fourth to go with Sergeant Meddars to the right, I would go with the first and second to the left. I told them to stay ten to fifteen meters inside the jungle, to watch for any sign of an ambush in or near the clearing. I had everyone check watches, and we would push off in fifteen minutes and maintain radio silence unless attacked, so we wouldn't tip off anyone who might be listening.

Once we were set, the platoon moved out in a column formation. I was up front with the point on the left. We moved very slowly, watching 360 degrees around us. After about twenty minutes, the third squad RTO called to alert us of their discovery. Several NVA, to their left, could be seen looking into the clearing. I told them to try to find their last man forward and move in and engage. We would hold our position here and block any one trying to escape through the clearing to the north.

POP, POP, POP, POP.

Rapid firing from M-14s, toward our direction, started the counter ambush. Several AK47 shots where heard but not many.

BUMP, BUMP, BUMP.

Grenades went off close to us in the clearing. The enemy was running away from the ambush into their own boobie traps set for us. My men were ready for any NVA that appeared; none did. The third squad RTO called to declare the ambush over and request we search toward their position.

135

I formed my two squads into a line formation and swept through the clearing. We found two NVA bodies in the middle near the trail, killed by grenades they had set along the trail to be set off by our point after most of the platoon entered the kill zone. Six more NVA were found on the south side of the clearing. We took their weapons and any documents. The bodies were left for the Americal Graves Registration unit to take care of. Most likely the bodies would be found by NVA in the area and removed before the infantry arrived.

I told the platoon to get formed up and move out rapidly. We probably alerted other NVA in the area, or they would be coming to check on their people. In this area you never knew how many NVA or VC you could expect. The platoon formed up and moved through the jungle, finally breaking through the tree line above the beach. The water looked inviting, but it was mid-day, and we had to make our way back to LZ Debbie. I told the point to move out along the tree line and keep an eye on the inner jungle.

We formed into a column, keeping a five- meter spread from man to man. Working along the tree line let us move faster and about 1600 hours (4 PM) we were even with the mountain of the Americal Division. The point turned left heading into the sunset toward LZ Debbie. My RTO called the base camp communication center and advised them we were coming in from the east, and to alert the perimeter guards. Apparently they did: no one fired on us. We crossed in front of the south wire and entered the base camp at the west gate.

When I reported to *Tommy Two Bars*, he said all the confiscated weapons and documents were to be turned over to the battalion staff. A sergeant from the battalion headquarters came down in a jeep from LZ Thunder taking the rifles, ammunition, and documents. I was hoping to get a chance to test fire one of the AK47 rifles.

Several days later, a directive came down from battalion headquarters forbidding the firing of any AK47 rifles or other NVA weapons. No explanation was given for the directive. Later, through the grape vine, we heard one of the battalion staff officers had test fired an AK47 and a round exploded in the chamber.

He was seriously wounded in the face, neck, hands and arms. He was medevaced to Chu Lia and then to Japan. Rumor had it NVA weapons were inferior to ours, repeatedly misfiring and exploding in the owners face. (Thirty years later, through the freedom of information act, and declassification of *MACVSOG* documents, it was disclosed that defective ammunition had been smuggled into the NVA by our government.)

CHAPTER 19
AGENT ORANGE

When we came back from the sweep and ambush, I had noticed brush was growing rapidly in the outer perimeter wire. I mentioned this to *Tommy Two Bars*, recommending a weed pulling party. Several days later a chopper, with extension arms closed on each side, landed outside our gate. Inside the cargo deck were metal drums of Agent Orange liquid defoliant. The chopper crew extended the arms, which had sprinkler heads attached on the end. The arms were locked out at a 90- degree position from the body of the chopper.

The pilot wound up his rotors and rose up about six feet above the ground. He slowly flew up and down our perimeter while spraying Agent Orange. I was standing on the top of our berm watching. The rotor wash was causing the liquid spray to swirl in a large round vortex.

No one on the chopper was wearing respirator masks, and on one particular close run to us, we were covered by the spray. I don't remember any particular smell or taste from Agent Orange and thought to myself, at least this stuff doesn't smell like the weed killer my dad and uncles used on the ranch.

Inside days the green was gone. (Since I was placed on the Battalion roster among the living, I have received requests for confirmation on exposure to Agent Orange from fellow veterans who have been having trouble convincing the VA of the exposure to the agent, and other physically damaging chemicals while in Viet Nam.)

Within days several of us who were watching came down with flu like symptoms. I was laid up for five days. I didn't eat the entire time. One night during a monsoon rain, the first since we move to LZ Debbie, I could hear a commotion down at the perimeter.

I called out for my platoon sergeant. No answer. Suddenly, there was *Tommy Two Bars* at my bunker entrance.

He began yelling at me, "Lieutenant, why aren't you down there with your platoon directing them on the emergency work?"

I leaned up and looked at him through bleary eyes. He turned and left. I crawled out of the bunk and got dressed. Every step was painful. My muscles and joints ached all over.

I left the bunker, and started down the slope, in the driving rain. I could see that the run off water had backed up behind the perimeter berm and was flooding the living- fighting bunkers in my platoons area.

Lieutenant Steve was directing the front loaders to cut through the berm giving the water an outlet to the rice paddies below our level. The front loaders were working with their lights on and several trucks had been positioned to flood the area with their lights. Lieutenant Steve looked around and saw me coming. He came up to me and told me to get back to my bunker. I was in no condition to be out in the driving rain and the hell with *Tommy Two Bars*, who wasn't out there either.

I stumbled back to the bunker and stayed several more days. Finally, one afternoon, several of my men came up to the bunker with a bottle of booze and a steak for the barbecue. By then I was starting to feel better, the smell of the cooking steak and the sound of the men talking brought me out of my stupor. I got out of my bunk, got dressed and joined them around the barbecue. After several drinks of the booze, I started to feel like myself.

I saw that the cut in the berm had been filled. Lieutenant Steve filled me in on what happened. Once the water ran through and the level dropped, a culvert was put in position and the berm was closed up. Several pieces of rebar were welded on the inside end of the culvert, to prevent Charlie from crawling through the culvert and entering the base camp. Don't think he didn't try it.

CHAPTER 20
CONVOY AMBUSH, DEATH CANYON

The next day I was back on mine sweep. It felt good being up and around, even if it was in the free fire zone. The heat during the day was getting unbearable. Several days the temperature was reported at 130 degrees. That's hard to believe, but being there, and feeling the pressure from the humidity made me a believer. That evening, at dusk, we heard a ferocious ambush from the direction of *Death Canyon*.

Black smoke was rising from the canyon and drifting over the hills on the breeze. The booms and machine gun fire went on and on. About thirty minutes later, just before dark, a convoy rolled passed our LZ. Several trucks stopped at our gate and yelled they needed help with wounded.

We had a new medic, who just arrived, and he ran out with his bag. The first man off loaded on a stretcher was covered in blood. The medic reached down to the head to check for a pulse. When the medic touched the neck, the head rolled off the stretcher.

The medic jumped back, becoming very pale, before vomiting in the ditch. He recovered fast and went to the others who were still alive. A M60 tank rolled up and stopped while the rest of the convoy continued north. The tank commander, a sergeant, told me what happened. The soldier with the decapitated head had been a machine gunner on a personnel carrier. He was hit in the back of his neck by a B40 rocket. When the rocket hit the neck, it exploded through, making a clean cut.

The convoy got a late start from Qui Nhon and had to stop at LZ Charlie Brown to pickup several fuel tanker trucks that had been off loaded from Navy ships in the bay. The fuel was needed at Duc Pho by the choppers. As the convoy was running through *Death Canyon*, Charlie hit several of the fuel trucks with B-40 rockets. The trucks burst into flame and ran off the road. Some dropped down the embankment. Others jack knifed at the north end of the canyon. The roadway had been paved, finally, and there were quite a few Vietnamese traveling with the convoy in various vehicles.

Once the ambush started, driving through the tight canyon was hairy. Several lambretas and motorcycles were hit by trucks and run over by the tanks and armor personnel carriers. The vehicles and occupants were flattened. Charlie was on both sides of the road throughout the canyon, and every curve had a streak of orange coming from different angles. Burning trucks and dead were left on and off the road. Several armor personnel carriers were left off the road. The tanks had to push the two burning jack knifed trucks off the road. This allowed the rest of the convoy through.

Finally the medevac choppers came for the wounded and dead, and the tanks left for Duc Pho. It was dark, and looking south, the hills were lit up by the burning trucks. All night the trucks burned. The next dawn our company was ordered to check the remains after mine sweep. I asked *Tommy Two Bars* if he was coming and got, "Just do your job!"

At least on this mine sweep, *Tommy Two Bars* deemed it necessary to have two platoons. Lieutenant Steve took the point with his first platoon. My platoon conducted the mine sweep, with them on guard. I was walking point with my platoon, as usual. The transport trucks were following. We had several armor personnel carriers and duster tanks on this trip. The smoke had gone from the trucks, but the heat still rose from their skin.

The first platoon passed the two jack knifed trucks and continued on. As we approached, my point man turned and said, "Hey Lieutenant, isn't that a claymore mine?" He was pointing in the direction of the jack knifed truck wheel wells. I moved closer, about ten feet away, and saw several mines set in the wheel wells of the hot trucks. Brush was set in front for camouflage. I yelled for everyone to get off the road. I ran around to the east side of the trucks. I saw several como wires leading from under the trucks down the road side and out to the rice paddies.

The wires looked as big as ropes to me. I yelled for everyone to get down. I could hear the cranking of the detonator, somewhere in the rice paddies. A squad leader came up to my side while I was trying to separate the wire to cut, he asked, "Can I shoot?"

I looked at him and said, "Hell yes you can shoot!"

He started shooting in the direction of the rice paddies. This started the others. I managed to separate the two wires and cut them, one at a time, with my Bowie Knife. Luckily, none of the mines blew. As the firing began to build, we were hit by an ambush on the other side of the road from the cliffs above. The Americal infantry unit that was expected to be up there had been wiped out the day before, either during the convoy ambush or before.

I called our company communication center and asked for help. The sergeant told my RTO to stand by. Lieutenant Steve was also calling and getting no reply. After several minutes of waiting for a decision from *Tommy Two Bars*, I switched radio frequencies calling the American Division on Thunder Mountain. Several minutes later two Cobra Gunships arrived, and I directed them to the cliffs above us.

They streaked in, one at a time, and plastered the sand bag bunkers Charlie was hiding in. Apparently, these were the bunkers the American infantry platoon had built into the rocky boulders. The bags went flying down as rockets hit their targets. Several NVA fell down to the canyon floor.

Charlie Company finally showed up, and everything died down. One of my men had been wounded. He was shot through the wrist. The man was a FNG and had been in country only a few days. (Twenty-five years later I was told that man had shot himself during the firefight.)

We spread out, and while the Cobra Gunships circled, we checked out the damaged trucks and the dead inside. The drivers and passengers were burnt to dust, lying on the burnt floorboards. There was nothing to collect. When touched, the bones just crumbled to ash. The mines were collected. The Vietnamese that had been run over by the tanks were flat as the road. The metal of their vehicles was flat and ground into the pavement. They weren't even up enough to cause a bump in the road. I had never seen anything like it.

The machine guns from the armor personnel carriers were collected, along with the dead bodies inside. The American Division sent a company of infantry by helicopter, landing on the road northwest of us. They headed west, into the hills, and after a brief firefight with escaping NVA and VC, made their way to the cliffs above us. The company commander called to say their platoon had been overrun, and there were no survivors.

About that time a light observation helicopter landed just west of the railroad cut where I had been shot. Out jumped the battalion commander and the command sergeant major in full battle gear. I walked toward them to report the situation.

"Morning, Colonel," I said.

"Morning, Lieutenant, where's your company commander?"

I told him *Tommy Two Bars* wasn't here and was taking care of the base camp. The colonel said when the order was given for this patrol Bravo Companies captain had been strongly advised to be on it.

He also wanted to know what *Tommy Two Bars* response had been to my request for help. I told him I didn't receive a response for several minutes. After several requests, I switched to the American radio frequency and asked for support.

141

This was the proper procedure we had been advised to use. The Chain of Command was to go through our own communication center to the Americal communications. The colonel had no problem with me making the command decision, with the lack of response from my own captain.

The colonel, command sergeant major, and I again surveyed the carnage. A medevac chopper landed to take my wounded soldier to Chu Lia. The colonel decided there was no more to do there. The Americal Division would be sending a Graves Registration team and wreckers to clear the damaged vehicles. The colonel and command sergeant major walked back to their chopper and left.

I ordered our two platoons to regroup, and head for LZ Debbie. I took the lead in my jeep. During the ride back, Shit Head, our platoon dog, decided she would ride on the hood of the jeep. The front windshield was down and the dog, usually riding in the back of the jeep, walked between the driver and me up onto the hood. After standing like the hood ornament, Shit Head calmly jumped forward into space, and disappeared under the jeep. The driver slammed on the brakes, and I expected to see Vietnamese dinner lying on the road. Nope. Shit Head was running back to the jeep like it never happened. For the rest of the trip, she quietly sat in the back.

CHAPTER 21
STUPID OCS WONDER!

Upon entering the base camp, the first sergeant came over to my platoon area. He said the captain wanted to see me at the command post.

(Our command post wasn't like the bunker we had at LZ North English. It was a general purpose medium tent, about 15 feet by 30 feet, with six-foot high sidewalls placed over wood flooring, similar to the command post and orderly room in the M.A.S.H. show. The company commander's office was a framed in room, inside the tent.)

I entered and was sent by the orderly specialist to the office. *Tommy Two Bars* had on his pissed off face, and told me to close the door.

He wanted to know, "Who do you think you are calling the Americal Division, going over my head in the Chain of Command."

I explained the lack of response from the communication sergeant, after several requests. He waved me off with one hand to shut up.

"You're just a stupid OCS wonder, who won't amount to anything in the Army, and have no right ignoring my command," he yelled.

Knowing I had the approval of the battalion commander, I said, "Captain, I am the executive officer of this company and was in charge of the patrol this morning. I made a decision under the circumstances and feel it was right."

"Did you?" he said, "What were you and Lieutenant Tomlinson doing on the same patrol? I told you two to stay apart!"

"Captain," I said, "my platoon was ordered to take part in that patrol, as was the first platoon. My responsibility is to my men in the second platoon and the men of this company when the company commander is absent."

"Don't you tell me your responsibility, Lieutenant, I know what your responsibility is."

At this point, he handed me several legal sized sheets of paper to read. Before I could get through the first sentence, *Tommy Two Bars* grabbed the sheets out of my hands, and began *yelling* the contents.

"I order a general court-martial against you, Lieutenant Suffern, for insubordination and disobeying a direct order. You're dismissed. But, before you go, I expect a salute," he said, "and you had better hold your salute until I return it."

I came to attention and saluted, and started to laugh. I couldn't help it. The situation was too unreal. *Tommy Two Bars* didn't see the humor. By this time he was so mad, he was nearly frothing at the mouth. I turned and left before he completed his salute.

The first sergeant was standing in the orderly room. He had a smile on his face and saluted me as I walked through. I went down to talk to Lieutenant Steve and fill him in on the situation. He was fit to be tied and ready to get after *Tommy Two Bars*. Once he finally calmed down, I told him about my conversation with the colonel, and besides, if I was court-martialed, and sent to Long Bien Jail (referred to as LBJ by the troops) he would assume his most desired position, that of second in command of the company. We both had a good laugh.

While we were laughing the communication sergeant walked up and had this to say. When Lieutenant Tomlinson and I had called for help, he notified the captain, who came running. The captain just stood there, muttering, "What do I do? What do I do?" while banging his head against the wall of the connex. The sergeant asked several times what his orders were, and he got no response. That's when they lost radio contact with the patrol. He wanted me to know. I thanked him and sent him on his way.

CHAPTER 22
BURNING BRIDGE

Later that morning, I was assigned a mission to rebuild a blown bridge several miles north of LZ Debbie on QL-1. The material had arrived from Qui Nhon, and together with a crane that had been brought up from LZ Lowboy, my platoon moved up to survey the damage and start the project. A company of local ARVN troops were sent to guard the bridge during construction and after the completion.

When we arrived I saw several ARVNs milling about village hootches but not a company. The crane was set up to drive piling for the timber trestle bridge. The rest of the day was spent driving piles and cutting the tops square to accept a cross timber for the base on which the trestles would set. As daylight faded, a jeep approached. A captain of the local ARVN command arrived, and in English, told me a platoon of men would be setting up a perimeter around the bridge that night, and the materials would be safe to leave.

I had my platoon form up, and we returned to LZ Debbie. I was called on the way in to report to the command post as soon as I got back. I entered the orderly room expecting to see two MPs ready to take me to the Americal Division Stockade. Instead were the senior NCOs and Lieutenant Steve. *Tommy Two Bars* told everyone we were to be on 50 percent alert tonight. Battalion Intelligence had called to say there was a possibility of attack by a regiment of NVA who were lurking in our area.

After the meeting and chow, Lieutenant Steve and I decided to have a few drinks. He had introduced me to Cherry Herring, and I had grown quite fond of the dark red liquid when we could get it. He happened to have several bottles, so we kicked back and toasted what ever we could think of. By nightfall, we were both a little tight. I didn't think Charlie would try anything this night because there was a full moon and clear skies.

Around midnight I was on the perimeter berm talking to one of my men. I scanned the perimeter with my binoculars and saw nothing out of the ordinary. Then I smelled smoke; heavy creosote smoke. The sky was filling with the haze, coming from the north on the other side of the mountain.

I told my platoon sergeant, "I bet that's the bridge material we left this afternoon."

About then muffled swishes and bangs popped on the other side of the mountain. A major firefight started on the Americal Divisions north perimeter. Everyone figured there was no way Charlie would try getting up that way. It was steep, rocky, and heavily covered by bunkers along the cliffs.

The explosions continued, and soon we were notified Charlie had breached the lines, and were running through the Americal Divisions base camp above us. I sent a runner to get *Tommy Two Bars* who was asleep in his bunker. I ordered the headquarters platoon to reinforce the north side of our perimeter where we had only one bunker defense and no wire.

I told *Tommy Two Bars* of the situation, and he questioned the seriousness of it. I told him to call Battalion Command Center if he didn't believe me. I turned and went down to the latrine for a deserved break. I had been having a problem with diarrhea, later diagnosed as scurvy, and needed a hasty retreat to the treatment center.

While sitting on the one holer, I was gazing up looking at the moon through the upper screen watching the smoke pass by. Bullets started hitting above my head. They were coming from the east, passing through the thin, tin metal siding, and exiting through the screen. All hell broke loose up on the top of the mountain.

Charlie had tossed several satchel charges into the Americal Division's ammo dump. Artillery and mortar rounds were cooking off. Charlie must have been done there and was coming down the access road toward our base camp. Several of our perimeter guards began firing. Off to my right, I heard headquarters platoon cut loose, in wild cracking thunder, up the road.

I quickly cinched up my trousers, and getting my helmet and rifle, broke out of the latrine. We had just recently been issued brand new M16A1 rifles, and they were beauts. I walked to the living fighting bunkers of the third platoon. I approached the door and yelled, "It's me; I'm coming in." I entered and asked how they were doing and got the reply I expected. Ok. Entering a living-fighting bunker at night while under attack was risky business.

The policy was not to enter under any circumstances, because if Charlie had penetrated the perimeter, he would go to these bunkers and toss in satchel charges. Anyone entering could be mistaken for Charlie and shot. I was either to intoxicated to worry about that, or felt I knew my men well enough for them to recognize my voice. Maybe luck had something to do with it. I wasn't shot that night or any other.

The men were firing at silhouettes of Charlie as he veered off to the east, toward the beach. Some firing came back our way, but not aimed. After several minutes, every thing on our perimeter quieted down. The ammunition dumps up on the mountaintop continued to blow until after daybreak.

Later that day I heard what happened. *Someone* ran off the ARVNs who were guarding the bridge we had started the day before, and burned the creosote dripping timbers we'd left behind. The black smoke drifted up to the mountainside, up and over.

Under the cover of smoke, the NVA made their way to the mountain cliffs and up to the bunkers perched there. Firing B-40 rockets at the bunkers, everything was destroyed, and the guards were killed. The NVA just walked into the main base camp and started shooting. The sappers went directly to the ammo dumps, tossing their satchel charges in before leaving on the south side road, down toward us.

After mine sweep, I led my platoon to the bridge, and found burning timber and pilings. Evidently Charlie didn't want that bridge rebuilt. Several weeks later the bridge was built, after we installed a perimeter fence for defense, so the ARVNs were more secure about staying there. That was the reason given for failing to guard the bridge that night.

About this time, a friend of mine from OCS, First Lieutenant Donald Lambert, showed up at the battalion. He had just left the helicopter school in the states (without finishing) and was assigned to Delta Company. Boy was it good to see him. He said the reason he didn't finish the school was the method of discipline for errors during flights. The training pilots would tap on the student pilot's helmet to punish him for an error, or slow response to the helicopter.

Lieutenant Donald Lambert, Delta Company Platoon Leader, 1969.

Lieutenant Lambert wasn't objecting to the punishment, but in the way certain instructors chose to dish it out. Lieutenant Lambert had discussed this with the commander of the helicopter school and the commander of the section he was assigned to.

One afternoon after conducting an auto rotation procedure and safely landing, the instructor, a warrant officer, smacked Lieutenant Lambert rather hard on his helmet. Lambert responded with a backhand fist to the instructors face. This knocked the instructor out. So, not wanting to confront the instructor in the air, Lieutenant Lambert waited until he regained consciousness. The instructor said to return to the airfield. After landing, they both walked to the office of the commanding officer.

The instructor demanded Lieutenant Lambert be court-martialed for striking a junior officer, as well as dismissal from the school. Lieutenant Lambert was given an option. Either voluntarily leave the school and accept immediate orders for Nam or be court-martialed and face a possible term in Fort Leavenworth prison.

He chose the first, and a letter of reprimand was issued to his file. Later in Lieutenant Lamberts' tour, he was shot through the legs while on a patrol and spent a month in Chu Lia and Japan hospitals. He returned to the battalion and won a Silver Star for his heroism under fire.

CHAPTER 23
HASTY RETREAT

That night we were again placed on alert, this time 100 percent. Charlie's regimental size force was to hit us again with a ground attack. A storm had been brewing all afternoon and as night fell, the clouds were dark and low. Fog drifted in from the South China Sea, and visibility was limited to several feet out front of the perimeter. I was moving up and down the berm, checking on the men and using my binoculars to try to see.

I happened to be in the center of the berm, facing south, over the area the drainage culvert ran. Several trip flares activated in the middle of the wire out front of us. We could only see a blur of light, no one in the wire or on the ground. The fog, and now rain, made it very difficult to see.

I shot a hand flare up into the fog hoping to get a different angle of light. Once it popped and ignited we could see forms on the ground. Some were right up to the culvert entrance. Firing started and continued for a while. When we started, Delta Company began, and we had a Mad Minute. They couldn't see anything, but shot down into our perimeter, using predesignated markers for their machine guns.

The American Division must have been resupplied with mortar rounds. They began dropping rounds around our outer perimeter. After several minutes, *Tommy Two Bars* came running down from his bunker yelling, "Cease firing, there's no enemy out there. The flares were tripped by the dogs."

Where he got that idea, I'll never understand. By this time I was down with the first platoon, watching their grenadier fire at NVA we could barely make out in a ravine, several hundred meters south. As the grenadier fired, one of the platoon members would hand him another round from a box of M-79 grenades.

It appeared he was hitting amongst the NVA. *Tommy Two Bars* came running down to the position yelling to stop firing and wasting ammunition. The grenadier probably didn't hear the order and fired another round. *Tommy Two Bars* picked up a handful of sand, and threw it in the grenadier's eyes. Everyone there turned on the captain with rifles aimed. I stepped between the men and *Tommy Two Bars*. I turned to *Tommy Two Bars* and said he better leave. He turned and made a hasty retreat to his bunker.

I turned and calmed the men down. They were all for following *Tommy Two Bars* and ending his suffering. Lieutenant Steve and I talked them out of doing anything they would regret. The rest of the night we peered into the darkness and fog. Periodically hand flares were fired, but the fog and rain were so thick nothing could be seen beyond ten meters.

The next morning the first and second platoons assembled on QL-1 for mine sweep. The third platoon had made a sweep of the perimeter, finding several bodies in the wire, and lots of blood and pieces of flesh in the ravine the grenadier had fired into. I ordered everyone to lock and load weapons. *THUNK.* A grenade launcher fired.

I said, "Who's was that, where's it going?"

The grenadier, who had his eyes sanded by the captain, said he had closed his breech and the weapon misfired. He was pointing the barrel up and didn't know where the grenade went. Everyone just stood there for a few seconds and finally, *WHACK.* The grenade exploded next to *Tommy Two Bars* bunker. I looked up at the bunker, several hundred meters away, and watched a plume of black smoke drift away.

I went over to the grenadier, and looking him in the eye asked, "Was that an accident Specialist?"

"Yes, sir," he said.

I said. "Well, next time aim the weapon away from the base camp before loading, is that clear?"

"Yes, sir, very clear, sir."

Several minutes later my RTO, motioned me over. The communications sergeant was on the radio, *Tommy Two Bars* wanted to talk. I took the radio handset and acknowledged my call sign. *Tommy Two Bars* began demanding an explanation. I told him, "The firing was an accident, over and out." I handed the set back to the RTO ,and we went on mine sweep.

When we returned to the base camp, I was called to the command post for a chat. *Tommy Two Bars* demanded to know who fired the round and wanted a report from me for a court-martial charge to be issued. I told him there was no need for a charge. The specialist had been talked to by me, and the incident was an accident. Besides, if he was trying to hit the captain's bunker, he would have. I refused to fill out a report otherwise and would not back up a charge against the grenadier. *Tommy Two Bars* again had his little discipline talk with me, and finally I was dismissed with the normal formality. That night was quiet, and Lieutenant Steve and I killed a few Cherry Herrings.

CHAPTER 24
DEJA VU

The next morning, at first light, the first platoon was assigned mine sweep alone. My platoon and the third were to stay in the base camp. At dawn I heard an ambush with lots of bangs and firing coming from the south. I went to my radio on the jeep, turned it on, and heard calls of help from Lieutenant Steve. The first platoon was being butchered by a large force of NVA.

I called for my platoon and yelled for the third to get moving. Within minutes we pulled out onto QL-1 and headed south. Several miles down the road we got a call from the communications sergeant. I chose to ignore the call, knowing it was probably *Tommy Two Bars*. The third platoon sergeant answered the call and was ordered to return to the base camp immediately.

We, out in the field, had a way of communicating off channel, and I contacted the sergeant. He said he had too much time in the Army to risk in disobeying a direct order. I told him to return to the base camp.

I continued south finally coming to the scene of the ambush. I stopped my formation about 100 meters north, and had my men dismount and take the right flank of the first platoons position. They ran to the railroad berm, working their way south, firing as they went. The NVA broke and ran down a draw into the hills. Several NVA were killed and wounded.

Lieutenant Steve was busy calling for medevac, and regrouping his men. Before I could get over to his position on QL-1, a light observation chopper landed. It was the battalion commander and command sergeant major; again, decked out in their combat gear, ready for action.

The colonel came up to me, and looking around asked for my captain. I told him where the captain was, and the orders he had directed my way. The colonel and I went over to the carnage.

As the mine sweep was heading south, several B-40 rockets were fired into the trucks. One hit at the right front of the lead truck and penetrated the cab. The rocket crossed in front of a FNG sergeant, peppering him with shrapnel. The rest of the rocket hit the driver in the right thigh. The rocket went through his right leg and nearly took off his left at the hip. By the time everything was quiet the driver and sergeant had nearly bleed out. Several inches of sticky red blood was covering the floorboard, and when the driver's door was opened, blood flooded.

About half the platoon was wounded. A medevac chopper arrived, and transported them to Chu Lia. The driver was the grenadier who *Tommy Two Bars* assaulted with sand. I told Lieutenant Steve to get his platoon reorganized and back to the base camp. I took over the mine sweep, and the colonel flew over us for the rest of the sweep.

When we returned to LZ Debbie, the first sergeant was waiting at the main gate to talk. He said, "Lieutenant, all of the NCOs here will back you up, 100 percent."

I said, "What are you talking about?"

He said *Tommy Two Bars* was waiting for me up at the command post, and I was to report *immediately*.

I dropped my gear at my bunker and walked up to the command post. When I arrived the captain said, "God damn you, Lieutenant. You stand at attention and listen to what I am about to say."

Tommy Two Bars was very agitated and appeared to be in a state of hysteria. He handed me several pages of court-martial forms. I began to read it, but he suddenly grabbed the forms out of my hands. He wanted the pleasure of reading me the formal charges. *Deja vu!* (Haven't we been here before?)

Tommy Two Bars read the charges, then said I was under arrest and confined to my bunker. "Do you have anything to say?" he said.

"No, I don't give a shit what you do, Captain; I'm done here," I replied, as nasty as I could.

I was ready to shoot him myself. Luckily, I had left my side arm down at my bunker. I was dismissed and didn't bother with the salute protocol. For this, I was yelled at to return and "Salute your superior officer." I just kept walking.

I got to my bunker and told my platoon sergeant what had happened, and told him to notify Lieutenant Steve he was now the executive officer of the company. Before he could leave, a jeep was driven up to my bunker. It was the battalion commander's driver, a staff sergeant, who told me the colonel wanted to see me. I told him I was under arrest and couldn't leave. The sergeant said he had a direct order from the colonel to come get me.

So, I got my gear and left with the driver, going to the Battalion Headquarters up at LZ Thunder. The day was clear and sunny and getting hotter. I had a headache, was thirsty, and figured it couldn't get any worse than it already was. We arrived at the command bunker.

Out walked the colonel. I saluted, a man I highly respected, and he returned the salute. He said the Group Commander Major General Walker, had flown in by chopper, and wanted a briefing on the ambush. I told the colonel I was under arrest for disobeying a direct order, confined to my bunker, and he should be talking to Lieutenant Tomlinson whose platoon had been hit.

The colonel said to consider myself unarrested, and *I* was the officer he wanted to brief General Walker. So, into the bunker I went, with heart pounding and palms sweatier than during an ambush. I had never been called to see a General before, and never given anyone in Viet Nam, above a colonel, a briefing.

I walked into a room full of brass. I don't recall the briefing and was glad to get out alive. The brass had several questions about what had been done, what Lieutenant Tomlinson had done, and what my company commander had done. I was glad when it was over, and I could leave.

The colonel said not to worry about my captain and to carry on with my duties. As I left, I noticed *Tommy Two Bars* jeep was parked out side the bunker. I didn't see him anywhere. I got into the colonel's jeep and was driven back down to LZ Debbie. Lieutenant Steve and all the NCOs of the company were waiting for me. I told them about the briefing and that I was no longer under company arrest. The first sergeant said they had already heard and welcomed me back.

I asked Lieutenant Steve how the grenadier was doing. With an anguished look, he said they heard he died on the operating table in Chu Lia. I needed a drink and started then and there. By that time it was mid afternoon, we didn't go on another mission for that day.

That evening, while Lieutenant Steve and I were eating chow in the mess tent, the orderly room clerk came down with a form for Lieutenant Steve to check over and sign. *Tommy Two Bars* had prepared a material lost form, with everything he had signed for on his arrival in the company that wasn't in the company now.

He wanted the material to be listed as lost on this ambush. Lieutenant Steve became very irate, and swore he was going to kill him. I, and several sergeants, grabbed him and calmed him down. The events of the day were a bit much for all of us, and *Tommy Two Bars* was stepping over the line here. I took the form and went up to the command post.

Tommy Two Bars was in his bunker eating. I tossed the form onto his bunk, telling him if he wanted it signed, he was going to have to do it and would get no backup from anyone in the company. I turned and left with no comment from *Tommy Two Bars*. That night we again were on alert.

A flotilla of navy patrol boats was brought up from the south and placed off shore to shell the jungle south of our LZ. The Americal Division had a battalion size force who were going to push from the south up to our position to get the NVA regiment who were hiding somewhere in the jungle.

We watched as choppers crossed back and forth over the jungle. At midnight, the navy boats began shelling the jungle about one mile south. The shelling walked its way north to the tree line south of our position. As the shelling stopped, we saw a large size force crossing from the east side of QL-1 to the west entering into a village. The artillery up on LZ Thunder Mountain began firing and landing at the road and into the village. From this village, we would receive green tracer sniper fire at night. The artillery continued to walk west. After several hours of shooting in various parts of the jungle, silence returned to the darkness.

155

CHAPTER 25
BOOBIE TRAP

The next morning the first and second platoons were assigned mine sweep. *Tommy Two Bars* told us the battalion intelligence officer said to be very alert, watching for any movement from the regiment that the Americal Division had encounter that night. So nice of him looking out for our safety!

I took the point and Lieutenant Steve took the rear guard. We had several armored personnel carriers and duster tanks for security. About half way to *Death Canyon*, we took a break. After several minutes, my first squad leader came over and said they may have found a boobie trap.

I walked over to the left flank squad. The point man had moved off the trail when we stopped and sat on a log. When he looked down, he saw a wire, like fishing line, leading from under the log across the trail up ahead at a diagonal. I looked at the wire and carefully uncovered brush where it disappeared under the log.

I found the wire to be tied to the ring of a grenade pin. The grenade was waxed into the nose of a 155mm howitzer shell. If the point man of the first squad had continued down the trail, he probably would have caught the wire with a boot, pulling the pin on the grenade. The resulting blast would have killed, or wounded, the entire squad and probably half the mine-sweep team. I had my RTO notify the company communication center on the find and that we were going to detonate the shell in place.

I placed a quarter pound block of TNT on the shell and used timer fuse. I told everyone to get down. A FNG sergeant in the first platoon, who was about 200 meters north chose to stay seated on a concrete abutment to watch the explosion. I yelled for him to get down. No reaction.

The artillery shell exploded and the sergeant was knocked off his seat. When the medic arrived the sergeant was lying in the streambed, blood covering his face. He was unconscious. After several minutes, he regained consciousness, having only a gash on his chin. I told him that didn't warrant a purple heart, and the next time he didn't listen might be his last mistake.

After the sweep was over, my platoon was ordered to stay in the area of *Death Canyon* looking for a 500-pound bomb, which had not detonated the night of the sweep. The bomb had been dropped by a navy jet on a hillside north of the railroad cut. I had several squads sweep the hillside, which consisted of brush and flat terraces stepped up the side. After several hours, the bomb was found.

The skin of the bomb had been hammered, and was dented. The bomb wasn't opened. I had my sergeant place a pound of TNT on the nose of the bomb and set a twenty-minute time fuse. I called the Americal infantry platoon, up on the hills to our southwest, advising them to get down in their foxholes. They were about half a mile away. We pulled back to the cut in the railroad berm using it as a shield. When the bomb exploded, it threw shrapnel over a mile from its resting place.

After the shrapnel quit falling, we rounded the berm to inspect the damage. A call went out from the infantry platoon RTO for a medevac. Several of the men had decided they would watch the fire works and got caught in the open. I couldn't control everyone in the area, I asked the infantry RTO if they could use our medic. They declined the offer. A few minutes later, the Dust Off chopper landed for the wounded.

After the detonation, we were to remain in the area to help secure the road. That morning a soldier, who had been court-martialed before I came into the company, returned from Long Bien Jail. He was told by the first sergeant to clean up the company area. He told the first sergeant in extremely colorful language where to go. So he left that afternoon, back to Long Bien Jail for another stay in the stockade.

When I returned to the company that night, I was told this man would be back, and he was to be in my platoon. One of my men asked to chat. He told me the man had been with them at LZ Max and had gone to Hawaii for R and R to see his wife. She didn't show up. He called his parents, and they had a private investigator look into her disappearance. He returned to LZ Max and was very distraught. After several weeks, he received word she had been found in Mexico, with several men.

The man (I'll call him Wally) was a truck driver with the company. He asked the previous company commander for an emergency leave to go home. He was denied the leave. Wally went berserk and drove his truck up and down QL-1, trying to hit a mine. He also refused to obey direct orders and was considered nuts. That's why he was court martialed and sent to LBJ. I was grateful for the information.

I went up to the Battalion Headquarters and had a talk with my friend, the chief warrant officer, in personnel. I explained the circumstances, and he said he would see what he could do. Later that evening, while relaxing in my bunker, the headquarters platoon orderly clerk, a specialist, was trying to start a make shift barbecue, using gasoline.

He had bought charcoal from the local barber outside the gate. I heard a commotion and yelling up by the command post, then the running of someone approaching my bunker. It was the supply sergeant. He was excited, blurting out the clerk had caught fire and was badly burned, and could I come quick.

I rushed up to the medic's first aid tent and saw the clerk sitting on the examination table. His clothes had been burned off, his hair was singed and smoking. The eyebrows were gone and skin was hanging off his body in sheets. He was shaking uncontrollably; the medic was trying to keep him from going into shock. He looked in shock already. A medevac chopper had been called for. The clerk wasn't responsive to any questions.

I went to the men who had been at the barbecue when the accident happened. Two of the men were my platoon squad leaders who were credited with saving his life. This is what they said happened. The clerk had started the charcoal with gasoline. After several minutes the fire went out, but the charcoal was smoldering.

The clerk poured more gasoline into a coffee can, tossing the gasoline onto the charcoal. The gasoline exploded, flames shot back to the clerk and engulfed him, catching his clothing on fire. A shrill scream came from the clerk, and he began to run. My squad leaders knocked him down, rolling him in the powdery dirt, extinguishing the fire. He was lucky they were there.

Tommy Two Bars was called to the medic tent and told of the accident. By then the medevac chopper was landing outside our gate, and the clerk was air lifted to Chi Lia. The next day I was ordered to go to Chu Lia to investigate the accident, and determine if the clerk should be charged with a court-martial offense, for a self inflicted wounding.

By the time I arrived at Chu Lia, the clerk had been flown to Japan. I sent a message to our company communication center requesting I follow to Japan. That request was denied. After spending several days at Chu Lia, discussing the war with fellow officers, we returned to LZ Debbie.

My after-action report, much to the dissatisfaction of *Tommy Two Bars*, was this was an accident, which could have been prevented, by the non use of gasoline to start charcoal fires.

CHAPTER 26
CHANGE OF COMMAND

A week later, Wally returned to the company. I happened to be there and had a talk with the man. I told him he would stay in the base camp at the bunkers, and I was working on getting him transferred back to the states. Several hours later, two of my squad leaders came to say they had taken two grenades away from Wally, who was telling others he was going to frag the company commander and first sergeant.

I told the leaders to take Wally to the supply connex and lock him up. I went up to the Battalion Headquarters and talked to the chief warrant officer. He understood the gravity of the situation and had orders cut with-in the hour.

The next morning, I had my squad leaders escort Wally to the supply truck and gave him the orders to go home. He left and later that day, the returning supply sergeant reported Wally took off running as soon as they got to Qui Nhon. No one knew where he was, and while convoying down, he constantly vowed to kill the captain and first sergeant. This information was relayed to *Tommy Two Bars*.

The next day my platoon was assigned another bridge building mission. This one was at the north end of *Deadman's Pass*, just south of Duc Pho. Also, that day was the last day any of us saw *Tommy Two Bars*. He decided to take a ride with the supply truck down to Qui Nhon. He never returned. The battalion commander notified me, upon return to the company, I was now the company commander. But I'm getting ahead of the story.

The Battalion Heavy Equipment Company sent a crane and operator to assist in the construction of another timber trestle bridge. We set up on the south side of the bridge. The pass was laid out with rocky hills on the west side, and open rice fields on the east side. The roadway was dirt and wide enough for traffic to pass either direction.

Deep ditches ran the length of the pass on both sides of the road, and vegetation had grown up enough to allow concealment from observation from the road. I had second squad on the railroad berm, on the west side, for security. They were above the roadway and could see southeast over the entire pass including the rice paddies on the east side of the road. Everything went ok for most of the day.

159

We were going to spend the night at the site. By late afternoon, I had the RTO call the company, reporting on our status. I looked around the terrain and noticed the Vietnamese in the fields were running back toward their village.

I pointed this out to my platoon sergeant as I looked south, seeing a cloud of dust. A convoy was coming. I didn't like what I was feeling, and yelled to the security squads to watch out. No one up on the berm could see why the Vietnamese were leaving.

Usually they were in the fields until after sunset. I didn't have Shit Head to consult, *Tommy Two Bars* had Shit Head and Star disposed of after the night attack in the rain. *Tommy Two Bars* still wouldn't acknowledge we had been attacked, even with the evidence, and believed the dogs set off the flares.

A lead MP jeep approached, turning down the west bypass road at our point and continuing north. Several supply trucks passed, with an armored personnel carrier approaching. *SWISH-BANG!* A B-40 rocket hit the armored personnel carrier on the left side. The carrier continued a few meters, belching black smoke, with men piling off on the east side, away from the rocket penetration.

The rocket had started a fire inside the carrier, and the ammo started to cook, exploding violently. The carrier was stopped dead center on the road, forcing the other trucks to pass, right or left. Luckily, the road was wide enough to do so. The driver of a large ammo truck was hit and drove right up to our point. I thought he was going to drive right off the bridge.

Guns were firing at a furious pace, the NVA were on both sides of the road. Several security chopper gunships were with the convoy, flying back and forth, shooting along the ditches. Some of the door gunners were shooting at my men. I got on the radio and warned them off. I advise the pilots if my men on the berm were shot at again, they would be our next target. Finally, they got the message we were friendlies on the railroad berm, out in the open. No one was wounded or killed.

The rest of the convoy accelerated, passing the disabled armor personnel carrier on both sides. The men who bailed out of the carrier made their way to us. Several were wounded and I called for a medevac. The ambush went on for a few minutes and then stopped. Our Delta Company, at LZ Thunder, was called to respond to the ambush.

Delta Company was being used as an infantry unit now, since our entire Battalion was north of the I Corp II Corp border and we had more companies than engineer work to do. Delta Company arrived at the south end of

Deadman's Pass. They moved out to the west side of the hills, pushing west, trying to cut off the enemy.

Lieutenant Lambert was in charge of the Delta Company troops, directing his men into a position to intercept the NVA. An ambush was set and sprung on the NVA in the rice bowl area west of *Deadman's Pass*. Most of the enemy were killed, wounded, or captured.

Back at the south end of the pass, I discovered the trailing MP jeep and its occupants had been wiped out by the NVA at the start of the ambush. Several drivers had been hit and had to stop their trucks in the pass. With the fast response of Delta Company, the enemy was not allowed to press their ambush, and kill more men. The wounded were flown out of the pass. The supply trucks were moved by drivers, who were brought back from Duc Pho, which was only a mile from the pass.

That night we stayed on alert and had no problems. The next day, after the bridge construction was complete, and deemed passable, we headed back to LZ Debbie. When we arrived, I was met by the first sergeant explaining *Tommy Two Bars* hadn't returned from Qui Nhon, and no one knew where he was. I was to go up to the Battalion Head Quarters and meet with the battalion commander.

I was told by Colonel Andrews, the battalion commander, to take charge of the company while the captain was gone. We never saw *Tommy Two Bars* again and never were given a reason for his absence. Rumor had it the AWOL Wally had stolen a rifle and shot *Tommy Two Bars* in Qui Nhon. This was not confirmed by anyone at the staff level of the battalion.

I must say that the morale in the company changed after *Tommy Two Bars* left. This left only two officers in the company. Now Lieutenant Steve *was* the executive officer. The next morning, first platoon and third platoon went on mine sweep south. After the sweep, first platoon was ordered to stay in the hills northwest of *Death Canyon* to pull security.

About mid day, I was called to the communication center. Lieutenant Steve was calling for a medevac chopper and requesting assistance with the security. I had the communication sergeant call the second platoon to respond, and I left in my jeep to follow them there. (I continued to use the second platoon jeep until the chicken plates could be removed from the company commander's jeep.)

When we arrived, Lieutenant Steve told me what happened. After getting to the hills, he had deployed his platoon over two hillsides. One of his FNG troops had walked between brush, crossing from one terraced level to another. A trip wire was stretched across the opening, and because of his inexperience, the troop pushed his way through the resistance.

This information was gathered from another troop behind him. The trip wire was attached to a directional mine, large enough to kill a tank or dozer. The trooper was cut in half. When the mine blew, several other men were injured. Running to help, the FNG sergeant who had been knocked unconscious a week earlier, (when I detonated the 155mm boobie trap), stepped on an anti-personnel mine, blowing off the front half of a foot.

After the dead and wounded were medevaced out, I ordered the first platoon back to the base camp to regroup. I called the communication center to let them know I was staying in the hills for the rest of the day. I had the second platoon check carefully for any more boobie traps, and suspicious ground disturbances for anti personnel mines. None were found. The rest of the day was uneventful.

CHAPTER 27
DISOBEYING MY OWN ORDER

That evening, the battalion communication officer radioed our company saying the battalion would be on 100 percent alert. Intelligence had received notification of a possible attack to LZ Debbie, by a force of 2,000 NVA. They were intending to use gas.

When I assembled the company executive officer and NCOs, I told them to tell the troops, making sure they had their gas masks handy. The mess sergeant said in a choked voice, "Why do they have to use gas?" I told him I didn't know, but in the past, I hadn't heard of gas being used by anyone, but us.

The sergeant was an E-7, who had been in the Army in World War Two, Korea, and several tours in Nam. He was getting close to the end of this tour, and I could see the fear in his face. This was to be his last tour of duty before retirement.

That night, I walked the perimeter with Lieutenant Steve. We checked up and down the perimeter with each living fighting bunker, and berm bunker, to make sure the men were alert and ready. About 0200 hours I heard, *THUMP, THUMP. THUMP*, mortars being fired from the south jungle.

Lieutenant Steve and I yelled, "INCOMING" and ran for the nearest bunker. Seconds later the mortars hit the base camp. *BAM, BAM, BAM.* Several men on the berm began firing out into the perimeter. I looked out through the firing windows of the living-fighting bunker. I didn't see anything, and yelled for the men down the line to cease fire, until they had a target.

I left the bunker after several minutes hearing no additional mortar sounds. As I was walking to the third platoon area, again I heard, *THUMP, THUMP, THUMP.* I ran up to a bunker in the berm, and dropped down with the men on guard duty. We crouched there until the mortars hit. *BAM, BAM, BAM.*

Just then I realized I didn't have my gas mask. I looked at the guard and said, "You don't happen to have two of those do you?" He said he didn't, and I began to laugh. Here I was disobeying my own order. I figured Lieutenant

Steve would have to issue court-martial charges on me if Charlie did hit us with gas.

After the last explosions, I watched the smoke from the mortars drift away from me, and out the west perimeter. I yelled for confirmation of no gas. No one was giving a damn about the gas. I left the bunker and walked to the west end of the base camp, sniffing the air.

I had been through tear gas (CS) and nauseating gas (CN) and knew what it smelled like. I was hoping they wouldn't use nerve or mustered gas. All I smelled was the smell of cordite explosive.

When I got to the west end, I went up to a perimeter bunker and took a look. Everyone was calm and watching for movement. The night was dark, with starlight only, but clear. No movement was seen. That was the extent of the mortars, and the rest of the night was quiet.

At dawn, I went back to the command post to confer with the first sergeant, and get some chow. When I approached the tent, the motor pool sergeant asked to chat. We went to my bunker, and he told me what was on his mind.

During the night, when the first mortars were heard, the headquarters platoon was gathered up at the command post, their usual place to be, and the mess sergeant put on his gas mask in a panic, crouching down in the corner of the post. He refused to move from that position the entire night, and wore his mask until dawn.

The motor pool sergeant was concerned for the mess sergeant's sanity. I told him I would look into it. I went up to the command post and had a chat with the first sergeant. Because of the closeness of the mess sergeant's DEROS (Date Estimated Return from Over Seas) from Nam, and his retirement from the Army, we decided it would be in the best interest of the Army, the men of the company, and the mess sergeant, if we could get him an early DEROS.

I went up to the Battalion Headquarters at LZ Thunder, and had a talk with my friend, the chief warrant officer in personnel. He said if I, as the commanding officer of Bravo Company, recommended the processing to begin ASAP on this sergeants retirement, and early DEROS from Nam, he would talk to the battalion commander.

I returned to LZ Debbie and called in the mess sergeant. The first sergeant and I told the sergeant what we were planning, asking him if he would like to leave Nam a little early. He said that was ok with him. I called the chief warrant officer. He said the sergeant could take the supply truck to Qui Nhon

164

that day, and the paperwork would follow him to the Group Headquarters tomorrow. The sergeant was packed in minutes and left on the truck with a convoy by noon.

The rest of the day was quiet. That night we were again on alert, but we had no incoming mortars or sniper fire. The next morning the battalion commander called to warn us of expected movement of the regiment of NVA some where in the south, and west of our base camp. He ordered a platoon to patrol back from mine sweep on the west side of the road, no more than 200 meters into the hills and jungle.

CHAPTER 28
DIVISION AMBUSH

I decided to take my platoon on the mine sweep and patrol. The third platoon went as guard for us on the sweep, and was sent back to LZ Debbie after the sweep was over. The day was clear and getting hot. There was a slight breeze from the northwest, placing us in a down wind position on the way back.

I missed the dogs being on the patrols. So did the men of the platoons. I was walking up front, several men behind the point. My point man stopped, raising his hand. He was looking left, off to the northwest, at something I couldn't see. His posture was still and tight. The smell of sweat and dirt hung in the air.

I slowly moved to his side. He whispered, "Do you smell that?"

I sniffed the air. A definite pungent odor was on the breeze. The air was moving slowly, so I placed my index finger in my mouth to get moisture. When I took it out, I could tell the breeze was still coming from our left front, northwest.

"Do you recognize that smell, sir?" the point man said.

"No," I told him.

He said it was marijuana. The locals grew it and sold to the GIs. I hadn't seen any in our company, but it may have been there.

The smell was faint, and after several minutes, seeing nothing moving, I decided to move on slowly. The terrain to the left front was open rice paddies, broken by bamboo hedgerows along the dikes. The hedgerows were staggered and not connected. I stayed up front with my point man. We went on for about 500 meters. The odor became more prominent, the farther north we went.

Suddenly, the point man raised his hand again and then gave the *get down* sign. Everyone dropped to the ground, and looked around. I crawled the five meters up to the point. He pointed to something to the northwest. There, about 500 meters away, was a column of NVA moving north. Immediately, the adrenaline began flowing.

We could only see a small section of troops as they moved north, passing between bamboo hedgerows. Our position was blocked from their view by several bamboo hedgerows on our left giving the platoon concealment. I crawled back to the RTO and called our communication center.

The communication sergeant relayed the information to Battalion Headquarters communication officer. The battalion communication officer called, wanting to know the strength of the NVA unit. I told him we had seen several hundred cross the opening, but didn't know what the entire size was. I waited while they communicated with the Americal Division. Several minutes later, I was ordered to stay put. The Americal Division was sending several companies of mechanized infantry to make contact with the enemy. When we saw them arrive, we were to support their command.

I acknowledged the order and passed the word to the platoon. I hoped we wouldn't get into something lasting to long, we were not prepared to get into an extended battle. Everyone had the normal amount of ammunition, but you never knew what was coming. I called the company communication center to confirm they had monitored the battalion order. They had. I ordered the first and third platoons to remain on alert, as backups, if they were needed.

I could see the dust flying up on the mountaintop, above LZ Thunder, and watched as the mechanized infantry, in their armor personnel carriers, dropped down the mountain on the access road. About twenty minutes later, my RTO received a radio call from the commander of the mechanized unit. He wanted to know where on our maps I had seen the NVA, and if we could still see them. I moved up to the point. I could still see the NVA moving northwest. I called and gave him the grid co-ordinates and location of the NVA movement.

I told him I would estimate about 1,000 NVA had passed the opening. He sounded pessimistic in his confirmation of my assessment. I was ordered to move north, and marry up with the last platoon of armor personnel carriers, as the rear guard. That sounded fine with me. I figured once the mechanized unit started west, the NVA would run west and disappear into the jungle, which is what usually happened.

I had the platoon move to the east, to QL-1, so we could make better time. By the time we got to where the mechanized infantry had moved west, we were about 1,000 meters from the rear platoon. I had my platoon move as fast as we could, with out getting too winded.

We caught up with the last armor personnel carrier; they had to stop for the front of the company to change into a battle formation. The platoon leader was glad to see us and said to keep to the rear and watch their backs.

Just then, loud bangs and gunfire broke out up front. The formation began moving forward. Swish sounds, from B-40 rockets were heard, but I couldn't see anything. Visual conditions were limited due to too much bamboo hedgerow in front of us, and jungle here and there. The rice fields were dry, which enabled the armor personnel carriers to maneuver. The further we got into the valley, the more firing came. Confusion rained down on the entire battlefield. Mortars started to rain down from the south hills. We were being drawn into a triangle enclosed, flat area, bordered by hills on the south, and a river on the west and north.

The farther we moved, the worse it got. With so much vegetation separating the rice fields, I couldn't tell where the enemy was. Then we saw NVA to our rear. We had walked over spider holes in the ground, and after passing, the NVA came out armed with B-40 rockets. They fired the rockets into the rear of the personnel carriers, trying to knock out the engines, disabling them. Several were, and the crews, who were not dead or wounded, had to join us as walking infantry.

I watched as NVA climbed out of the ground, several hundred meters away, and walked right at armor personnel carriers. The machine gunners on the carriers would be firing as fast as they could to stop the NVA before he could fire the rocket. I watched NVA get hit many times, but keep coming. Rockets were fired and hit the front shields of the machine guns, glancing up into the air off the slanted surface.

As the day wore on, many of the barrels of the machine guns became red hot from all the firing, and became useless. The lands and groves in the barrel would melt, causing the bullets to fly out of the barrel in a wide arc, not in a direct line. Many tracers arced to nowhere near the targets. That's when the NVA would get bolder in their attack. My platoon was able to pick off most of the NVA coming toward the platoon we were with.

Jets and choppers were called in to help. The commander of the mechanized unit was trying to knock out the mortars to our south, and bunkers he had discovered on the far side of the river just in front of his position. The NVA were everywhere among us.

The only place the jets could drop bombs and napalm was on the south hills, and across the river. The area we were in died down a bit, and I watched as choppers tried to land for the wounded. Several got to tree height and were fired at by B-40 rockets. The chopper pilots would accelerate and go around. One chopper was hit in the belly by a rocket. As the pilot veered to the right, smoke pouring from the deck, it lost power and fell tail first to the ground. The chopper burst into flame as it hit.

The jets changed their direction, and began their runs from south to north, trying to hit the mortars, who had the front of the formation pinned down. A jet came in low right toward us. The pilot dropped a napalm canister. I watched it drop into the jungle in front of us.

Then I watched it come back up, over the jungle trees intact, heading for us. I yelled to get down and watched, and heard, the canister as it tumbled over us and hit well behind and exploded. Boy, that was close. The platoon leader, of the armor personnel carriers we were with, called to request a different flight path from the jets.

More jets came in the same way and blasted the hills. No more napalm bounced over us. We dodged another bullet. The daylight was fading. The unit commander ordered everyone in his command to assemble into a tight circle with him. This was dead center of the battle.

We had no choice; we were surrounded. All the personnel carriers, that were mobile, moved to the center and created a circle, like the covered wagons in the old west. Here we were in the middle of a nasty fight. The mortars had been stopped, so at least we didn't have that dropping in. The NVA were determined to over run the unit.

Chopper gunships circled and shot for hours. As light left and darkness engulfed the jungle, jets constantly flew over, dropping large magnesium flares, making the area daylight bright. Snoopy, the navy aircraft gunship with many miniguns, showed up and circled our position all night, firing a curtain of red tracers down into the jungle and rice fields around us. The command chopper, several thousand feet above, could still see the NVA trying to work their way to us.

As I lay there, next to a personnel carrier, I thought back to the previous week. A colonel from the pentagon had arrived in our battalion, to interview officers (recommended by the battalion commander) for promotion to captain, with extension of eighteen months in the Army.

I had been interested in going to helicopter training, and was told if I extended, I could go to a duty station of my choice, and then to flight school. If I became a pilot, of helicopters, I would have to extend my enlistment to another four years. I was seriously considering the promotion, and going to Fort Belvoir to help train candidates at the Officer Candidate Regiment until there was an opening for chopper school. This, the colonel assured me, was no problem to arrange.

I had several weeks to sign the necessary paper work. This night made up my mind on furthering my military career. Not a chance. I guess I had been getting over confident again, as I had been before I was shot. Now I was thinking, I probably wasn't going to get out of this pickle. My adrenaline level was high all night; I didn't feel the need for sleep. Several hours before daybreak, the NVA stopped trying to attack. The jets continued to drop flares, but there were gaps of darkness and no shooting from Snoopy, who was still circling.

At daybreak, several companies of infantry were ordered to break through to our location. By mid morning the official battle was over. Then, the order was given to get a body count of the NVA killed.

At first, very few bodies were found around the perimeter. Then someone discovered a shallow grave. We started probing the soft ground, and in the end, found over three hundred bodies and their gear. The NVA had buried their dead and gear, leaving with their wounded. Many blood trails led across the river and into the hills.

The Americal Division was licking its wounds too and didn't have the heart in pursuing the NVA in an unconfirmed direction. No one could be sure how far they had traveled, and with the many tunnels in the hills and jungle, they could be right under our feet at that time.

I was ordered to take my platoon back to LZ Debbie. Everyone got through the ordeal without a scratch. We were hungry and thirsty. I set the platoon up in a diamond formation, just to be careful, on the way back. No telling where Charlie was.

We made it back to LZ Debbie with no problems. By this time, I had been in Nam for over eight months, and my R & R was close at hand. I was so ready to get away from this.

CHAPTER 29
HAVE A LOOK?

For several days, the mine sweeps and missions went well, with no problems or enemy contacts. Then one morning as the mine sweep was starting, the 19th Engineer Battalion Commander, riding in a Light Observation Command Helicopter (LOCH) landed on the road behind the sweep. He asked me to join him for a ride in the chopper.

I turned the sweep over to Lieutenant Steve and went back to the chopper. A light observation chopper is small and usually has only a pilot and observer. There is a seat behind the pilot, on the left, with the ammunition for a minigun on the right behind the observer.

The colonel sat in the right front seat, and I was in the seat behind the pilot. We took off and flew about 500 feet above the ground. I was wearing a headset, so I could communicate with the pilot and colonel. We flew over the sweep and continued south. The colonel pointed out a unit of the Americal Division who were working the hills west of *Death Canyon*. We were going to fly up the canyons for a look.

I thought, *Have a look?*

I knew that was Charlies' fun place, and where they usually came from when they ambushed the mine sweeps and convoys. I trained my M16 out the opening to the left, and watched the hills get closer. We flew straight up a canyon with the hillsides straight out in front of me as I looked out to the left.

We were only twenty to thirty feet from the ground, and if some crazy Charlie should pop out of a tunnel in the brush he could very easily rake the chopper. We were flying at a fast speed, swinging up and down, like we were on a roller coaster. My stomach wasn't keeping up with the ups and downs, and I was thinking I really didn't want to barf now.

At the top of the canyon the pilot did a 180 degree turn, and ran back down into another canyon the same way. Back and forth we went. I was beginning to think we were trying to get Charlie to shoot. And that's exactly what he did. Charlie probably was trying to rest after the all nighter we had several days earlier, and here was this buzzing, annoying machine, keeping him awake. I didn't see where the bullets came from, but the noise from the hits had me convinced, we were under fire.

The chopper swung right, then left. The pilot started doing things rapidly; no one was talking. We were flying in the direction of the Americal Division troops, and they weren't far away. The pilot managed to perform auto rotation to the ground with a fairly soft landing compared to the one I had been on eight months earlier.

Our troops were on us before I had a chance to climb out. A recovery chopper was called for from Duc Pho, and in only minutes it arrived, and the light observation chopper was lifted out of the brush. The rear rotor had been damaged, causing a lack of stability.

I went back to the mine sweep. The colonel flew back with the recovery chopper and crew. My men wanted to know how was the ride.

I said, "Great, I could do that everyday."

The mine sweep had been east of where we went down, and out of sight, so I didn't mention it to them. I was the company commander after all and supposed to be tough as nails. Even though, I felt I needed a drink to calm my inner nerves. We went back to LZ Debbie.

As we rode back, all I could think about was something that happened about six months earlier. While my platoon was working on a road project, south of Bong Son, we watched a light observation chopper being flown right on the road, at a very fast speed. The pilot was doing acrobatic maneuvers, as he approached our work sight. He flew under the branches of several trees in the distance as he approached. After passing us in a flash, he tried to fly under the next tree limbs.

The rotor blades hit the limbs. After getting to the other side, the chopper went straight up, and came straight down on its tail, from a height of several hundred feet. The chopper crumbled tail first off to the left of the road.

We raced up to the crash. The pilot and passenger climbed out with only complaints of minor pain in their backs. The passenger was hopping mad at the pilot, who had been showing off the maneuverability of the chopper. The pilot, using our radio, called his base of operations and requested a recovery chopper to pick them up and the crumpled chopper.

That night Lieutenant Steve and I tied one on, having a very good time. The next morning, again the same chopper landed behind the sweep. The battalion commander walked up and asked me to ride again. How *could* I refuse? If he was game for the ride, so was I.

We flew into the same canyons, the same way, only this time we did a few more ups and downs as we went through. We didn't draw any fire, as far as I could tell, but I was expecting to get shot the entire time. We circled the sweep until it was done, and followed the trucks back to LZ Debbie, where the chopper landed to let me off. The next day I left for Da Nang and R and R.

CHAPTER 30
HAWAII FOR R&R

I arrived in Da Nang in the late morning. My former roommate, Russ Clark, was stationed there with the Air Force working in their CID unit. He had written when he arrived in country and was looking forward to a visit for a few days, before I went to Hawaii. As I walked from the turboprop aircraft to the terminal building I was amazed at the size of the airfield and base camp. I was used to small strips, or no strip. All the activity of jets coming and going was overwhelming. Getting closer to the terminal building I caught a glimpse of a small white building down the road. It had an Ice Cream Cone sign.

I had been craving ice cream and hamburgers for months. I checked in at the terminal, and they pointed out a bus route to get me to Russ' barracks and where I would go for pre flight processing for the flight to Hawaii in the morning. I left the terminal and went immediately to the ice cream stand. I had several shakes for lunch before I felt satisfied. I was still having troubles with scurvy and had to seek out a latrine before getting on the bus.

I finally found the barracks. Everyone there was watching for me, for Russ. He was still at work and would be back at the barracks by mid afternoon. The barracks were two story, like stateside, with a concrete wall about five feet high running around the entire building. On each end, where the entry doors were located, was a gap with a five- foot high wall several feet in front of the gap. This prevented any shrapnel from entering the lower level during a rocket attack.

I was shown an empty bunk in his cubicle and dumped my gear. I took a nap. Several hours later Russ arrived, and we had a good time catching up on the last few years. He explained the evacuation procedure during a rocket attack. The rockets here were 125mm to 145mm in size, fired from several miles away in the jungled hills, west of Da Nang.

We left the barracks and went down to his off duty job, running the base movie theater. So I got to watch all the movies from the projection booth. After the double feature, I wandered over to the Air Force Officers Club, called the *Dooms Day Club.*

The hard liquor drinks were selling for 25 cents each. So I sat at the bar and consumed my share of the last eight months. I don't remember how I got back

174

to the barracks, but I did. During the night, the base siren sounded, and all the airmen in the barracks ran out to a bunker at one end of the building.

The bunker was dug into the ground and offered protection against close rocket blasts. I happened to be in the latrine, at the end of the barracks, with my scurvy problem and sleeping. I heard the swish of the rockets as they came in. They flew over the building and hit on the runway. Charlie was shooting at several jets taxiing for a takeoff.

After the all clear, I heard the airmen coming back to the barracks. They were saying they didn't know where the lieutenant was, and yes, they'd seen me in the barracks. Russ went around looking and finally popped into the latrine. There I was, sitting on the pot. He asked if I was ok. I said yes, I would be spending some time here. He was concerned for my safety during a rocket attack. I assured him I had been through much worse, besides, there was a concrete wall above my head level and unless there was a direct hit, I would probably be ok.

The next day I went to the R&R orientation. There, the Provost Marshall warned every one of the dangers of trying to carry anything out of Viet Nam that was prohibited, such as weapons, or drugs. We all were processed and given a date and time for the flight, to whatever place we were going. I had several days before my flight, so I spent most of it in the *Dooms Day Club*. I exchanged war stories with the pilots and REMFs who never saw combat.

Finally, it was my day to leave. The air was clear and bright and the temperature was promising to be another scorcher. We all lined up and walked up the rolling stairs to the Freedom Bird. Every plane going out of this country to anywhere else was called a Freedom Bird. As we cleared the runway and turned east, everyone yelled a cheer of approval. On the way, we were all served a large steak and potato, along with small bottles of booze, limit two.

The flight was over in a flash, I was so anxious to see Ellen. We landed in Honolulu just before dawn; rode a bus to Fort De Russe and were taken to the R&R Center. There she was, as pretty as ever. She was shocked to see my appearance. I had left nine months ago weighing around 200 pounds. Now I weighed in at 135 pounds. I was so anxious to talk to her; she didn't have much chance to ask about my health.

We went over to the Reef Hotel and straight up to our room. After taking some time to get to know each other again, we decided to go have breakfast. We went down to the hotel restaurant and I ordered a hamburger and french-fries.

I took one bite of the hamburger and broke into a sweat and started shaking. I couldn't stomach the food and had to get back to the room. The hotel management was concerned and refused to charge us for the breakfast.

With Ellen's help, I got back to the room and into bed. She tried to get me to tell her what was wrong. I finally described the scurvy problem, and she suggested I go to the Fort De Russe Hospital. No way. I had heard of guys on R&R getting sick and spending the entire time in the hospital. Not me.

So Ellen went down to the street fresh fruit vendor and brought back a fresh pineapple. By then, I had slept several hours, and after eating half the pineapple and downing several Mai Tais, I started to feel ok. The fresh citrus fruit knocked out the scurvy quick.

The rest of the time we spent touring the island and relaxing. One of my fellow OCS graduates was meeting his wife at our mid week. He had extended his enlistment to obtain an early Captain's promotion, and got his R&R after only two months in country. It was good to see them again. The week went awful fast. Ellen brought 8mm movies of our daughter, and we watched them over and over. We also spent alot of time at the Don Ho's show and drinking various local drinks.

The next thing I knew, I was back on a flight to Da Nang. We landed in late afternoon and the heat hit us like a ton of bricks. Oh the good old smell of burning shit. Russ had left for his R&R to Bangkok or some such place, so I had the cubical to myself. I wasn't in a hurry to get back to the combat zone and enjoyed the *Dooms Day Club*.

For several mornings, I would go to the terminal and get a pass for a flight to Duc Pho. I would sit there and watch the flight come in and then leave. After the plane was taxiing to the runway, I would catch the base bus for the *Dooms Day Club*. The fourth day I was sitting there, trying to get up to the plane, when up walked our battalion executive officer.

Boy was he glad to see me. The feeling wasn't mutual. He said the battalion had been transferred out of I Corps and down to Camp Smith in III Corps, about 85 miles northwest of Saigon. My company was to be the lead company, going the next day to relieve the National Guard unit leaving for home. *Wonderful*! I thought to myself. This meant we were going back to the 173rd Airborne Unit and into the Central Highlands.

CHAPTER 31
LZ CAMP SMITH, BAO LOC

The morning was hot, hazy, and humid beyond belief. I had become acclimated to the Hawaiian drier heat and breezes. We landed in Duc Pho, and fortunately, there was a jeep waiting for the battalion executive officer. So I hitched a ride to LZ Debbie to prepare for the move. Most of the company was already packed, and my gear had been stored on a deuce-and-a-half for the trip tomorrow.

Lieutenant Steve's platoon, and mine, the second, were out on mine sweep, so I was left with nothing to do but be reminded of how dry my throat was. All the beer and sodas had been packed and moved to LZ English, so the only liquid available was what I had avoided all the tour, the drinking water supplied from the water treatment truck. In the command post, we had a five-gallon water bottle. I decided to take fate into my hands and have a glass of the wonderful Army water.

Within minutes, I developed a stomachache. This quickly turned into a severe abdominal pain that had me doubled up on the floor. The clerk specialist came in, and I told him to go get the medic. Our medic rushed over to the command post, bringing a drug that, within minutes, cleared the pain. He said there was a parasite in the drinking water and to avoid it at all possible costs. I had been told by NCOs in the states the same thing and had avoided it until now.

Lieutenant Steve returned with the mine sweep team and offered me a beer. Boy did that taste good. The battalion commander called and sent me down to LZ Lowboy to see the battalion adjutant officer. I left with a convoy heading south. When we arrived at LZ Lowboy, there was a commotion at the rock crusher. We stopped to investigate. The NCO in charge said one of his men had fallen into the crusher while directing a backing dump truck with a load of boulders for crushing. Before anyone noticed, the rocks and crusher had done their gruesome job; another casualty of war.

I went over to the Battalion Headquarters. As I walked in to the command bunker a captain began to verbally assault me. I recognized the voice, and when my eyes adjusted to the gloom of the room, here was one of my upperclassmen from OCS, Captain O'Neil. He said he had arrived in country while I was gone on R&R and was assigned as the Adjutant General of the Battalion to oversee any violations of the Uniform Criminal Code. I had been charged several times by *Tommy Two Bars* for various offenses. He wanted an explanation.

We went to his office, which was a desk in the corner of the large open room. I began to explain the problems the company was having with *Tommy Two Bars*. After only a minute or so, he raised his hand to stop me from continuing.

He said, "This is what the colonel and battalion executive officer think of the charges." With a big grin on his face, he picked up the thick file folder and tossed it into the round file.

"Now, with that out of the way, let's have a drink," he ordered. We went to the Officers Club and had several beers. After catching up on our duty stations, since OCS, I left for the afternoon convoy back up to LZ Debbie.

Charlie must have known we were leaving, so he left us alone. Lieutenant Steve and I caught up on what happened while I was gone, while downing a fifth of Cherry Herring. Half of my platoon had already gone to LZ English, preparing several tents for the company, while waiting for our flight to Bao Loc and LZ Smith.

I walked with the first and third platoons on my final mine sweep here in I Corp, and the rest of my platoon followed the sweep down to *Death Canyon*. I was sure glad to say goodbye to that canyon. Once the sweep was over, I ordered Lieutenant Steve back to LZ Debbie to close the base camp and wait for his departure to LZ Camp Smith. The remainder of second platoon and I married up with Charley Company and made our way back down to the *Pacified Zone* and LZ English.

The Asphalt Company had made pretty good progress over the last nine months of my tour and had paved QL-1 about one mile north of *Death Canyon*. The goal was to pave QL-1 all the way to Chu Lai. I don't know if that was ever accomplished. By this time in the war, the American troops were starting to be pulled out of the country.

We arrived at the airstrip at LZ English by midday. The platoon had raised several large GP Medium tents, about 15 by 30 feet in size, for the platoon to rest for the night. Since we were in a *Pacified Zone* assurances were made by a captain from the 173rd Airborne, who was in charge of our transport, that we wouldn't need shelter from incoming rounds.

After talking to my men for a few minutes, the captain told me to come with him to his company location. I rode with him to his company. I didn't feel good about leaving my platoon out at the runway. The captain told me this was the arrangement by our battalion. I ate night chow there and was shown were to bunk that night.

The next morning, before I could get a ride back to the airstrip, a jeep drove into the company, at a dust kicking speed. Out jumped my battalion executive officer hotter than a wet hen. He chewed my ass for five minutes over leaving my platoon out on the tarmac by themselves, and said the plane ride for Bao Loc was being delayed because of me.

Then he ordered me to walk back to the tarmac with my gear. He drove off in a cloud of dust. I guess there wasn't any hurry to get back to the plane. The captain, who had brought me to his company, had seen the chewing and said that was the officer who told him to bring me here, and no one had a clue when the flight would be scheduled.

I caught a ride out to the tarmac, and there was a plane running up the engines and getting ready to take off. I hurried to the cargo deck. The crew chief tossed my gear on and showed me to my seat, on the deck with everyone else. We sat on our duffel bags, eight men to a row, with a wide web belt draped across everyone from left to right. The belt was locked down on each end. This kept us all locked in for the flight, just like so much cargo. The ride was about one hour and not very comfortable.

The runway at Boa Loc is considered a short runway, so the larger planes had to make a steep assent and take off. When the drone of the turbo props slowed down and we started to drop our elevation, I expected a normal landing. Suddenly the nose of the plane dropped sharply and the engines throttles were cut to nothing. All we could hear was the rushing of the air and every face I could see had the same look. Sheer terror, thinking we were going down. Not to land but to crash. We hadn't been warned of this procedure.

Of course, we couldn't see out the porthole windows, so there was no telling what was going on. I caught the crew chief looking bored; so decided this must be the normal landing. Suddenly, the plane was leveled off, and we hit the runway. The runway was on a hill, so the plane landed on the down side and ran up to the top and down the other side. The runway was built out of pierced steel planking over red clay dirt. Apparently it rained over night and spray from standing water was shot back along the sides of the plane and through open portholes.

We taxied to the small Quonset hut terminal. There, waiting for us, was the National Guard company commander I was to replace. He was glad to see us. We piled into the several deuce-and-a-halves waiting and rode to Camp

Smith. This was a large camp, twice the size of LZ North English. The camp was built over several hills, and a small river ran through the middle.

Our camp was on the south hill, with an asphalt company to our west. We would be responsible for the south and east perimeter to the main gate entrance. A Quarry Company, Light Equipment Company, Heavy Equipment Company and Alpha, Bravo, Charlie and Delta Companies would be based here. The Battalion Command Center, with the Headquarters Company, was located in the center of the base camp.

Our view from the hill was jungle on the north side, QL-20 ran along the east and south perimeter wire, with jungle across the road and thick jungle to a mountain several miles to the east. The captain of the National Guard Unit was to leave in several days, with the first of his unit to go back to the states. He took me to meet his battalion commander.

CHAPTER 32
PLANE RIDES

I was introduced to the colonel who suggested I be taken to the Air Force Forward Air Controllers base at the airstrip for a chat about the terrain here and the procedure for calling in air support in the event of an attack while out on the road. Our mission here was to upgrade the airstrip to an asphalt runway and to maintain QL-20. I ordered my platoon to get settled in, and my platoon sergeant to talk to the first sergeant about the enemy conditions here.

I piled in the captain's jeep for the short ride back to Bao Loc. We went there alone; the captain didn't seem too concerned saying the chance of ambush here this close to the town was low. *Whoopee!* Another non-combat *Pacified Zone*. Didn't turn out to be that way. Later, I found out the reason for the lack of combat here was the lack of work being done by this unit. Once we started to take on projects, things got hotter, quick.

The jeep driver drove back to the airstrip, entering a small base camp. There were two small L-19 fixed wing aircraft parked near a revetment. The captain led me to a concrete bunker and introduced me to the two captains from the Air Force, who were the Forward Air Controllers (FAOs) for the jets coming from several large air bases on the coast. The lead captain asked me if I would like to go for a ride and see the terrain from the air. Sure, why not.

The National Guard captain said he would send the jeep driver back to wait for my return, if I made it back alive. Ha, ha, just kidding! The L-19 is a small, narrow plane, with a seat behind the engine firewall for the pilot and a seat behind the pilot for a spotter. The plane reminded me of a piper cub the Army used during World War Two. May have been the same. I walked around the plane with the pilot. He asked if I had ever flown in a small plane. I said yes, with my college roommate. He was glad to hear that, he wouldn't have to worry about airsickness or all out fear from his passenger.

The day was partly cloudy and fairly clear. I took my camera to get some shots. I had been sending all my rolls of film home. Ellen had them developed but wouldn't look at them until I got back. I got into the back seat (where else), and we were off, taxiing down the bumpy pierced steel planking. I noticed many potholes from damaged planking. Captain Good, the pilot, said the potholes were from mortars Charlie pitched in at night.

Repair of the runway and aprons of the field would be one of the 19th Engineer Battalion responsibilities. He hoped we did a better job than the unit we were replacing. The plane was maneuvered to the north end of the runway, which was down at the bottom of a hill. When we turned to face south, Captain Good ran the engine up. We were forced back in our seats, like we were going straight up.

Here, because of the short runway and steep hill, the engine would be run up with the breaks on, and after a short wait, the plane lurches forward up the hill. Once we were on the top of the hill, the plane wings took air, and we were off. Captain Good kept us a few feet off the ground until the air speed increased enough to climb. The hill dropped away to jungle on the south side. By then our altitude was higher, and we weren't in any danger of crashing into any trees. Captain Good pointed out power lines running from west to southeast from the mountains.

These used to be for power coming from hydroelectric dams, west of Bao Loc. The larger, multi-engine aircraft had to really watch for the lines as they took off. Captain Good mentioned that a C 130, like the one we came in on, took off several days earlier and crashed trying to avoid the lines. They didn't look that close to me, but because of the altitude here and the conditions of the weather, the larger planes had a problem making altitude on take off.

We flew northeast following QL-20. As we went, Captain Good pointed out the various Special Forces Camps along the road. After an hour of flight, the captain turned west, and we flew away from the road and were over triple canopy jungle. Many rivers cut through the mountains here and how anyone up here could see anything on the ground was a mystery. The captain took me on a joy ride close to the rivers; following their path with the jungle so close I could smell it.

He showed me the open grass valleys, where the shit really does hit the fan for the infantry units working here. A large deer was grazing near a small lake in the middle of one of the valleys. Captain Good dropped to within several feet of the elephant grass and buzzed the deer. I was expecting shots to come from Charlie at any time. I kept looking over the ground to the right and left. The windows, on either side of the plane, were locked up in the open position.

During the pre flight walk around the plane, Captain Good pointed out the rockets mounted under the wings. These were white phosphorous (willie peters) used to mark the enemy on the ground. This gave the fast movers in the jets a good look at their targets. Captain Good followed the Dung River for a ways. It was a yellow color. As we passed over an area where an Arc

Light run had been made (B-52 bombing run), I suddenly saw a column of NVA crossing the river. A sand bar in the middle made it easy for the men to cross.

I called to the captain, and he turned around to take a look. Sure enough the NVA were still crossing. At this time, we were up several thousand feet above the mountaintops. Captain Good said he never saw them as we passed. He circled and told me he would be off the intercom for a while. He was calling the fast movers from the coast to join him in the hunt. When he came back to the intercom, he said the fast movers would be here in a few minutes. They were coming from a base south in the Saigon area.

The jets arrived a few minutes later and began to circle several thousand feet above. I wasn't ready for what took place next. We circled several times, dropping down as we went. Suddenly, Captain Good went into a dive, right at the NVA who were now scattering into the jungle. I was hanging out the window on the right to get a shot with my camera. *SWISSSSH*. Captain Good fired a rocket under the right wing. I thought a B-40 rocket had been fired at the plane.

The rocket flew down into the jungle. Captain Good swung us around, and he fired another rocket. He did this several times until we had the NVA in a bracket. Then we pulled up and watched as the fast movers came in to drop their ordinance. Time and time again the jets made their runs. Black smoke from the bombs rose up through the jungle, mingling with the white plumbs of the willie peters. Once the fast movers were done, they circled while we dropped down for a closer look. This I wasn't too keen on. Lower and lower we went. Slower and slower the captain flew. Finally, he cut the engine, and we leaned out the window listening; for what? *GUN FIRE!* Not a peep.

We circled around for an hour looking for any sign of Charlie. Couldn't really see anything down in the triple canopy anyway and the daylight was beginning to fade, with more clouds coming in. A storm was brewing from the mountains to the west. Finally, Captain Good released the fast movers, and we headed home; none to soon for me. I'd seen enough.

We approached the landing field at Bao Loc with rain starting to drop. Captain Good wasn't coming in for a glide landing; he was coming in for a short field landing. We were about 1,000 feet above the field when he cut his engine and put down his wing flaps. We dropped like an elevator. I thought it was all over. Captain Good seemed to be having a good time. (Years later, when I took up flying, this was the best kind of landing for sheer fun). Just as we were to hit, Captain Good, pulled back on the stick and we leveled out to a soft landing.

As we taxied to the revetment, the rain came down in buckets. Here in the central highlands the rain fell much harder than on the coast. Once stopped, we were drenched running to the bunker. I was treated to a great Air Force meal and drinks for several hours. I was invited to go up any time.

Captain Good said he hadn't had a good contact all month and with me spotting we would make a good team. All I had to do was ask for a transfer to their unit, and he said he would make it happen. I decided I had pushed my luck about as far as I was going to be allowed to so far in my tour, so I declined the offer.

I was a little concerned about the daylight when I left for Camp Smith. The driver didn't seem too concerned and said not to worry. As we cleared the gate, the guards began closing up for the night. That's the first time I noticed the perimeter lights. This I didn't like. We drove up to the command post. Another thing I wasn't too keen on was the living accommodations. The company was set out like we were state side, with stick-framed buildings lined up in rows; the buildings surrounded by sand bags up to about the four-foot level. The roofs were tin, with no false roof to detonate any incoming mortars. *Not to worry* was the everyday comment by the company commander.

CHAPTER 33
MONKEY MOUNTAIN

The National Guard captain asked me if Captain Good had told me about the mountain to our east. He hadn't, so over a few beers the captain explained why the mountain was called Monkey Mountain. This mountain stands at 4,009 feet and dominates the jungle below. The entire mountain is covered in triple canopy trees and very dark and forbidding. It seems in the past the Army Helicopter unit near by flew missions called Sniffer Missions.

I looked at the captain like he had been drinking a little too much, or he was too glad to be getting out of here alive. The captain saw the look and stressed the correctness of this story, getting the other company officers to agree. So I listened. (Many years later, from reading books written by chopper pilots, I found this tale to be true.)

One chopper was installed with a device to detect the smell of human urine. Several gunships would accompany this chopper as it made its way around the mountains and valleys sniffing for human concentrations. The Special Forces, with their Long Range Recon Patrols, would report movements of large NVA forces; the powers to be at MACV needed to make a more believable confirmation than the eyes of their own troops. I later found out MACV didn't always listen to the Special Forces, because they weren't conventional troops.

So, in they sent the Sniffer chopper. Several years ago, a large NVA troop movement was reported in this area. The choppers came. After several hours of scouting, the sniffer chopper homed in on the mountain to the east. *WOW!*

The amount of urine detected was unbelievable. There must by a whole North Viet Nam Army Corps there. The chopper was told to circle several times to confirm the find. MACV command also wanted the machine to be checked for calibration by the operator. He was located in the deck bay of the chopper with all the sophisticated equipment.

Finally, MACV was convinced and ordered an Arc Light mission to attack the entire mountain. They were going to get the highest body count to date and show the NVA who was boss. Within the hour, a flight of B52s was on the way from Guam. The sniffer chopper was to remain on sight until the last possible moment before the drop of the bombs. MACV command didn't want Charlie slipping off to another mountain. The chopper and its escort circled and circled.

Finally the B52s were on their final approach, so the choppers were ordered to retreat to their base. The mountain lit up with the ordinance dropped and the ground shook. The run was from the south to the north straight across the top of the mountain. Several sorties had been ordered, so the entire mountain and its slopes were hit. MACV didn't want any NVA soldier to get away. After the last bomb blasted the jungle, the mountain was covered by dust. Even at night, the dust could be seen hanging in the air.

The next morning, teams of Special Forces went in to check on the carnage and get a body count. The scene the Special Forces encountered was horrendous. Reports of body parts everywhere were heard over the radio. The MACV commanders flying high overhead wanted to know more. How much equipment was found? What NVA units could be identified? Any survivors? The brass just couldn't wait to gloat. Finally, one of the Special Forces captains reported the bodies were not human.

Not human!

"What are you talking about?" was the terse reply from the MACV Commander, riding in a chopper at 2000 feet above the mountain. The Special Forces captain said there were thousands of monkeys lying everywhere. Must have been a whole army of the species. No weapons or equipment found, only dead or dying monkeys the size of a small human. The MACV Commander relayed the finding to MACV headquarters; another victory for Charlie? From then on, the mountain was called Monkey Mountain.

The same species of monkey could still be seen crossing through Camp Smith almost every night. The first time I saw them I thought they were Charlie. The monkeys were tall and ran on their hind legs. They had black hair and at a distance looked human. They would cross through the perimeter wire without slowing down. Apparently this was one of their trails to the mountain, and they weren't about to deviate for an invading army of humans. I suppose we were lucky the monkeys didn't turn on us and wipe us out.

The first night was a shock to my system. The temperature dropped into the sixties, and I had to break out my field jacket. I certainly was glad I kept it and didn't leave it at the supply depot. It was a bit musty, but felt good. With being used to the heat on the coast at 125 degrees during the day and around 100 degrees at night, this was different. Most of us from the 19th Engineer Battalion caught colds the first week of the change.

During that week, I was introduced to the local beetles that were the size of a large baking potato. Some were horned and looked like prehistoric insects. Some had a wing-span of twelve to eighteen inches. At night, they made a terrific racket. They also warned us of approaching enemy in the jungle. When the beetles quit their sound, you could expect company.

CHAPTER 34
SHORT TIMER

I was beginning to feel *short* in my time in Nam. No more was I the FNG. I hadn't felt like an FNG since the second week into my tour of duty. I could see the light at the end of the tunnel. I had been told by veteran NCOs and officers that the most critical time in country was the first few weeks and the last few weeks. If I was able to make it through the first, my chances of making it through the entire tour were high. The last month is a time of anxiety in anticipation of going home.

I was the only Officer of our Battalion for a week and took advantage of checking out the countryside via plane rides with Captain Good almost every day. The three other times we went aloft were boring compared to the first; just the same terrain and no contacts with Charlie. No calls for the fast movers and no marking rockets. I took more photos of the different camps up and down QL-20.

The last day I had to go flying, Captain Good called and said to hurry over. The other FAC captain had been up looking for a large NVA unit and had been shot down. I had the company driver race me over to the airstrip and in minutes we were off. We flew for fifteen or twenty minutes before Captain Good pointed out the location of the other L-19. It was crash landed on top of a thick pine forest. The plane was perched on the top of several high trees.

After flying through, a hail of bullets fired up from the ground, the L-19 engine quit and the pilot had been hit in both legs. The pilot was able to dead stick his plane to the forest, away from the enemy and stall the plane into a fairly soft landing on the top of the trees. Our mission was to locate the plane, direct our troops to it, and keep the NVA away.

The crashed L-19 was heading southwest at the time of the crash, so Captain Good continued west and circled several miles away. He even fired several willie peter rockets into the jungle to mark the false location. Hopefully, this would draw Charlie to the false spot and away from the crashed L-19. A company of infantry were flown in and dropped near the crash site for perimeter protection in case Charlie didn't take the bait.

The choppers that dropped off the troops then made several false drops around the area and circled with us waiting to pick up their troops. A medevac and recovery choppers slowly made their way to the crash site. Once there, they hovered over the plane and a medic lowered by cable to the plane to get the pilot out. Once the medic was down to the pilot, he bandaged the pilot's legs and helped him get out of the cockpit and into a harness for the lift.

The medic chopper stayed over the plane, just meters above, for a fast extraction. Once the medic was up into the chopper, the medevac was gone and on it's way to Phan Rang to a hospital. The plane recovery chopper then moved into position and dropped a crewman down by cable to attach a sling around the wings of the L-19 to lift it out of the trees and bring it back to the airstrip for repairs. The Forward Air Controllers didn't have a spare plane, and it was hard to get replacements. The operation went well, and once the L-19 was up and heading back, the troops on the ground moved to an open area for pickup.

The NVA in the area were nowhere to be seen. The troops were picked up while we circled for support, in case Charlie decided to make an appearance. He didn't! Once the mission was coming to a close, I remembered I had forgotten to bring my camera. DAMN! In the excitement of the mission, I hadn't even thought of it.

We circled for about an hour, hoping to get a glimpse of the NVA in the area we assumed the L-19 had been hit. As far as I was concerned, we were flying much to low. There were four fast movers, also circling, several miles to the east, just in case we made contact. The Army gunship choppers were also circling. Nothing was seen and a nasty black-clouded storm began rolling in from the coast. So we headed back to the airstrip and landed again in a down pour. It was good to be back on solid ground.

Again I enjoyed a meal with the air controller, and his partner was reported as doing fine. He wouldn't be back anytime soon, and another pilot would be sent out within the month. This position was a voluntary position, and the Air Force was short on volunteers. After spending another hour with Captain Good, talking about other missions, I decided I had better get back to LZ Camp Smith.

Good thing I did. Once there, I was called to the Battalion Headquarters to meet with my battalion executive officer, who just flew in. *LUCKY!* The major wanted to know how things were going and if we were getting settled in. The bulk of Bravo Company was to be landing later this day, so everything was ready. As they landed, the National Guard Unit was to leave for Cam Ranh Bay and a flight home.

As the company arrived and the first sergeant got there, everything began to get back to normal. The next week a new captain was assigned as the company commander, and I was dropped back to executive officer. The next day two second lieutenants, just recently commissioned from ROTC, arrived and were assigned to Bravo Company. One took over my platoon, and the other took over third platoon. The third had not had a lieutenant for the better part of five months.

Captain Bishop was the new company commander. He had come from Germany and just happened to come from my hometown, Orange, California. He also happened to know a good friend of mine from high school. Captain Bishop had lived on the other side of the city and went to different schools. What a coincidence.

The morale of the company was very high with this change and the new personnel. Our mission at this time was to repair the airstrip as needed and to dismantle the 173rd Airborne Division basecamp, LZ Rocky Road. Since I was now officially only the executive officer, I was free to go to all the work sites, and marry up with the platoon of my choice in the field. I started the two new lieutenants off with as much information as I could think of for their education here in Nam. The second platoon leader was very receptive to my advice. The third platoon leader didn't seem to need any advice from a mere OCS commissioned officer.

After several weeks of trying to help both, I concentrated on the second platoon leader. Possibly more so because he was the leader of my own platoon, and it was hard for me to let go of what I felt were my own men. I worried every day I wasn't with them for their safety. I did spend more time with the second platoon than with the first or third. The second platoon had the mission to disassemble the bunkers at LZ Rocky Road. The camp was large, and it took a great deal of work by the dozer operators to clear the sand bags and timbers.

Some of the timbers were to be taken to another camp. They were stacked in an area to be lifted by sling from a Chinook helicopter to the new camp. During one day of work, a load was to be taken. The load was quite large, and I watched as the men hooked the sling to the belly of the chopper. As the chopper began to lift, the engine began to labor. The rotors began to bend trying to pick up the load. The noise of the rotors cutting through the air was deafening. WHAP, WHAP, WHAP. The rotors bent more and more. The men below the chopper started to run in every direction.

I managed to get some shots of the chopper on film. After trying for several minutes, the engine began to overload, and the pilot let off on the throttle. The load was released, and the men on the ground had to restack the

190

timbers to a smaller load. I certainly didn't want to see the chopper come down in a heap because of an over loaded cargo. After taking several timbers off the load, the chopper was hooked up, and the pilot tried again. This time the chopper was able to lift the load several hundred feet above ground and take off for the other camp.

While cutting and removing the sand bags from around the bunkers, the dozer operators and men working around them had to watch out for snakes and scorpions. Several times a nest of scorpions was uncovered. Hundreds of white baby scorpions scrambled from their opened nests. Stings from the babies are just as nasty as the adults. The same was true of the snakes. Most of which were poisonous. Several times a large cobra was unearthed ,and every one scrambled to get out of its way. The cobras were very fast, and no one wanted to get bit.

The rain was off and on every day. While working on LZ Rocky Road (which was located on the side of the air strip) I would walk to the west side of the strip and watch the planes landing and taking off. The atmosphere was mostly clear here, and because the strip was on a high hill I could see for miles, in any direction. Most of the time the sun was shining and the air moist and hot. The ground would be bone dry in seconds after a rain. Many times I could see a single dark cloud circling around the valley, with rain streaking down at a slant as it was being moved by the wind. It could be calm at the airstrip, and as the cloud moved closer, the air would begin to stir and get faster and faster as the rain wall approached.

Once the rain hit, it was so hard I couldn't see more than ten meters in any direction. This was hard rain, no fog. This would last for a few minutes and then taper off as fast as it started. Once the cloud moved off the sun came out, within minutes, the ground would be dry; quite a difference from the coastal area.

One day, while watching the second platoon, I decided to ride with the dozer operator. I had been raised on a ranch and driven a dozer for many years. So after a while, I asked the operator to let me drive. Of course, while I was doing this, the company commander showed up.

He waved me off the dozer, and in a firm manner reminded me I was in middle management and not authorized to operate the dozer. I was caught. I knew this and took the chance and acknowledged the error of my ways and took the chewing. It wasn't like the chewings I took from *Tommy Two Bars*; maybe because this captain was an OCS commissioned officer or because he was out there with us all the time.

191

Later, the operator came over and asked if I had been reprimanded. I told him yes, he was correct in objecting to me operating his dozer. We had a good laugh, and he went back to work. I went back to being bored. So the next day I decided to go out to the first platoon to see how Lieutenant Steve was doing with a large culvert and bridge project. The road had been washed out northeast of Bao Loc, and he had finished the culvert installation and was in the process of repairing the approach to the bridge.

Water was everywhere around the area because of all the rainfall runoff from the mountains. This was a small flood. I stayed with them the rest of the day. The next morning I decided to walk with the third platoon on their mine sweep. The roadway here was paved, and the only checking had to be the potholes, culverts and unguarded bridges. It was hard to get used to the difference in caution here. The attitude of the quarry company was like they were in the states and Charlie was nowhere around.

I warned the third platoon leader he should walk with the point men until he became convinced there was no danger. He would ride in his jeep towards the center of the grouping of trucks and let the platoon sergeant handle any problems. The quarry company would follow the mine sweep for about a mile to the quarry. During the sweep, the quarry company officer would constantly call to try to push the sweep faster. *A BIG MISTAKE!*

Several times I got on the radio and told the quarry officer to get off the air, and the sweep was going as fast as I felt it needed to go. As soon as we passed the quarry, the quarry company would pull off to begin work.

QL-20 wound around the mountains and hills, having many switchback turns where a good ambush could be set up. In many stretches of the road, the jungle came right down to the road. Waterfalls hit next to the road at most of the hair pin turns and caused continuous maintenance problems.

CHAPTER 35
PURE ACCIDENT

After we had returned to the company, a call came into the communication center from the first platoon RTO. A truck had been involved in an accident, and they requested the company commander. Captain Bishop and I went out in his jeep. The driver was new and seemed to be a bit concerned about driving out here alone on these roads. I had the same feeling. As we rode north, from Bao Loc, I watched every clump of tree line close to the road for a good ambush site.

We came to a long sweeping curve that inclined as we went. This slowed the jeep and all I could think about was the Bravo Company lieutenant, who had been in the same situation north of LZ Lowboy, and was shot to death in a ambush. We made it to the first platoon site.

One of the five ton dump trucks had been backing up on the approach to the bridge and the back dual tires got too close to the side of the graded road. The weight of the load had caused the road to give way and the truck rolled over into the flooded area. The driver managed to escape from the truck before the entire cab was covered.

A wrecker was called from the heavy equipment company, and several hours later, the truck was back at the battalion being assessed for damages. Later, Captain Bishop asked me for my opinion on whether to hold the driver responsible for the accident or call the damage combat related. My feeling was we were in a combat zone (a free fire zone at that) and this was, in my opinion, a pure accident due to the roadway giving way to the load weight. The battalion brass thought otherwise.

The next morning, while I was trying to pressure the captain into encouraging the brass to reconsider, we got a call from the first platoon RTO for a medevac.

One of the men had stepped on a mine in the same location the truck had rolled over. Charlie found his opportunity to plant a few reminders he was still here. I asked the communication sergeant to identify who was hurt and how bad. It turned out the driver of the rolled truck had stepped on an anti-personnel mine that took off his foot and shattered his leg to the hip.

I reported this to the captain, and said it was my opinion he paid for the damage to the truck. He agreed, and recommended to the brass that the debt be covered as combat related. I don't know what the final decision was. The medevac chopper got to the bridge and managed to get the casualty to the mash unit before he died from shock and blood loss. Charlie was beginning to step up his pressure in this area.

CHAPTER 36
PERIMETER LIGHTS

At night, with the perimeter lights on, the guards were not on their toes. The bunkers, on part of the perimeter, were only a few feet from QL-20. Chain link fence was placed in front of the bunker to prevent Charlie from throwing grenades into the opening. These bunkers were not like the ones we were used to. There was a place to lie down and chairs with arm tables, like the ones found in schoolrooms. One night, while I was on guard command, I was checking each bunker for the guards' alertness.

I walked into one bunker and found the guard had fallen asleep. This was bad enough, in its self, but he had been writing a letter in candlelight and was sitting across from the opening to the outer perimeter; a perfect target.

I snuffed the candle and cleared my voice to waken the guard. The man was a FNG and had no idea what danger he was in. He didn't wake up. I shook him lightly; still no response. His rifle was lying there on the table. I picked it up and checked to see if a round was in the chamber. There wasn't and the noise from opening the chamber and dropping the bolt back didn't disturb him either.

I couldn't smell any alcohol to explain the behavior. I clicked off the safety and fired a round through the bunker opening out into the jungle.

This did get a *reaction*. The man sat straight up and grabbed my arm in a death grip. He sat there for several minutes with eyes wide open, looking straight at me. Finally, I asked him if he knew who I was. Yes, he did. I told him he was ok, and he started to calm down. Once he loosened his grip, and our ears quit ringing from the concussion of the rifle fire, I explained the danger he was in sitting in the chair with a candle on the desk front, illuminating his body, across from the opening of the bunker.

To this he said, "But what about the fence in front of the bunker? It will keep any grenades from coming in!"

I said, "Soldier, the fence isn't there to stop a bullet."

I told him to report the incident to the company commander in the morning. This happened to be the company commander's orderly room clerk. I felt it was up to the company commander to decide on the discipline of one of his headquarters platoon members.

The next morning I asked the captain if he had a talk with the clerk. He had and decided I had disciplined him enough with the rifle shot. The clerk said I had made an impression he would not forget. I hoped I did, for his sake. Here, we also had a tower on the east side of the perimeter, facing toward Monkey Mountain. I climbed the tower several times, and after that, decided there was no need for me up there unless we were on full alert.

As each day passed, I became shorter and shorter, and I began to hate the perimeter lights. Every time I checked on the guards, I would find them close to dozing. No one was actually caught sleeping since word spread about the clerk's experience. Especially if they knew I was on guard command. They weren't in the states now where the enemy only scared you. Here the enemy killed you and anyone they could get to.

By the end of September, all of the battalion had been moved in. A rumor was making the rounds that the company commander I had relieved had tried to smuggle an M60 machine-gun home in his footlocker. He had been caught with it at the Cam Ranh Bay airport and was currently cooling his heels in the Long Bien Jail.

CHAPTER 37
TOO SHORT FOR THIS

I was assigned a mission to go to the Long Bien Jail and meet with a man from Bravo Company who had gone "Absent without Leave" several years earlier. He had been caught working the black market in Saigon. My duty was to read the charges being brought against him.

When he came into the holding cell, he was in shackles and not too excited to see me. I did my duty and returned to the officer billets at Bien Hoa. I had a bad rash that I caught shortly after the move to LZ Camp Smith, and it was driving me nuts. I couldn't sit still and took the first chopper ride back to the base camp.

I went right to the battalion medics to have them check the rash. The battalion surgeon took one look and said it was a case of jungle rot, the worse case he had ever seen. Before he would administer medication, he had to have a photo.

So I sat there itching while he went to get his camera. I didn't think to send someone for my camera. He finally took several photos, both regular camera and Polaroid. Then it was cover me from neck to crotch with a sulfurous smelling, orange cream that burned when it came in contact with the rash. The rash was red and blotchy lumps, a bit raised on the skin. The worst areas were in the crotch and armpits. Anywhere there was a lot of hair and moisture.

Now, it's the first week in October. I was a few weeks from going back to the World in one piece. Lieutenant Steve was getting short too, and we partied every night in our billet. All four of us company Lieutenants lived in the same building, much like a one room, wood floored area, about fifteen feet wide and twenty feet long. All the bunks were lined up on one side, with the footlockers and wall lockers on the other side. In the middle on the locker side was a bar. Lieutenant Steve and I had a pretty good time remembering what we had been through and how short we were.

Lieutenant Steve Tomlinson on a blown bridge along QL-20 north of Boa Loc.

On October 5, 1969, after evening chow, several of my former platoon members came to our building and invited Lieutenant Steve and myself over to the enlisted men's club for a short timer drink.

Usually we would keep our helmets and flack vest with us whenever we went out side the building. This night we didn't. We were having a great time being short and especially appreciated the invite to the enlisted men's club.

While talking the short talk with the men, we heard *WHUMP, WHUMP, WHUMP*; the definite sound of mortars. Incoming mortars to be sure. We all froze and listened. Surely we must have heard wrong and they were out going from the other side of the base camp. *KABAM, KABAM, KABAM.* All hit inside Bravo Company's area. Then, *CRACK, CRACK, CRACK, CRACK, CRACK, CRACK*, the sound of a heavy weapon machine-gun. The perimeter guards started to open up.

Everyone scrambled for weapons. We weren't supposed to move about in the open, without the helmet or flack vest. Lieutenant Steve and I ran back to our building and got our weapons, helmets and vests. The other lieutenants were on the floor. I ordered them to get down the hill and to their platoons. This might be the beginning of a ground attack, and the men needed their officers there. More mortars were fired and hit closer to our building.

Lieutenant Steve took off, between mortar hits, running to his platoon on the west side of the perimeter. I ran to the command post to check on the captain and then to head down the hill for the perimeter. The night was dark; with the perimeter lights on, the reflection from the rain threw too much light back into the base camp to suit me. I left the command post and ran down the road to the bunkers on the perimeter.

Half way down the hill a mortar round hit to my left. I was dropped like a wet rag onto the mud. When I woke up, my ears were ringing, and I was lying face down in the rain-spattered mud. I looked around and saw my helmet lying several meters away. Beyond it was my rifle. I wasn't recognizing where I was and couldn't hear anything but the ringing. I felt like I was in a void and could see, but not move. Slowly, I began to hear rifle pops and mortars blasting in the distance.

Charlie was walking the mortars across the perimeter, and the last were outside the perimeter and in the jungle to the east. Where I was lying, my head was lower than my feet; I couldn't feel my lower legs. I stared out to the perimeter and watched the flashes from Charlie's guns in the jungle.

I was too short for this. *Why me, why now?*

I lay there for what seemed like a long time, but was only a few minutes, and finally got up the courage to feel for my legs. I feared I had lost both.

Slowly, I ran my left hand down the left leg; I got to my knee, it was still there. I went lower and so was my lower leg and boot. I rolled over to my back and sat up. I looked down to my feet and let out a holler.

199

Yes, I was still whole!

I forced myself to get up. My lower legs were numb from shrapnel wounds, but I could walk and had no pain. I picked up my helmet and rifle and ran down to the perimeter to my old platoon to check on them first. The FNG lieutenant was doing the right things, so I left to check on the first platoon.

I ran into one of my second platoon leaders who had been on guard duty in an elevated bunker on the west side. A mortar had hit the bunker, and his eardrums had been shattered. He was deaf.

I yelled at his ear, "Stay with me."

Another of my second platoon squad leaders came out of a fighting bunker in the perimeter berm and pointed out a line of NVA approaching the west perimeter wire. I went into the bunker and got a light anti-tank weapon (LAW) and went to the top of the perimeter berm

I opened the weapon and aimed for the NVA. The weapon misfired. The second platoon squad leader had brought another LAW weapon. This one I opened and again aimed and fired. This time the rocket swished out to the line of NVA, hitting just in front of their line, dropping a bunch in their tracks.

About that time, a FNG major, who had no combat experience, and had just relieved the battalion executive officer, showed up and chewed me out for using the LAW against the NVA and scaring our own troops.

I looked at the major and the two sergeants, who were with me, and just said, "Yes, sir."

He then turned and ran back up to the battalion command bunker. The mortars had stopped by then and the NVA had stopped their attack. Most of the firing on the perimeter had died down and Captain Bishop emerged from the third platoon bunker and yelled cease firing, cease firing, it's all over.

He walked over to me and pointed out the red on my legs. I explained about the mortar, and he ordered me to take the sergeant and myself up to the medical station for attention. Gladly!

I told the captain we would probably get hit again around midnight, which was Charlies' normal method of operation. I walked the sergeant to the aid station. Several men were already there with more serious wounds than me, so I went back to our camp across the river and went to the shower building to rinse off the mud and blood.

Once the fatigues were cleaner, I went back to the medics. They had me lay on a table, and I lifted up my fatigue trousers. There were several holes in the cloth and in my lower legs. The medics patched me up and said they were waiting on the medevac for the men who were shot.

THUMP, THUMP, THUMP. The mortars were back. Everyone scrambled. I ran back across the river to the company area. *BAM, BAM, BAM.* It was right at midnight. I ran back down the same road I had been hit earlier. *THUMP, THUMP, THUMP.* I made my way to the third platoon to check on the lieutenant. He was there and doing his job.

BAM, BAM, BAM. Charlie lobbed in twelve more to make that an even thirty-six for the night. After the last blast, everything went quiet. Only the sound of rain splashing on the false metal roofs and mud puddles was heard.

I stayed on the perimeter until 0200 hours. I felt if Charlie wasn't hitting then, he wasn't going to hit. I slowly walked back up the hill to the command post. I decided I wasn't going back to our building, so I sat in the rain on top of a bunker, near the command post, the rest of the night.

Every time I began to doze I would hear, *THUMP, THUMP, THUMP.* This woke me up fast. I would listen for the sound of the mortars flying through the air, to get a bearing on their flight.

Nothing!

The rain stopped, and the dawn came. I just sat there looking out toward Monkey Mountain. The second platoon and the quarry company took off for mine sweep. Lieutenant Steve and I watched as they made their way down QL-20 to the southwest. Captain Bishop had decided to go along. Lieutenant Steve and I were confidant the company had finally got a good leader in this captain.

When the sweep arrived near the quarry, a furious gunfight erupted. The sweep was engaged in an ambush. A Forward Air Controller was up above the sweep this morning because of the hit last night.

Within minutes, a fast mover was swooping down over the road and dropping bombs in the jungle. The firing stopped. I took some pictures of Lieutenant Steve and the men at the bunker. We watched the jets work over the terrain for several minutes, and then it was over. A fast mover turned and made a low pass over our base camp. He was so low we could see the pilot at our level on the hill.

The company clerk came up and told me I was wanted at the battalion command center. *NOW WHAT? Am I getting my ass chewed again by that major?* I slowly walked across the river to the command center.

That major was there, and he was who I was to see. The major introduced himself and *apologized* to me for his behavior the night before. He said he was new here, had never been in combat and got his ass chewed on by the battalion commander for his reaction to a veteran officer who knew what was happening.

Then he hit me with a *bombshell*. He handed me an emergency leave to go home early. He said the American Red Cross had called the Group Command and requested I be allowed to leave, due to a grave illness in my family. My dad was on death's door, and the battalion commander had granted me an emergency leave and early DEROS from Viet Nam.

I looked at him and couldn't respond. He said, "Are you ok, Lieutenant?"

I finally came out of my daze, "Yes, Sir. Will I be required to return to finish my fourteen days?"

Nope, my tour and active duty status was up. There was a chopper coming in from Cam Ranh Bay in a few minutes, and if I was ready, I could be on it to Phan Rang.

I thanked him, saluted, turned and ran back to the company command post. I gave all my personal possessions to Lieutenant Steve or whomever wanted them and packed only one set of fatigues and boots. I said my good-byes to Lieutenant Steve and wished him and the rest of the company well. I ran back to the battalion command center in time to watch the chopper land. They were delivering the mail and other dispatches.

I approached the chopper and the crew chief asked if I was the short lieutenant going home. "That's me," I replied. He motioned me on board and handed me a set of earphones. The pilots revved up the engine, and we lifted off. The pilot backed up a few feet and then after rocking back and forward we were off.

I watched the ground drop and said *thank you, thank you, thank you* to no one in particular. I watched as the clouds came down to the chopper, and we flew closer and closer to the ground. We were flying between the hills and the thought of the time I was shot down came back. I looked out front and saw the clouds getting lighter and the sky open to sunshine. A coastal town was straight ahead. The pilot said it was Phan Rang, our destination.

Once on the ground, the crew chief pointed to the terminal building and said to show the sergeant there the orders I had and I would get priority on any flight to Cam Ranh Bay for the flight home.

I walked over to the terminal and showed my orders to the sergeant. He immediately called the turbo aircraft pilots getting ready to taxi from the front of the building. The plane was held until I got on. The plane taxied to the runway and off we flew to Cam Ranh Bay.

The flight lasted only minutes. Once on the ground, I again went to the terminal sergeant, and he pointed to a freedom bird getting ready to taxi out. I ran to the rolling stair, just being backed off. The ground crew stopped, the jet door was opened, and a stewardess leaned out, motioning them back to the door. The ground crew took my bag and up I went. Once aboard, they put me in a front seat. The door closed, and we started rolling down the tarmac.

Within minutes we were racing down the runway, and once we were airborne, the passengers came alive with a rousing cheer. After we leveled out I fell asleep. I awoke to the wheels hitting the runway in Japan; the daylight was gone, it was around midnight. We were on the polar route to the United States.

The plane was to be on the ground for several hours for refueling and whatever. I got off to COLD, COLD, COLD! I was still wearing the same jungle fatigues I had on when I was wounded. My legs started to ache, and I went into the terminal looking for painkiller.

A soldier in the terminal came over and asked if I had just come from Viet Nam. I said, "Yes, how did you guess?" He laughed, and pointed at my soiled fatigues. He was heading to Nam for his second tour in the medics. Just the man I needed to see. None of the terminal stores were open that had painkillers. I asked if he had anything for pain and he did. Darvon. So he gave me several capsules to get me to the States. We talked for a while and then my plane was ready to go. I wished him well and returned to the plane.

I slept the rest of the flight and woke as we were circling over pine forests in the Pacific Northwest. It was mid morning, and we landed at McChord Air Force Base. After taxiing to the terminal, I was met by an officer from Fort Lewis who escorted me to a waiting car.

It was October 6, 1969. Once at Fort Lewis he took me to a barracks, where a tailor was waiting to out fit me with a new class "A" uniform. Once I was measured for the fit, I went outside to a pay phone to call my wife. It was so good to hear her voice. I told her I was back in the States and would be home as soon as I got the paper work done. She told me my mom had called that morning to say my dad had died that night. While I was coming home, he left.

CHAPTER 38
BRAVO COMPANY REUNION 1994

The turbo prop aircraft wheels hit the tarmac. We landed in Springfield, Missouri. I was back to the present and ready to face my men. I drove a rental car to Aurora, Missouri and checked in at the Aurora Inn Motel. The owner said, "Good, you're finally here." The host of the reunion, Don Munden, had been calling all afternoon. I had expected to be in around mid afternoon but had a delay, and now it was after six.

I went to my room and before I got a chance to call him, he was calling me. Don told me to wait right there, and he would send two guys to get me. So I waited only a few minutes. They must have flown down the road as far as they came. I opened the door to a knock. In walked Carl Enlow and Larry Curbow. I was greeted with a hug and welcome home. I was surprised by the affection from these men I hardly knew.

They escorted me back to Don and Melinda Mundens' farm, several miles out of town. When I pulled into the farmyard, there were several men standing around the tables. As I got out of the car I was welcomed in a similar manner by Don Munden, Paul Bialoncik, Alvin "Yogi" Presswood, "Jungle" Jim Hall, Paul "Rocky" Nawrocki, and Bob Horner. Today was July 1, and the main bunch of men were expected on the 3rd and 4th.

The evening was hot and muggy but no one noticed, we had so much to catch up on. When it was time for me to head back to the motel, it was late, and the fire flies were lighting all over. Most of the men, and their wives, were staying at the same motel, so we all convoyed back. Most of the men were from the first platoon and were very anxious to see Lieutenant Steve who was coming in on July 2nd.

The next day in mid afternoon, Lieutenant Steve and his wife Rose, arrived. There was much hugging and flowing tears. Over the next few days, we spent as much time together as we could. The rest of the men to attend were John Hollis, Richard Hatten, Paul Thomas, Richard Frick, Louis Saavedra, Steve Reeves, Darryl Mollison, Fred Enlow, John Rugg, Paul Gebhart, Richard Harsh, Steve McCracken and Henry Carpenter. Also present were many wives and children of the members of Bravo Company.

*Bravo Company troops at the first reunion, 1994. Left to right standing:
John Hollis, Yogi Presswood,
Richard Hatton, Gary Suffern, Larry Curbow, Steve Tomlinson, Paul
Thomas, Richard Frick, Paul Nawrocki, Louis Saavedra, Steve Reeves.
Left to right kneeling: Bob Horner, Darryl Mollison, Carl Enlow, Paul
Bialoncik, Jim Hall, Fred Enlow, John Rugg, Paul Gebhart, Don Munden,
Richard Harsh, Steve McCracken and Henry Carpenter.*

On the 4th of July, we had a memorial service for our buddies who didn't make it home. We gathered around the flagpole, which also flew the KIA-MIA flag and lit candles for our fallen friends...

My sincere gratitude goes out to Melinda Munden who worked so hard to get all of us together, and on the road back to our sanity. I have tried for years to get this part of my life down on paper and just couldn't do it. As the years go by since the first reunion, I have been able to talk more freely about the events in this book and feel I owe Melinda and Don Munden many thanks. We have met at their farm for three reunions and each has been more rewarding.

EPILOGUE

After Viet Nam, Gary and Ellen Suffern settled down in Fullerton, California. The family increased to four with the birth of another daughter, Randi, in 1971. Gary entered the field of law enforcement with the Fullerton Police Department chasing criminals for eleven years. He was in patrol for three years, traffic enforcement for four years and investigation for four years. A turning point came in 1981, and Gary took an early retirement to change careers into the electrical field.

After moving to Seattle, Washington in 1981 and working for five years in the electrical trade a partnership was made with his brother and Mads Electric Company was born on Camano Island, Washington.

Gary and Ellen have been married for 37 years and currently live on Camano Island.

After leaving Viet Nam Lieutenant Steve Tomlinson was promoted to Captain and returned to Fort Belvoir, Virginia. He was assigned to the Officer Candidate Regiment as a company commander. There he married his childhood sweetheart Rose and has been happily married for 34 years. They have two children, Buddy and Dianne.

The United States troop involvement in Viet Nam was being reduced, and the OCS program was terminated in 1972. Captain Tomlinson was reassigned to the Mine Warfare Department where he taught boobie trap detection to local police and foreign officers. He was reassigned to Fort Wainright, Alaska and worked with the Bureau of Land Management in their smoke jumpers unit being transported to the summer fires by Chinook helicopters and help the local firefighters on the fire lines.

In 1973, Captain Tomlinson became a civilian and joined the Penn Central Railroad. He was promoted to a supervisory position and in 1978 joined AMTRAK.

Steve Tomlinson became active in the Railroad Union and in 2002 was elected President and General Chairman. He currently represents union supervisors from Montreal to Michigan, Maine to Virginia along the east coast. He is also the vice president and board member of the National Lodge. While still active in safety work for AMTRAK, he won the AMTRAK

Presidents Service award for sustained excellence in 2002 and has been nominated for the Gary Burch Award in the transportation industry in 2004.

Steve and Rose currently live in the mountains of central Pennsylvania in Forksville, the best small town on the Loyalsock River.

TO ALL VIET NAM VETERANS WHO NEEDED A FRIEND

Written by: *Melinda Munden* **for her husband** *Don.*

I knew when we met that you were for me
I didn't know then, but I think now I see.
You were always surrounded by those you called friend
But none really cared, not one of them.
But then you found love in your life once again
With a girl who is now your wife and best friend.
You told her of heart aches, buddies, and pain
With tears in your eyes that fell like the rain.
You had finally found someone who you could lean on
And tell of your hell, in Viet Nam.
The months of fighting in jungles, mud and dirt
With no one back home who cared if you hurt.
You would wait for mail call and a few letters came
But you knew in your heart they all read the same.
Dear son, how are you? We're all doing fine
I'll close for now, until next time.
But you read those letters once, then again
'cause they came from a place you'd forgotten you'd been.
A place you called home where as a child you ran free
And now you're here fighting for them, and for me.
Some days you say it gets so damn hot
120 degrees in the coolest of spots.
Your body is drenched with blood, sweat, and tears
As you and your buddies share several hot beers.
Then there's the rains, that go on for weeks
You're covered with mud, from your head to your feet
But still you keep going, even though you need sleep.
From out of the darkness, a shot rings out
You yell at the men, "Take cover

We have a man down and can't lose another."
For what seems like hours, has only been minutes
Then all seems quiet, or really is it?
You never know what could happen after that
Did you get rid of them all, or did they just pull back?
You say that the dark can mess with your mind
That it happened to you, but only one time.
"I see the VC, hiding in the trees
But wait, now they're gone, I'm losing my sanity."
"I see them coming, I aim and I fire
But all that I've hit is sand bags and wire.
The doc told you that you need a break
Take R&R and get your life straight.
But you just couldn't go and leave all your men
For they needed you, and you needed them.
They helped you forget that dark lonely night
And you where able to go on and fight.
Side by side you all stuck together
Though names sometimes fail you, their faces live on forever.
So many years have gone by since then
And you reach out to hold your wife and best friend.
I say to my husband, "I feel your pain too
I hate the thought of the hell you went through."
"I want you to know and never forget
That I'm proud to be the wife of a Viet Nam vet!"

GLOSSARY

Arc light
B-52 bombing mission.
AK-47
Communist made 7.62 cal. automatic assault rifle. Primary individual weapon used by the NVA and VC troops.
ao da
Traditional Vietnamese female dress, split up the sides and worn over pants. Teachers wore white.
AO
A units area of operations.
APC
An armored personnel carrier, a track vehicle used to transport troops or supplies, usually armed with a .50 caliber and two .60 caliber machine guns.
Article 15
Punishment under the Uniform Code of Military Justice. Less severe than a general court-martial.
ARVN
South Vietnamese regular army: officially the Army of the Republic of Vietnam.
Autorotation
A procedure for landing a helicopter without engine power. The weight of the falling helicopter creates a "pinwheel" effect that turns the blades. The pilot gets one chance to use the "pinwheel" effect to safely touch down the helicopter.
AWOL
Absent Without Leave.
Bailey bridge
British designed, steel framed, assembled bridge; used to cross narrow gaps.
Battalion
A military unit composed of a headquarters and two or more companies, batteries, or similar units.
B-52
US Air Force high-altitude bomber.

B-40 rocket
An enemy antitank weapon.
Beaucoup
French word for "very many."
Berm
High, earthen levee surrounding most large, permanent US Military installations as part of the perimeter defense system.
Body bag
A plastic bag used to transport bodies from the field of battle.
Boom-boom
Slang for sex.
Bouncing Betty
A land mine that, when triggered, bounces waist-high and sprays shrapnel when exploded.
Brigade
A tactical and administrative military unit composed of a headquarters and one or more battalions of infantry or armor with other supporting units.
Butter bar
Gold colored bar of a second lieutenant, brown on field fatigues.
CA
Combat assault.
Chopper
Slang for any helicopter.
Clacker
Slang for electric firing device for a claymore mine or to detonate a blasting cap.
Claymore mine
Anti personnel mine; rectangular in size, containing 750 buck shot size pellets, impregnated into plastic explosives. Command detonated, designed to saturate an area six to eight feet above the ground and over an area of 60 degrees across its front.
CO
Commanding officer.
Cobra
An AH-1G attack helicopter; also known as a gunship, armed with rockets and machine guns.
Company
A military unit usually consisting of a headquarters and two or more platoons.

Concertina wire
Coiled barbed wire used as an obstacle.
Connex
Large steel container used to transport and store US Military supplies and equipment.
C-rations
Combat rations; canned meals for use in the field.
DEROS
Date of Estimated Return from Overseas.
Det cord
Demolition cord, made of plastic explosive.
Deuce and a half
Two and one half ton military transport truck.
di di or *di di mau*
Vietnamese phrase for "get out" or "go."
Dink
Derogatory term for the Viet Cong or NVA soldier
DMZ
Demilitarized Zone; the dividing line between North and South Vietnam established in 1954 by the Geneva Convention.
Dust off
Helicopter conducting a medical evacuation.
E&E
Escape and evasion.
EM
Enlisted man. Echo mike in radio terminology.
FAC
Forward Air Controller; a person who coordinates air strikes.
FNG
Fucking New Guy, slang term meaning an inexperienced soldier newly arrived in a combat zone.
FO
Forward Observer.
Fast movers
Jet aircraft.
Fire base
An artillery firing position usually secured by an infantry unit; also, fire support base.

Fire Fly
LOH scout helicopter mounting a search light and capable of dropping aerial flares.
Firefight
Small arms battle.
Fire mission
Directed artillery barrage.
Fire team
Two gunships in attack formation.
Flak vest
Vests worn by US soldiers to lessen the severity of torso wounds caused by shrapnel.
Frag
Fragmentation grenade.
Fragging
Intentional grenade attack against a friendly soldier, usually directed at officers or non-commissioned officers not liked by the troops.
Freedom Bird
Name given to any military or commercial aircraft that took troops out of Viet Nam.
Free fire zone
An area declared off-limits to all personnel. Anyone encountered within its confines was assumed to be hostile and could be fired on without verification or authorization.
G-2
Battalion intelligence section.
Gook
Derogatory slang term for Viet Cong or NVA. Also dink, slope and slant.
Go to cover
Move into heavy concealment.
Graves Registration
Section of the military service charged with reception, identification, and disposition of US Military dead.
Grunt
US Infantryman.
Gunship
An armed helicopter.

HE
High explosives.
HQ
Headquarters.
Hootch
A hut or simple dwelling.
Horn
Term used to describe radio communication.
Hot
Term describing an area of operations or a landing zone where contact has been made with enemy troops, and gun fire is being exchanged.
Hot LZ
A landing zone under enemy fire.
Howitzer
A short cannon used to fire shells at a medium velocity and with relatively high trajectories.
Huey
Nickname for the UH-1 series helicopter.
Hump (the)
The midpoint in a soldiers overseas combat tour, usually the 183rd day.
Hump (to)
To walk on patrol.
I Corps, II Corps, III Corps, IV Corps
The four military regions into which South Vietnam was divided, with I Corps the northernmost regions, and IV Corps the southernmost regions.
In country
Term used to refer to American troops serving in Viet Nam.
Indian country
The enemy infested jungle.
Jody
Universal name for the guy back home who tries to steal the GI's girl while he is overseas.
KIA
Killed in action.
Kill zone
The target area of an ambush.
Kit Carson scout
Former VC/NVA soldier, repatriated to serve as a scout for US combat forces.

Klick
One thousand meters.
LAW
Light Antitank Weapon; a single shot, disposable rocket launcher.
LOH
Light Observation Helicopter, also known as a **loach.**
LP
Listening post.
LRP
Long range patrol.
LZ
Landing Zone.
Lifer
A career soldier.
Lima Charlie
Loud and clear, a radio communication request, as, "How do you read me?"
Lister bag
A waterproof canvas bag providing water to the troops in the field.
Lock and load
Order to chamber a round in ones weapon.
M-16
Lightweight automatic assault rifle used by US forces in Viet Nam.
M-60
Light 7.62 cal. belt fed, machine gun used by US forces in Viet Nam.
M-79
Single shot, 40mm grenade launcher; also called a blooper or thumper.
MACV
Military Assistance Command/Vietnam; the main American military command unit that had responsibility for and authority over all US military activities in Vietnam based in Tan Son Nhut.
MIA
Missing In Action.
MP
Military Police.
MPC
Military Payment Certificate; funny money or script issued to US military personnel in Viet Nam.

Mag
Ammunition magazine.
Medevac
Medical evacuation from the field by helicopter; also called a dustoff.
Mikes
Radio designation for the letter *M*; usually means minutes, meters or men.
Miniguns
Similar to gattling guns, fires 6,000 rounds per minute.
Monsoon
Rainy season in the Orient.
Mortar
A muzzle-loading cannon with a short tube in relation to its caliber that throws projectiles with low muzzle velocity at high angle trajectory.
NCO
Noncommissioned Officer; ranks E-5 to E-9.
NCOIC
Noncommissioned Officer In Charge.
NVA
North Vietnamese Army.
Nam, or the Nam
Short for Viet Nam.
Nouc mam
Rotten smelling fish sauce used by the Vietnamese.
Number one
Slang, meaning the very best.
Number ten
Slang, meaning the very worst.
OCS
Officer Candidate School.
OP
Observation Post.
One-oh-five
105mm howitzer cannon.
One-five-five
155mm howitzer cannon.
One-seven-five
175mm howitzer cannon.

Op orders
Operations order.
Overflight
Pre-mission aerial scout of a recon zone for the purpose of selecting primary and   secondary landing zones and extraction points.
PAVN
People's Army of Viet Nam.
PF
Popular Forces; South Vietnamese irregular forces.
PFC
Private First Class.
POW
Prisoner Of War.
PRC-25 or Prick-25
Portable radio used by American combat troops in the field.
PSP
Perforated steel planking, used for airstrips, helicopter pads, bunker construction, and bridge matting.
PT
Physical Training.
PX
Post Exchange.
PZ
Pick-up zone.
Piastres or Ps
Vietnamese currency; 19 Ps for 1 MPC.
PIG
Slang nickname for the M-60 machine gun.
Piss tube
A 12 inch pipe or the shipping case for an 8-inch artillery round, with one end buried at a 60 degree angle and the other end projecting 30 inches above ground and covered with screen wire mesh. It served as a semi permanent urinal for the US troops in base camps.
Point
A unit's advance man in line of march, or the scout in a combat patrol
Pop smoke
To ignite a smoke grenade to signal an aircraft.

Psy Ops
Psychological Operations unit.

Punji stakes
Sharpened bamboo stakes, hidden in grass, vegetation, in covered pits, or under water, to penetrate the feet and lower legs of unwary troops. They were often dipped in feces to cause infection to the wounds.

Purple Heart
A US military decoration awarded to any member of the armed forces wounded by enemy action.

REMF
Rear Echelon Mother Fucker; slang derogatory term that combat troops called noncombat administrative and support troops getting combat pay.

R&R
Rest and relaxation; a three to seven-day vacation from the war for a soldier.

Recon
Reconnaissance; going out into the jungle to observe for the purpose of identifying enemy activity.

RPG
A rocket-propelled grenade; a Russian made antitank grenade launcher.

RTO
Radio telegraph operator.

Rappel
The controlled descent, by means of a rope, from a hovering helicopter.

Redlegs
Informal name given to artillerymen.

Revetment
Sandbagged or blast walls erected to protect aircraft from shrapnel.

Rock 'n' roll
A slang term used to describe the firing of a weapon on full automatic; as opposed to semi-automatic.

Rucksack
Infantryman's backpack.

SAR
Search And Rescue.

SFC
Sergeant First Class.

SOG (MACV)
Special Observation Group, Military Advisory Command Viet Nam, covert unit.

SNAFU
Situation Normal All Fucked Up, slang for some operations in the field, and command decisions.

Sapper
Specially trained enemy soldier, with the mission to penetrate the perimeters of US and allied military bases by stealth, and then to cause as much damage as possible using satchel charges.

Satchel charges
Pack used by the enemy containing explosives that are dropped or thrown and is generally more powerful than a grenade.

Shrapnel
Pieces of metal sent flying by an explosion.

Shit-burning detail
The most detested extra duty detail in Viet Nam. Some troops volunteered to this detail to stay out of combat.

Short or short timer
A term to describe a soldier whose time remaining in country was less than sixty days.

Sitrep
Situation report.

Six
Radio call sign for a unit's commander

Silver Star
A US military decoration awarded for gallantry in action.

Slack
The second position in a line of march or in patrol formation.

Slick
Informal name for a Huey transport helicopter.

Smoke
Informal name for a smoke grenade.

Snake
Informal name for a Cobra gunship helicopter.

Snatch
To capture a prisoner.

Spider hole
A camouflaged enemy foxhole.

Spooky
AC-47-large airplane with miniguns.

Stand down
A units return from the field for rest and resupply.
Starlight scope
A night vision device to artificially illuminate the area within its range of view.
Stars and Stripes
US military newspaper.
Strack
Term used to describe or designate the ideal in military dress, demeanor, and bearing.
TDY
Temporary Duty.
TL
Team Leader.
TOC
Tactical Operations Center.
Tanglefoot
Fields of barbed wire stretched tightly over a grid of metal stakes, approximately twelve inches above ground; part of a perimeter's static defense, and designed to discourage rapid and uninterrupted penetration.
Tarmac
A term describing the hard surface coating used to construct permanent airstrips, road, and helicopter pads; the word comes from "tar" and "macadam."
Toe popper
A small, plastic US made anti-personnel mine, designed to cripple rather than kill.
Tracer
A round of ammunition chemically treated to glow or give off smoke so that its light can be followed.
Tree line
A row of trees at the edge of a field or rice paddy.
Typhoon
An Asian hurricane.
Uncle Ho
Slang term for Ho Chi Minh, leader of North Viet Nam.
Victor Charlie, Mr. Charles, Chuck, Charlie
Viet Cong, the enemy.

WIA
Wounded In Action.
Wait-a-minute vines
Strong, thorned ground creeper vines that caught at the boots and clothing of American troops and retarded their forward movement.
Warrant officer
Military rank between commissioned and non-commissioned officers.
Willy peter
White phosphorus; an element used in grenades, rockets or shells for incendiary purposes and marking a target zone for jet aircraft.
World (the)
USA, the states, home.
XO
Executive Officer.
Zapped
Killed, slain in combat.